THERE IS A DREADFUL HELL,
AND EVERLASTING PAINS;
THERE SINNERS MUST WITH DEVILS DWELL
IN DARKNESS, FIRE, AND CHAINS.

Isaac Watts (1674-1748) *from Divine and Moral Songs for Children. 1720.*

YOU DON'T HAVE TO STAY ANYWHERE FOREVER.

Edwin Paine (1901-1914), *in conversation, December 1990.*

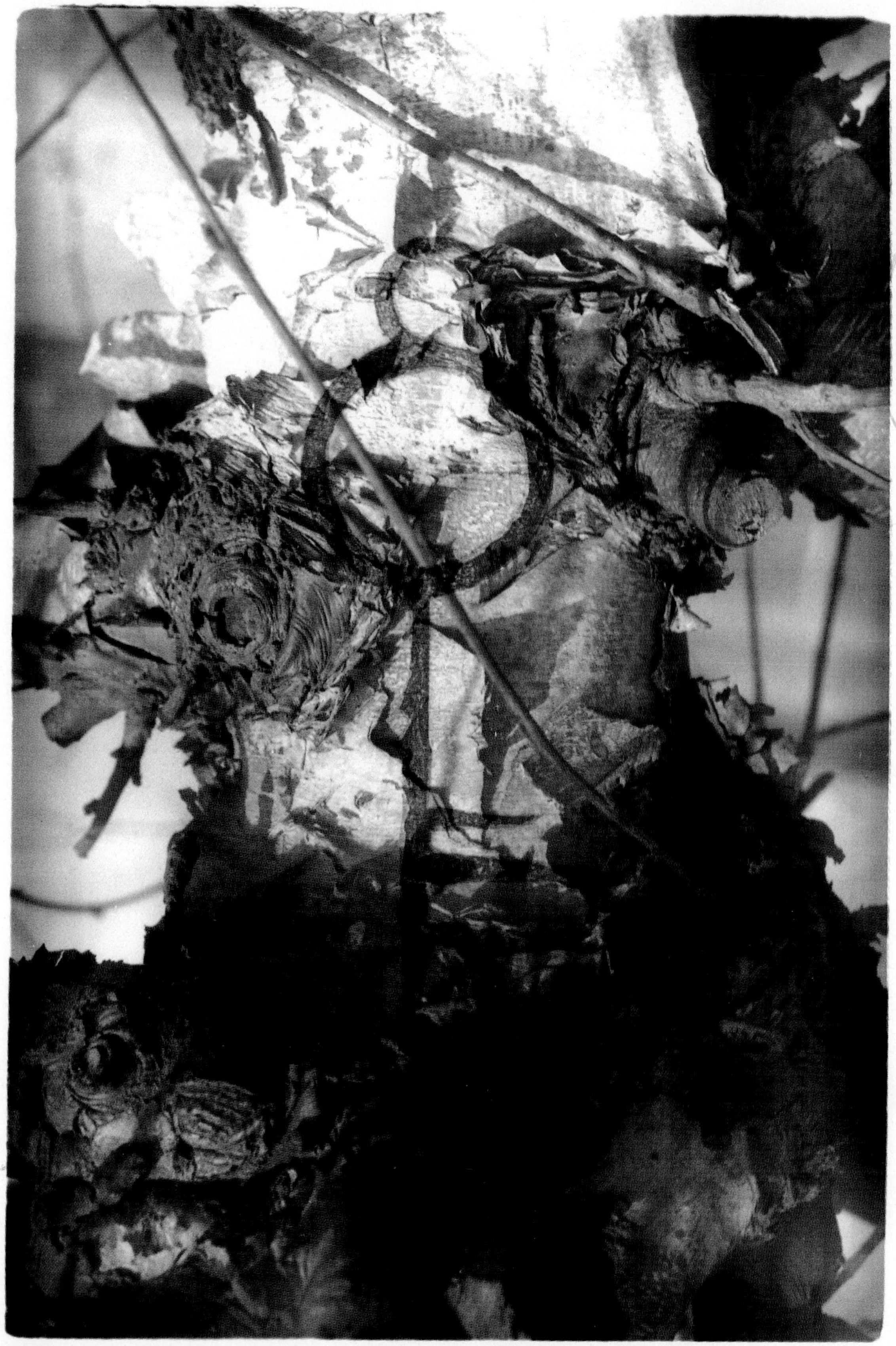

the SANDMAN

SEASON OF MISTS

writer	**NEIL GAIMAN**
artists	**KELLEY JONES**
	MIKE DRINGENBERG
	MALCOLM JONES III
	MATT WAGNER
	DICK GIORDANO
	GEORGE PRATT
	P. CRAIG RUSSELL
letterer	**TODD KLEIN**
colorists	**STEVE OLIFF**
	DANIEL VOZZO
covers	**DAVE McKEAN**

Introduction by
HARLAN ELLISON

Featuring characters created by
NEIL GAIMAN, SAM KIETH, MIKE DRINGENBERG

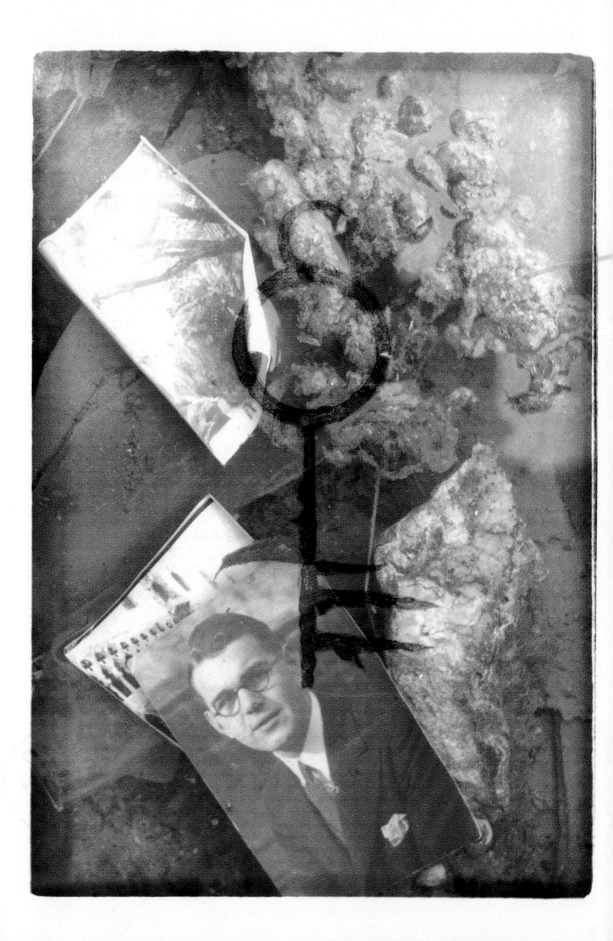

THE SANDMAN: SEASON OF MISTS

Published by DC Comics.
Cover and compilation
Copyright © 2010 DC Comics.
All Rights Reserved.

Introduction
Copyright © 1992 Kilimanjaro Corp.
All Rights Reserved.

Originally published in single magazine form as THE SANDMAN 21-28. Copyright © 1990, 1991 DC Comics. All Rights Reserved.

DC Comics, 2900 W. Alameda Avenue, Burbank, CA 91505
Printed by RR Donnelley, Salem, VA, USA. Seventh Printing.
ISBN: 978-1-4012-3042-5

Cover art, interior illustrations and publication design by Dave McKean.

Cover design by Richard Bruning.

PEFC Certified

Printed on paper from sustainably managed forests and controlled sources

PEFC/29-31-75   www.pefc.org

Library of Congress Cataloging-in-Publication Data

Gaiman, Neil.
   The Sandman. Vol. 4, Season of mists / Neil Gaiman, Kelley Jones, Mike Dringenberg, Malcolm Jones, Matt Wagner, Dick Giordano, George Pratt, P. Craig Russell.
      p. cm.
   "Originally published in single magazine form as The Sandman 21-28."
   ISBN 978-1-4012-3042-5 (alk. paper)
   1. Graphic novels. I. Jones, Kelley, 1962- II. Dringenberg, Mike. III. Jones, Malcolm, III. IV. Wagner, Matt. V. Giordano, Dick. VI. Pratt, George, 1960- VII. Russell, P. Craig. VIII. Title. IX. Title: Season of mists.
   PN6728.S26G454 2012
   741.5'973—dc23

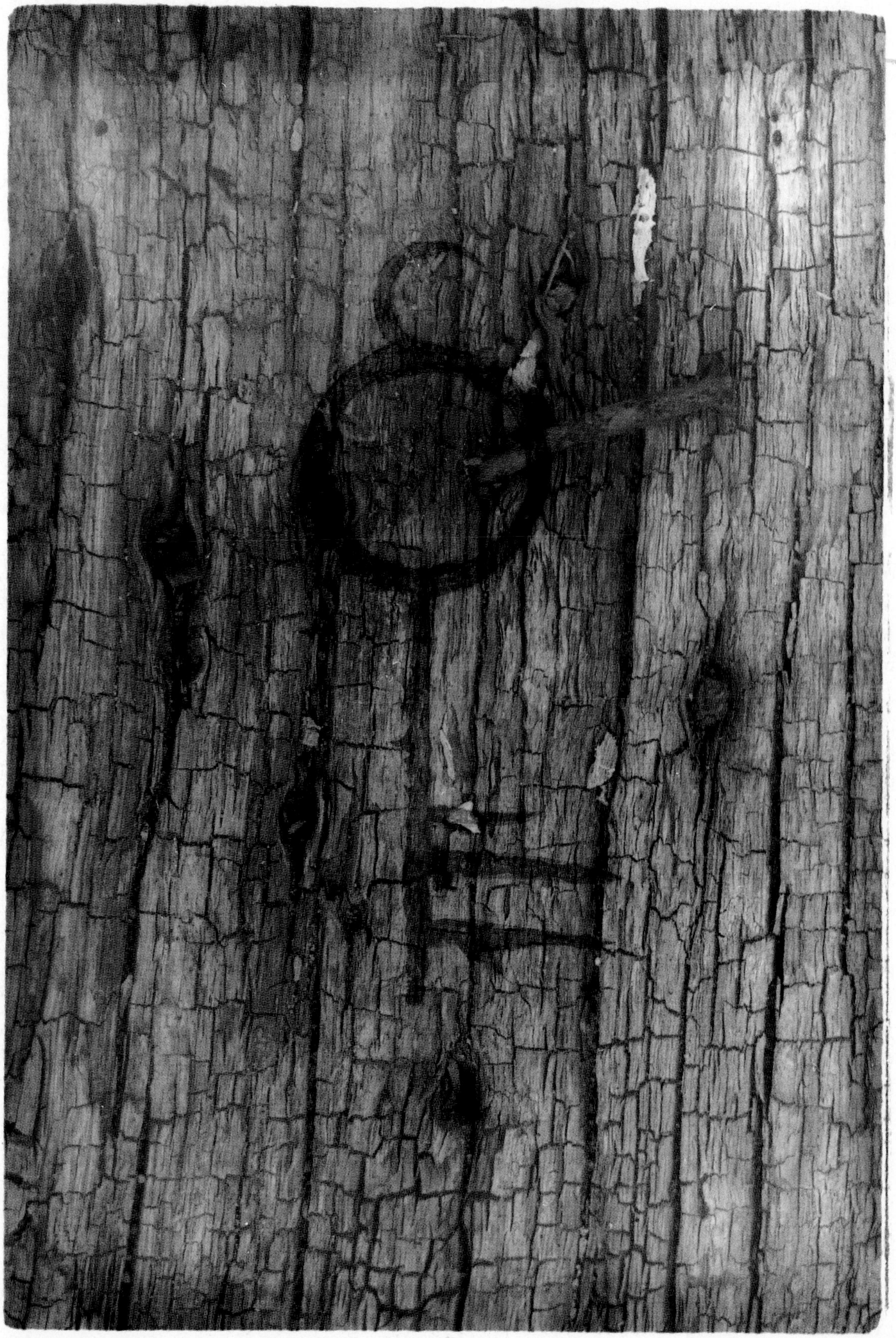

i n t r o d u c t i o n
by HARLAN ELLISON

Possibly the only dismaying aspect of excellence is that it makes living in a world of mediocrity an ongoing prospect of living hell. The subtle distressing perturbation.

Michelangelo wrote: "Trifles make perfection and perfection is no trifle." Hardly a sentiment for our times, for a world of assembly lines and buck-passing and litterbugs.

Perfection. Excellence. What a passionate lover. But once having tasted the lips of excellence, once having given oneself to its perfection, how dreary and burdensome and filled with anomie are the remainder of one's waking hours trapped in the shackled lock-step of the merely ordinary, the barely acceptable, the just okay and not a stroke better.

Sadly, most lives are fashioned on that pattern. Settling for what is possible; buying into the cliché because the towering dream is out of stock; learning how to avoid taking the risk of the dizzying leap. Miguel de Unamuno (1864–1936) wrote: "In order to attain the impossible one must attempt the absurd." So the paradigm becomes all the Salieri shadows unable to touch the Mozart reality, all the respectably-talented but not awesomely-endowed Antonios fulminating with frustration at the occasional Amadeus. Excellence in the untalented and ordinary produces pleasure and awe; but in the minimally-talented it produces hatred and envy that boils like sheep fat.

Excellence is its own master, owes no allegiance, bows its head to no regimen. It exists pure and whole like the silver face of the moon. Untouchable, unreachable, exquisite. But frustrating because it reminds us of how much mediocrity we put up with, just to get through the week.

The point being: Neil Gaiman's work on *The Sandman*.

In any field of endeavor, in any medium of the arts or sciences, an occasional talent will manifest itself and, through bare existence, we perceive how mundane has been the effort in that field or genre, that medium or category. Until Monteverdi, was there higher achievement than that of Palestrina, Wm. Byrd, Andrea Gabrieli? Before Mark Twain, what were the names of the writers at the pinnacle: Sir Walter Scott, R.D. Blackmore, James Fenimore Cooper? Prior to John L. Sullivan, can anyone make a rational comparison of excellence with any of the nameless bare-knuckle champions who spilled their blood in sawdust arenas? There was only one Machiavelli, only one Chaka Zulu, only one Alexander of Macedon. Name the highest and brightest and most accomplished till you get to Fellini or Billie Holiday or George Bernard Shaw; and compare; and recognize how much higher thereafter is the high water mark. Suddenly, there is more sunlight in the world.

The point being: Neil Gaiman's work on *The Sandman*.

This is remarkable work. Perhaps you know that already. Nonetheless, I tell you. A fact: do with it what you will.

It is not merely that Mr. Gaiman (who is midway between being a frequent acquaintance and a close friend of mine, something more than a pal but less than an intimate, and thus available to me as "Neil" rather than "Mr. Gaiman") has committed with these Sandman stories what is usually known as *macrography*, "huge writing," work that is to be examined with

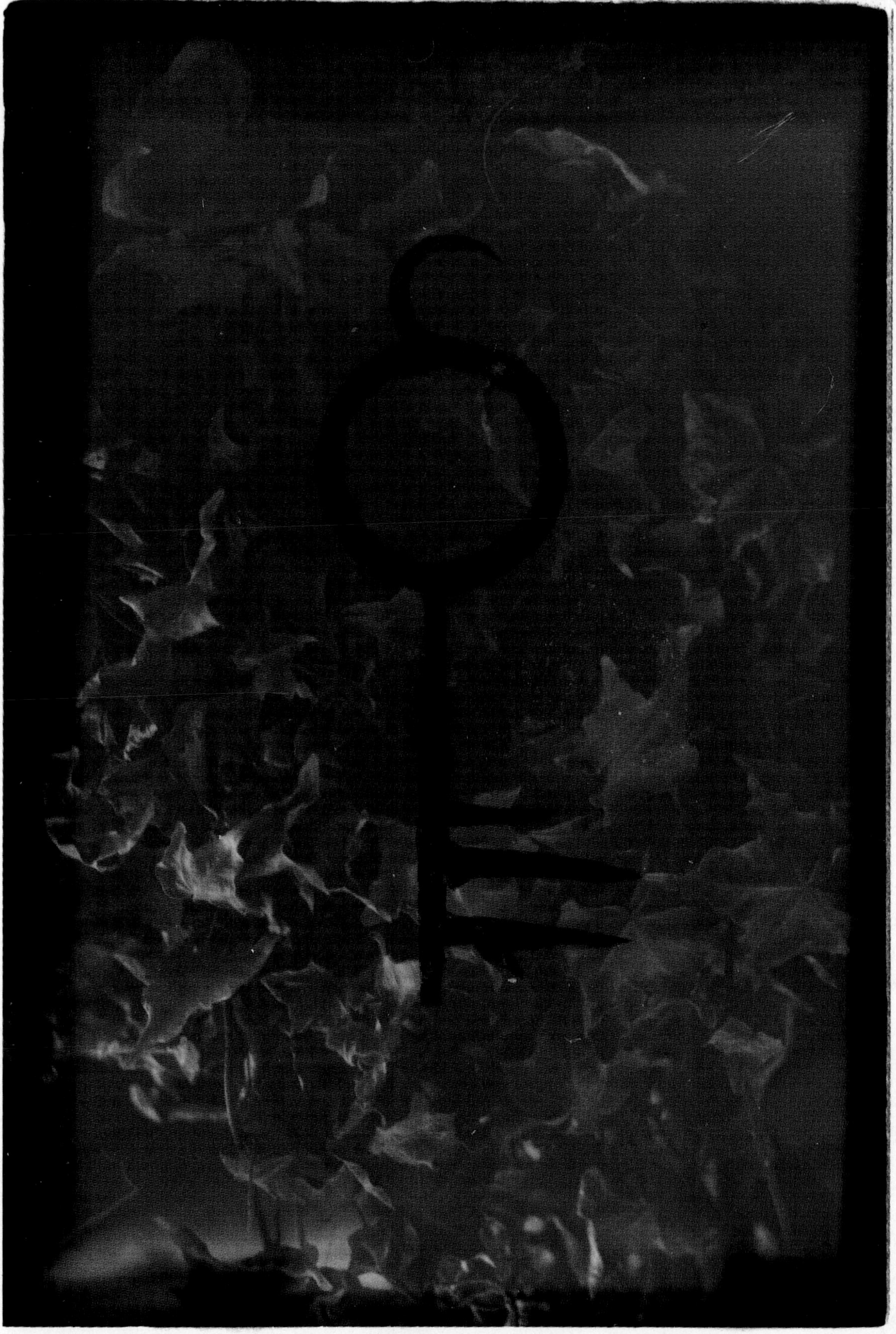

the naked eye, the opposite of *micrography*. Nor is it unique that Neil has created a compelling internally-consistent universe for these stories: a fully-realized cosmology with a pantheon of beings and godlike non-beings, a non-Aristotelian superimposed pre-continuum, a freshly-minted polytheism as compelling as it is revisionist. Hardly unique, because *every* fantasist builds a new universe each time s/he creates a new story. It's the way the game of "what-if?" is played. Some people do it better than others; and most people can't do it at all (which is why there are folks who believe actors make up their own lines, that truth is stranger than fiction, that one picture is worth a thousand words, and that we are regularly visited by far-traveling malevolent incredibly intelligent aliens in revolving crockery, who have nothing better to do with their time than snag couch potato humans so they can have unfulfilling sex with them and just for laughs give these lousy sex partners rectal examinations with mechanical appendages the size of oil pipeline caissons); and every once in a while a person does it so splendidly that it raises the high water mark and puts more sunlight into the world.

The point being: Neil Gaiman's work on *The Sandman*.

Notwithstanding the macrography and the new cosmology, the runaway excellence of what Neil has done with this character is wrapped up in the sense one gets, as one reads *The Sandman*, that what one is reading is *new*, is of consequence, and isn't as transitory (however entertaining) as most of what is done day-in-and-day-out in comics. If you have been following the progression of Neil as guiding intelligence on *The Sandman* —

(Available for the aficionado in three previous graphic novels — PRELUDES & NOCTURNES, THE DOLL'S HOUSE and DREAM COUNTRY — and even as a boxed set of the trio as THE WORLD OF THE SANDMAN.)

— you will have been snared by an outstanding intellect given to esoteric amusements and surreal re-viewings of the Natural Order. You will certainly (if you're one of the few surviving atavists who still read for the pure pleasure of intellectual invigoration) have been mesmerized by the sneaky wit and puckish nastiness of the Gaiman reformation of the received universe. I would praise his erudition, his frequent seeding of the stories with arcane facts and literary glyphs, but as it is a truism that it takes a *very* good con artist to con a very good con artist, so it is possible that Neil "Scam Man" Gaiman is no more widely-read and filled with erudition than the con artist who writes these words of introduction. And, knowing what a fraud *I* am, quoting here and there in Latin and colloquial French just to seem clever, *ignorantia legis neminem excusat*, like *n'est-ce pas*, I have my suspicions that Neil has as diverse and bellyful a library of references as I maintain just to drop in something obscure to remind the groundlings what a smart cookie I am.

Not to be diverted too long on that preceding point, but let me give you a f'rinstance:

Early on in the story of SEASON OF MISTS, when Morpheus sends Cain to deliver the message of his imminent visit to the nether regions, the emissary tells Lucifer what is about to transpire, and the fallen angel goes off into one of those wonderful rhapsodic panegyrics all mad scientists, despots, nitwit super-villains and televangelists indulge in for many odd-shaped panels. He culminates his paralogical blather by ranting, "Better to reign in hell, than serve in heav'n."

And just in case the reader hasn't seen the 1941 Warner Bros. adaptation of Jack London's THE SEA WOLF, in which Edward G. Robinson as the tyrannical freighter skipper Wolf Larsen quotes that quotation repeatedly, Neil bangs us over the head with the information that the aphorism comes from Milton's PARADISE LOST (1667). Leaf ahead to that page and take a look at it.

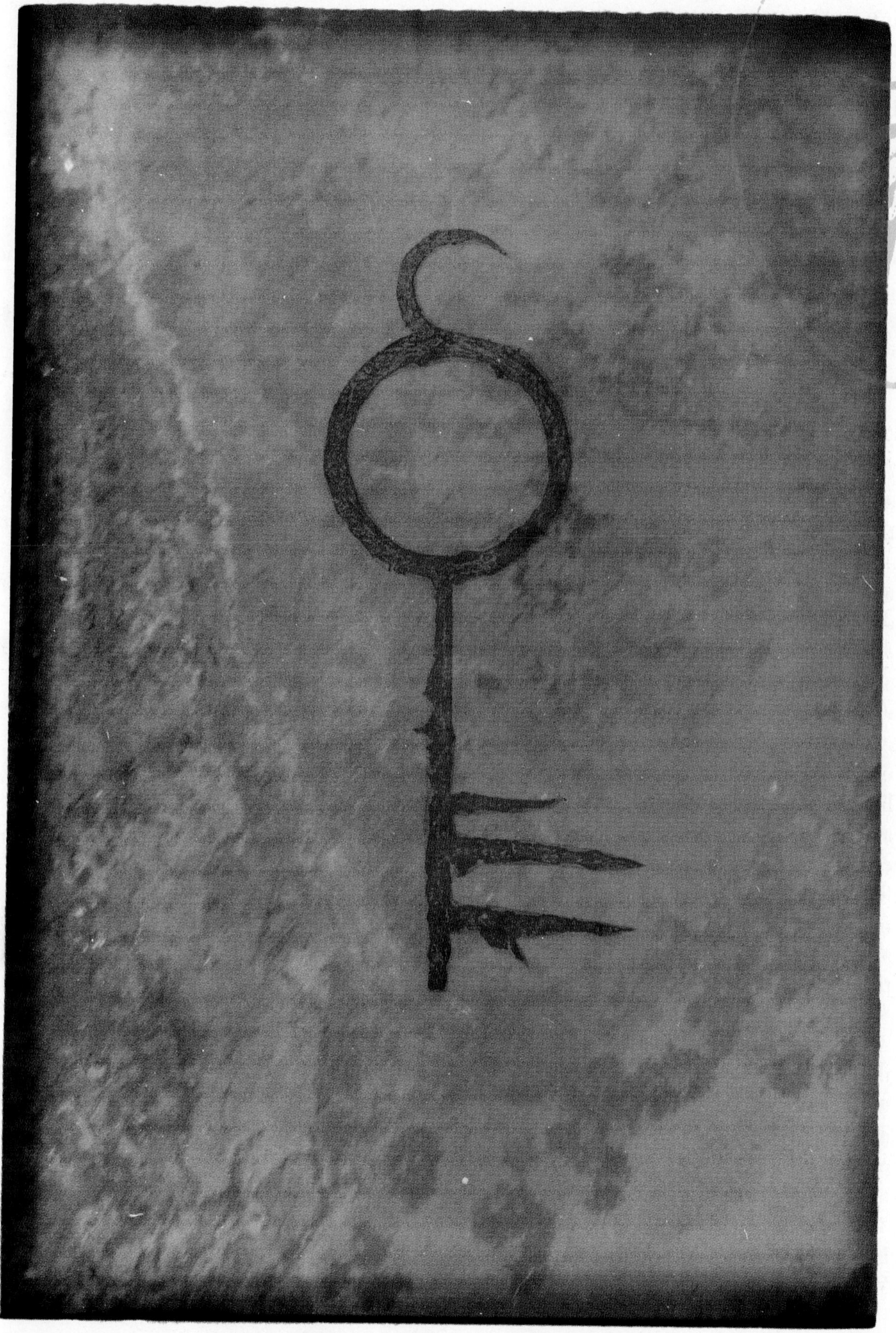

See what I mean? A *really* intellectual guy, secure in his own voluminous erudition, wouldn't have bothered making sure we know how goddam sharp he is. Now, I'm not saying Neil *isn't* as sharp as he wants us to believe he is, I'm merely suggesting that he is so intent on building all the buttressing into his fictional structure that he makes certain we perceive of what excellent granite is made the basement slab.

So excellent that one might quote yet again from Milton: "The mind is its own place, and in itself can make a Heav'n of Hell, a Hell of Heav'n."

The point being: Neil Gaiman's work on *The Sandman* is so excellent, so much a presentation of the new high water mark, that we realize as we read, that it is *about something*, that it is not merely an amusing entertainment. (Though it is *that*, of course.)

I'll not reconnoiter the story in this graphic novel … what originally appeared in monthly comic book format as sections 0 through 7, December 1990–July 1991. The story lies before you, and I wasn't engaged to restate the obvious. (As critic John Simon wrote in 1981: "… there is no point in saying less than your predecessors have said." Which is good advice that should be taken by all those who write Sherlock Holmes or Sam Spade pastiches.) Nor will I play the role of the carping bluejay, shrieking that Neil says in the earliest section of the story that Destiny casts no shadow, but Dringenberg has repeatedly scumbled in shadows only pages earlier. That sort of petty bitching is beneath me, a guy as clever as I am.

I will only repeat the theme of this preamble by reporting that excellence, as contained in the work of Gaiman's *Sandman*, has made the awareness of the mediocre world extremely painful for a great many people. I know this to be true, for I sat there at the 13th annual World Fantasy Convention in Tucson in 1991 and watched with devilish pleasure as Neil won the highly-prized FantasyCon "Howard Philips Lovecraft" trophy for the Year's Best Short Story … an issue of *The Sandman* "comic book." Devilish pleasure, I tell you, because all those artsy-fartsy writers and artists and critics sitting there expecting a standard-print short story to win, choked on their little almond cups as this renegade funnybook guy carted off the Diamond as Big as the Ritz. Much snorting through the nose. Much umbrage taken. Many dudgeons raised to new heights. And screams and cries of foul play at the polls. So infuriated were the Faithful at such a choice having been made by a blue ribbon panel of experts who couldn't be suborned or shamed into overlooking excellence, that the Great Gray Eminences who run the FantasyCon from behind their nightshadow veil of secrecy, have rewritten the rules so that, heaven forfend, no "comic book" will ever again be nominated, much less have an opportunity to kick serious artistic butt.

The point being: Neil Gaiman's work on *The Sandman* brings that perennial DC Comics character, whom I first loved in 1940 in the 96-page 15¢ *New York World's Fair Comics*, with his green business suit, his orange-colored snapbrim fedora, his fuchsia cape, his World War I doughboy gas mask and his deadly gas gun, into a refurbished state of rebirth, transmogrified for our angst-festooned era, not merely as a marvelous and entertaining myth-figure, but as the symbol of excellence in a world where mediocrity is our normal prison.

And how do we know that what Gaiman has done is excellence?

We know it because of something critic Susan Sontag wrote. She said, "Real Art has the capacity to make us nervous."

Nervous. You should've been there at the awards ceremony. Those suckers like as almost laid square bricks.

The point being: isn't this Gaiman just too cute for words!

In which a Family reunion occasions certain personal recriminations; assorted events are set in motion; and a relationship thought long done with proves to have much relevance today.

EPISODE 0

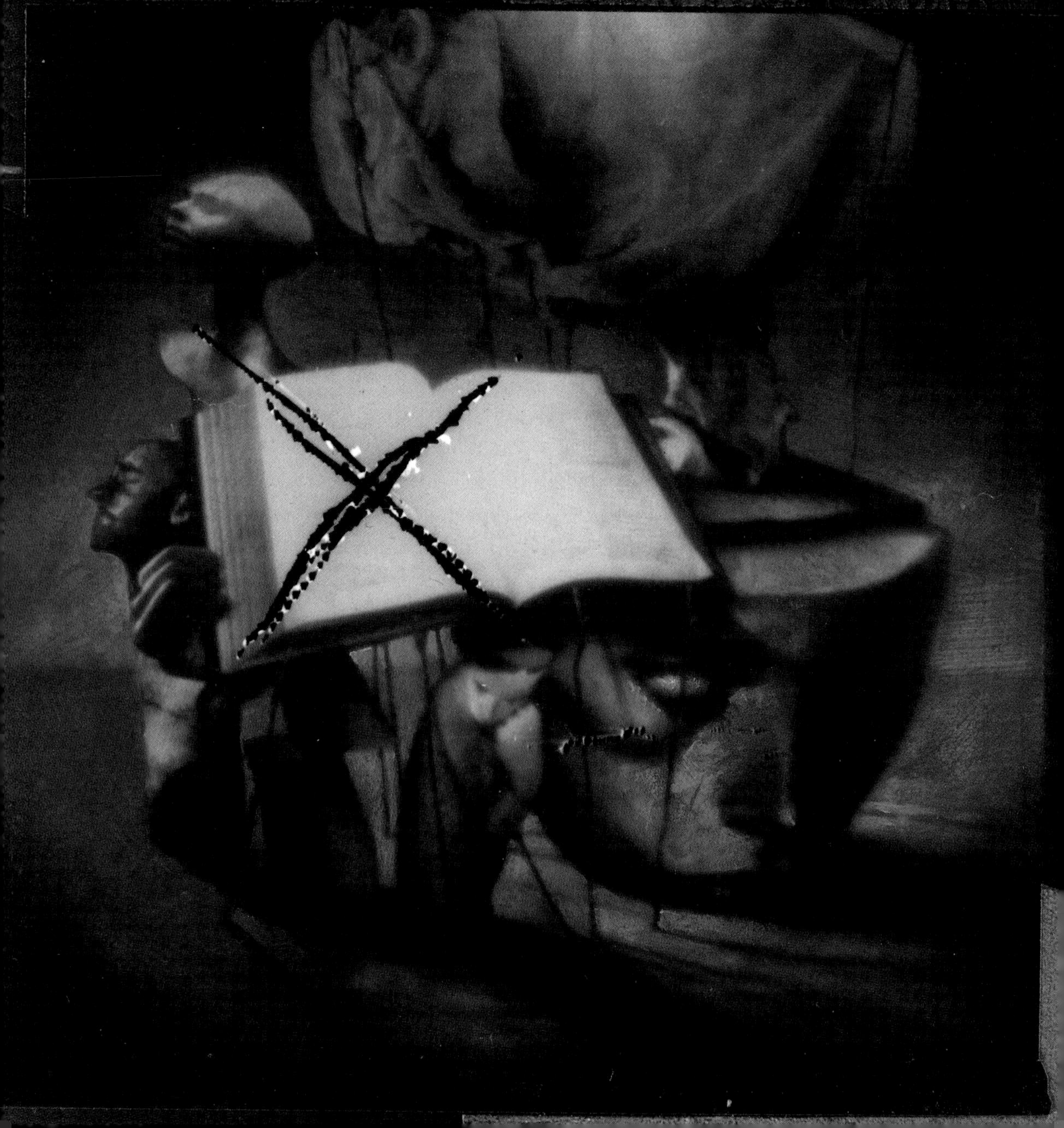

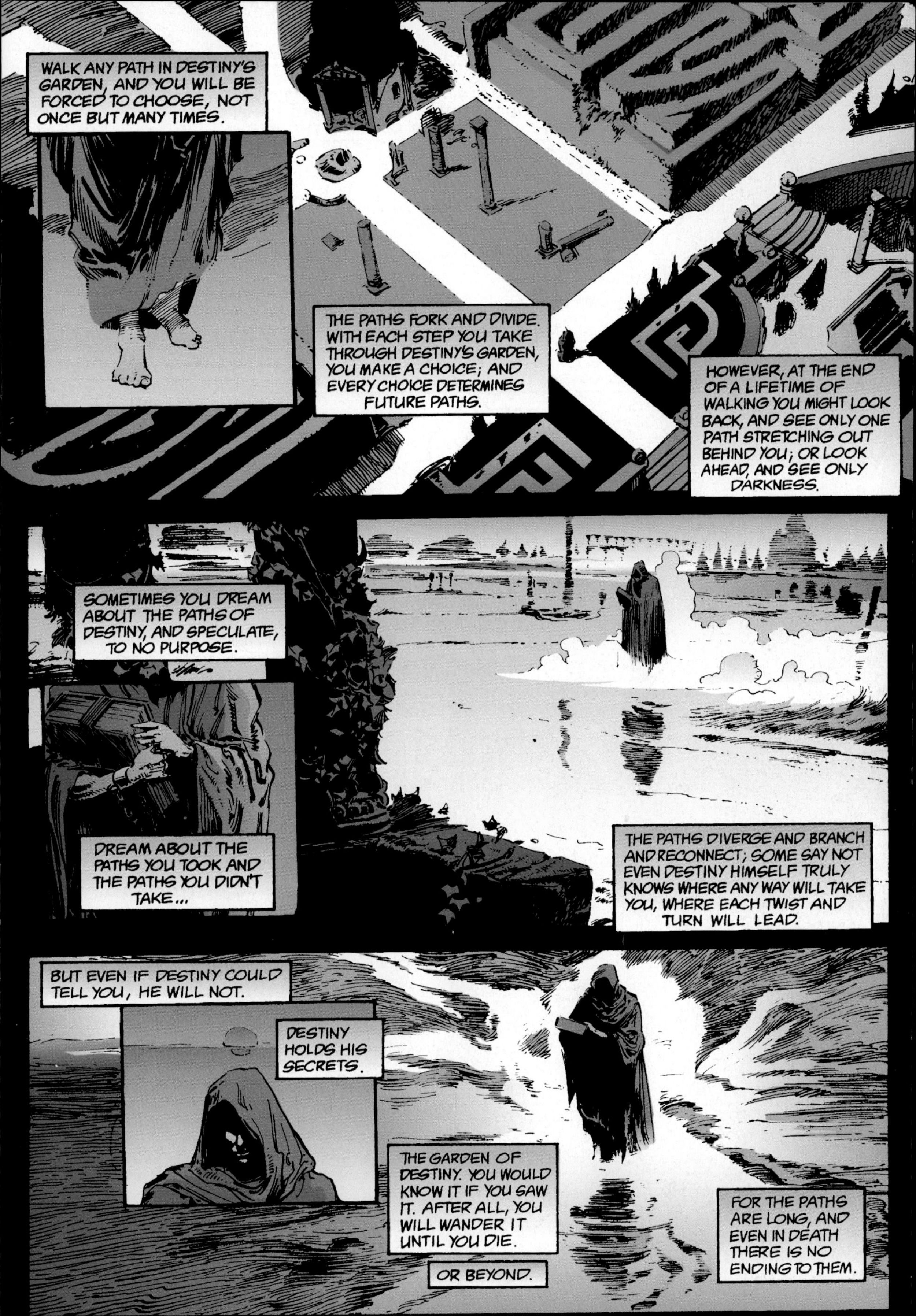
WALK ANY PATH IN DESTINY'S GARDEN, AND YOU WILL BE FORCED TO CHOOSE, NOT ONCE BUT MANY TIMES.
THE PATHS FORK AND DIVIDE. WITH EACH STEP YOU TAKE THROUGH DESTINY'S GARDEN, YOU MAKE A CHOICE; AND EVERY CHOICE DETERMINES FUTURE PATHS.
HOWEVER, AT THE END OF A LIFETIME OF WALKING YOU MIGHT LOOK BACK, AND SEE ONLY ONE PATH STRETCHING OUT BEHIND YOU; OR LOOK AHEAD, AND SEE ONLY DARKNESS.
SOMETIMES YOU DREAM ABOUT THE PATHS OF DESTINY, AND SPECULATE, TO NO PURPOSE.
DREAM ABOUT THE PATHS YOU TOOK AND THE PATHS YOU DIDN'T TAKE...
THE PATHS DIVERGE AND BRANCH AND RECONNECT; SOME SAY NOT EVEN DESTINY HIMSELF TRULY KNOWS WHERE ANY WAY WILL TAKE YOU, WHERE EACH TWIST AND TURN WILL LEAD.
BUT EVEN IF DESTINY COULD TELL YOU, HE WILL NOT.
DESTINY HOLDS HIS SECRETS.
THE GARDEN OF DESTINY. YOU WOULD KNOW IT IF YOU SAW IT. AFTER ALL, YOU WILL WANDER IT UNTIL YOU DIE.
OR BEYOND.
FOR THE PATHS ARE LONG, AND EVEN IN DEATH THERE IS NO ENDING TO THEM.

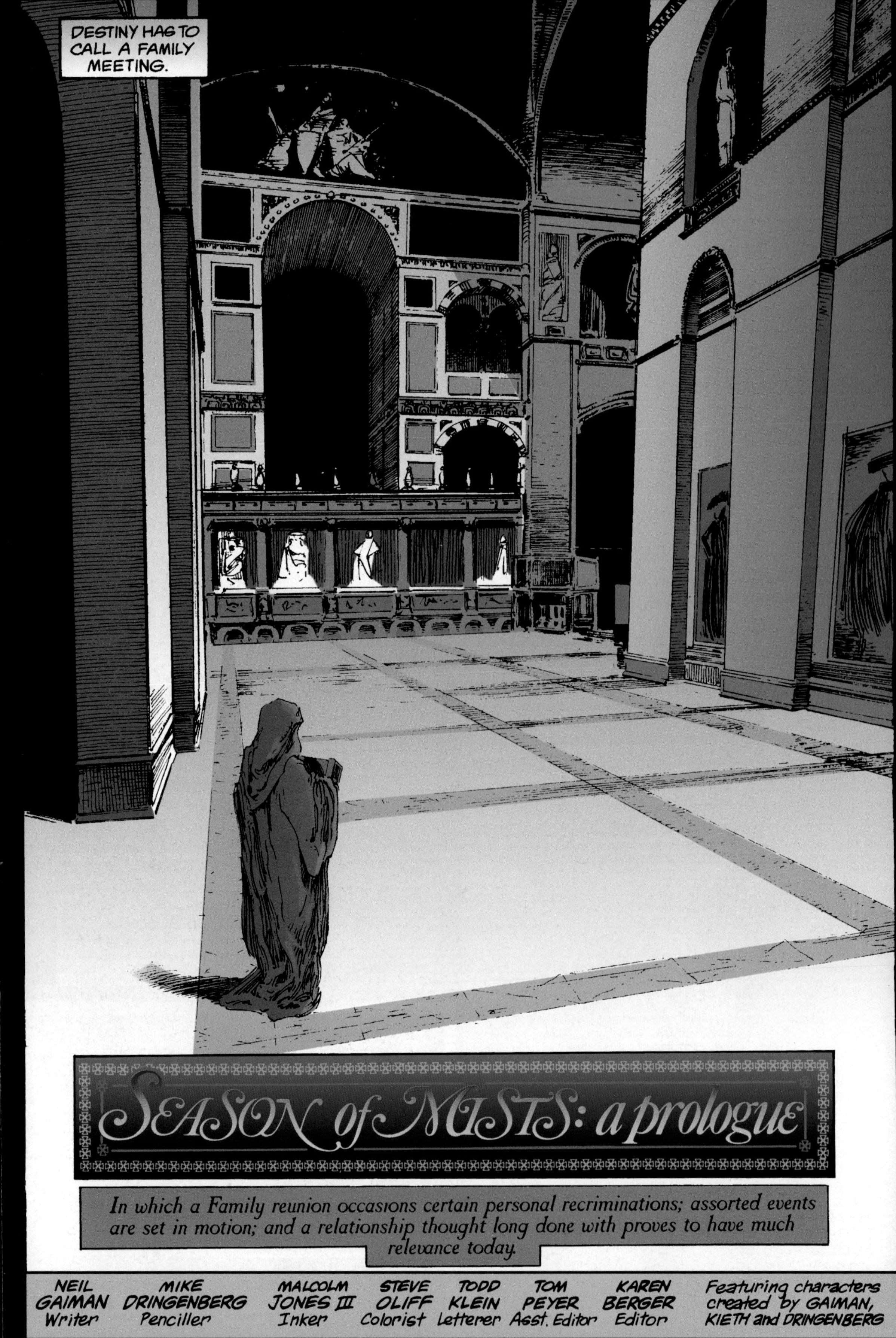
DESTINY HAS TO CALL A FAMILY MEETING.
SEASON of MISTS: a prologue
In which a Family reunion occasions certain personal recriminations; assorted events are set in motion; and a relationship thought long done with proves to have much relevance today.
NEIL GAIMAN Writer
MIKE DRINGENBERG Penciller
MALCOLM JONES III Inker
STEVE OLIFF Colorist
TODD KLEIN Letterer
TOM PEYER Asst. Editor
KAREN BERGER Editor
Featuring characters created by GAIMAN, KIETH and DRINGENBERG

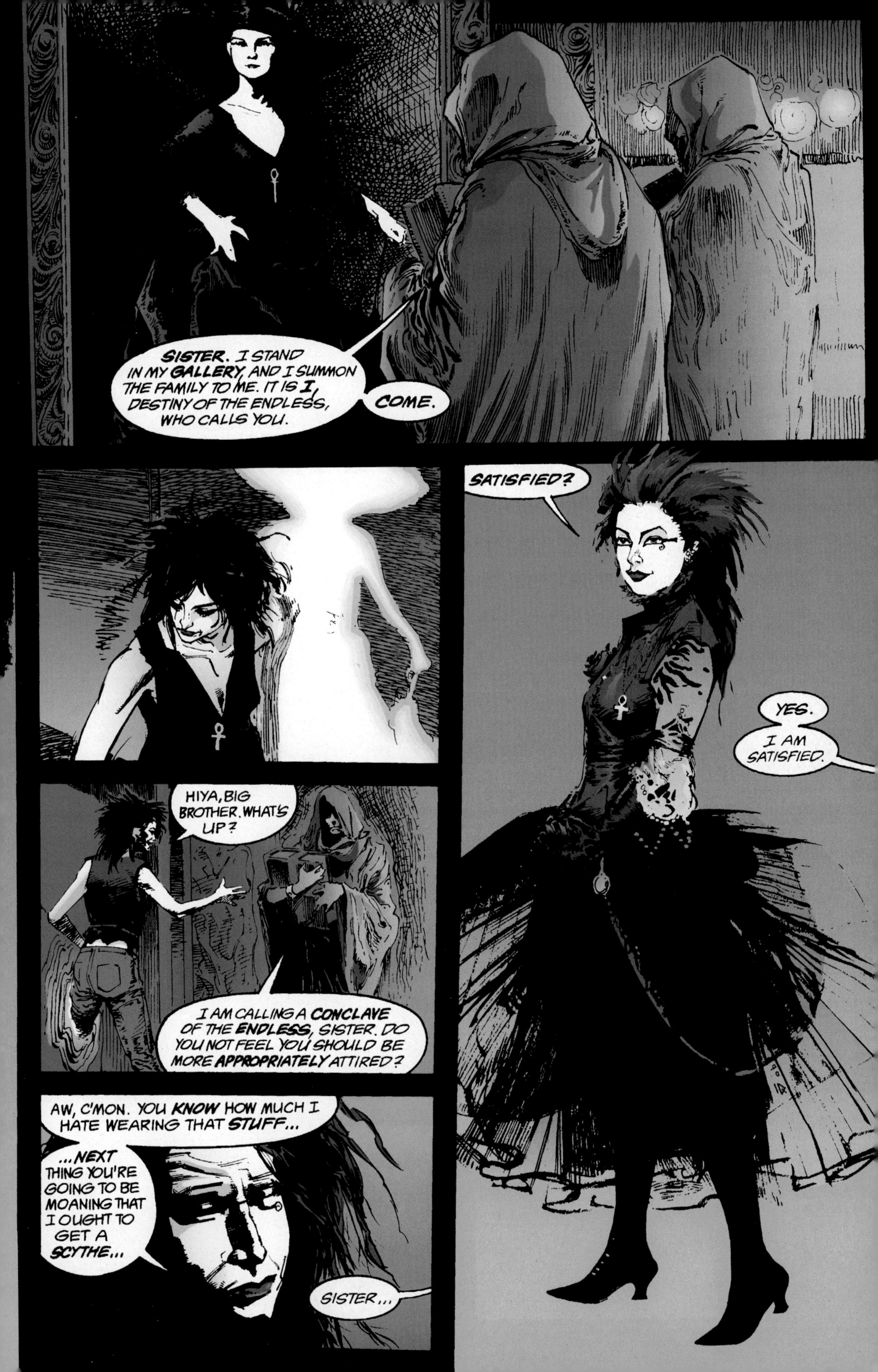
SISTER. I STAND IN MY GALLERY, AND I SUMMON THE FAMILY TO ME. IT IS I, DESTINY OF THE ENDLESS, WHO CALLS YOU.
COME.
HIYA, BIG BROTHER. WHAT'S UP?
I AM CALLING A CONCLAVE OF THE ENDLESS, SISTER. DO YOU NOT FEEL YOU SHOULD BE MORE APPROPRIATELY ATTIRED?
AW, C'MON. YOU KNOW HOW MUCH I HATE WEARING THAT STUFF...
...NEXT THING YOU'RE GOING TO BE MOANING THAT I OUGHT TO GET A SCYTHE...
SISTER...
SATISFIED?
YES.
I AM SATISFIED.

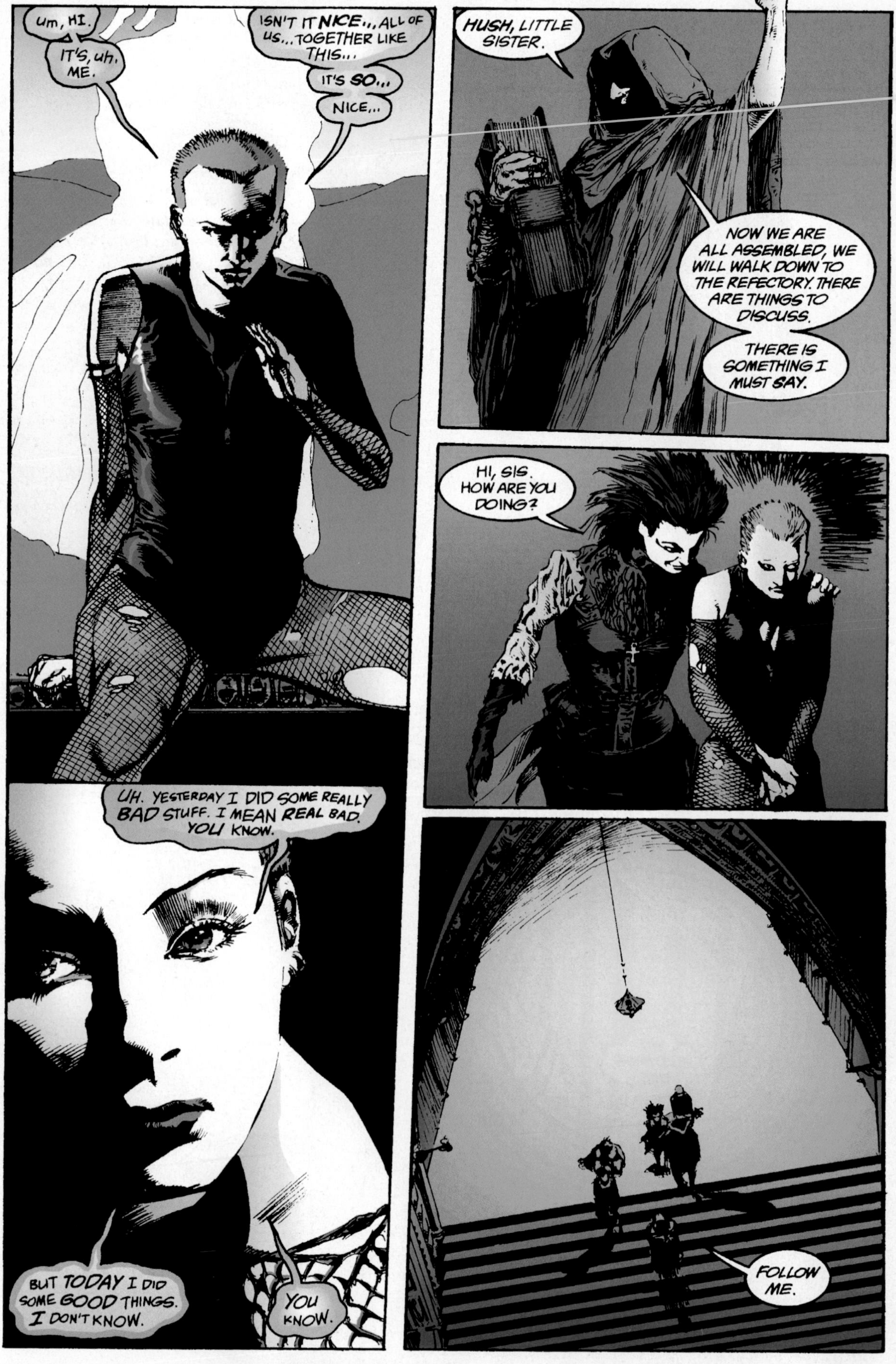
um, HI.
IT'S, uh, ME.
ISN'T IT NICE... ALL OF US... TOGETHER LIKE THIS...
IT'S SO...
NICE...
HUSH, LITTLE SISTER.
NOW WE ARE ALL ASSEMBLED, WE WILL WALK DOWN TO THE REFECTORY. THERE ARE THINGS TO DISCUSS.
THERE IS SOMETHING I MUST SAY.
HI, SIS. HOW ARE YOU DOING?
UH. YESTERDAY I DID SOME REALLY BAD STUFF. I MEAN REAL BAD. YOU KNOW.
BUT TODAY I DID SOME GOOD THINGS. I DON'T KNOW.
YOU KNOW.
FOLLOW ME.

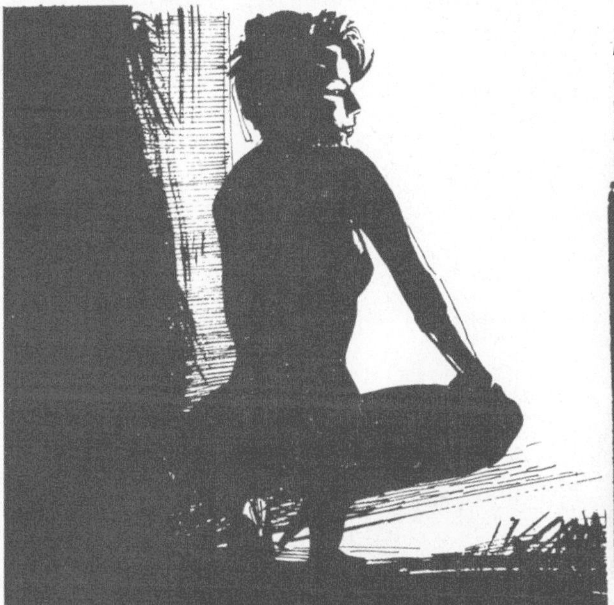

Let us pause for a moment, as they descend the grey steps toward Destiny's banqueting hall, to consider the Endless.

Desire is of medium height. It is unlikely that any portrait will ever do Desire justice, since to see her (or him) is to love him (or her),—passionately, painfully, to the exclusion of all else.

Desire smells almost subliminally of summer peaches, and casts two shadows: one black and sharp-edged, the other translucent and forever wavering, like heat haze.

Desire smiles in brief flashes, like sunlight glinting from a knife-edge. And there is much else that is knife-like about Desire.

Never a possession, always the possessor, with skin as pale as smoke, and eyes tawny and sharp as yellow wine: Desire is everything you have ever wanted. Whoever you are. Whatever you are.

Everything.

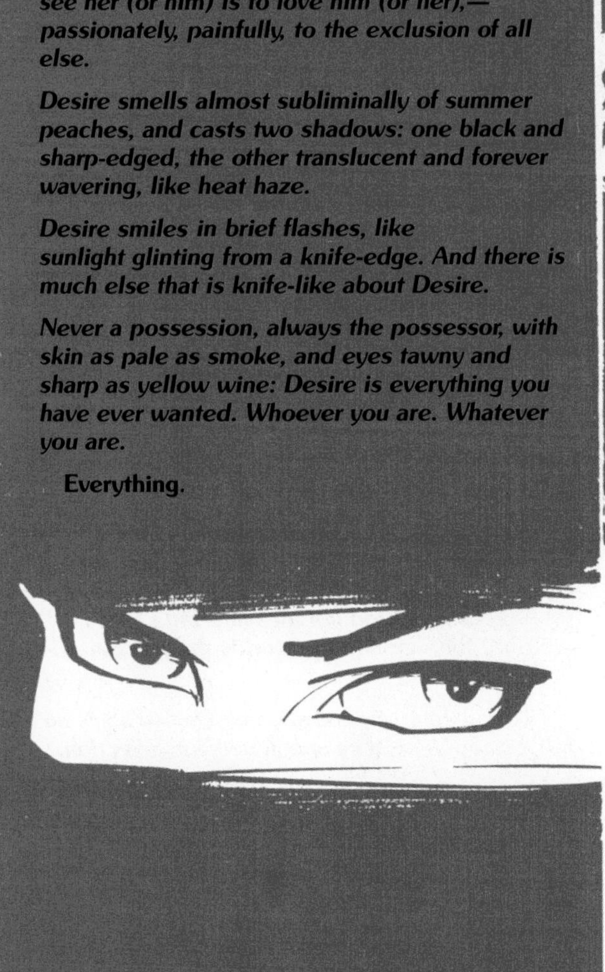

Despair, Desire's sister and twin, is queen of her own bleak bourne. It is said that scattered through Despair's domain are a multitude of tiny windows, hanging in the void. Each window looks out onto a different scene, being, in our world, a mirror. Sometimes you will look into a mirror and feel the eyes of Despair upon you, feel her hook catch and snag on your heart.

Her skin is cold, and clammy; her eyes are the colour of sky, on the grey, wet days that leach the world of colour and meaning; her voice is little more than a whisper; and while she has no odour, her shadow smells musky, and pungent, like the skin of a snake.

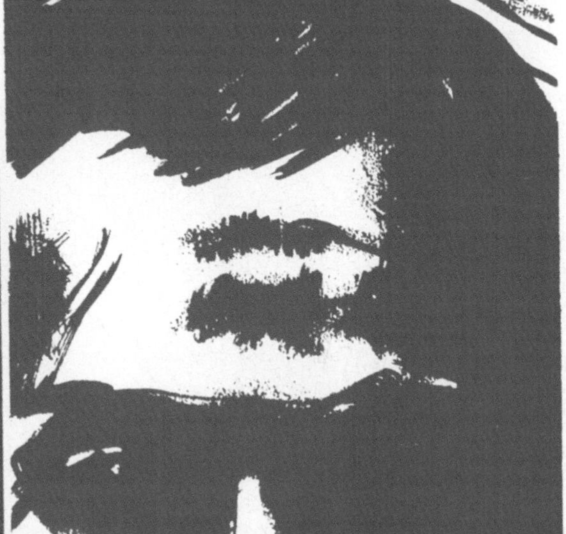

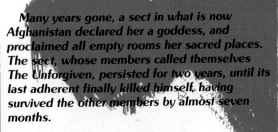

Many years gone, a sect in what is now Afghanistan declared her a goddess, and proclaimed all empty rooms her sacred places. The sect, whose members called themselves The Unforgiven, persisted for two years, until its last adherent finally killed himself, having survived the other members by almost seven months.

Despair says little, and is patient.

Destiny is the oldest of the Endless; in the Beginning was the Word, and it was traced by hand on the first page of his book, before ever it was spoken aloud.

Destiny is also the tallest of the Endless, to mortal eyes.

There are some who believe him to be blind; whilst others, perhaps with more reason, claim that he has travelled far beyond blindness, that indeed, he can do nothing but see: that he sees the fine traceries the galaxies make as they spiral through the void, that he watches the intricate patterns living things make on their journey through time.

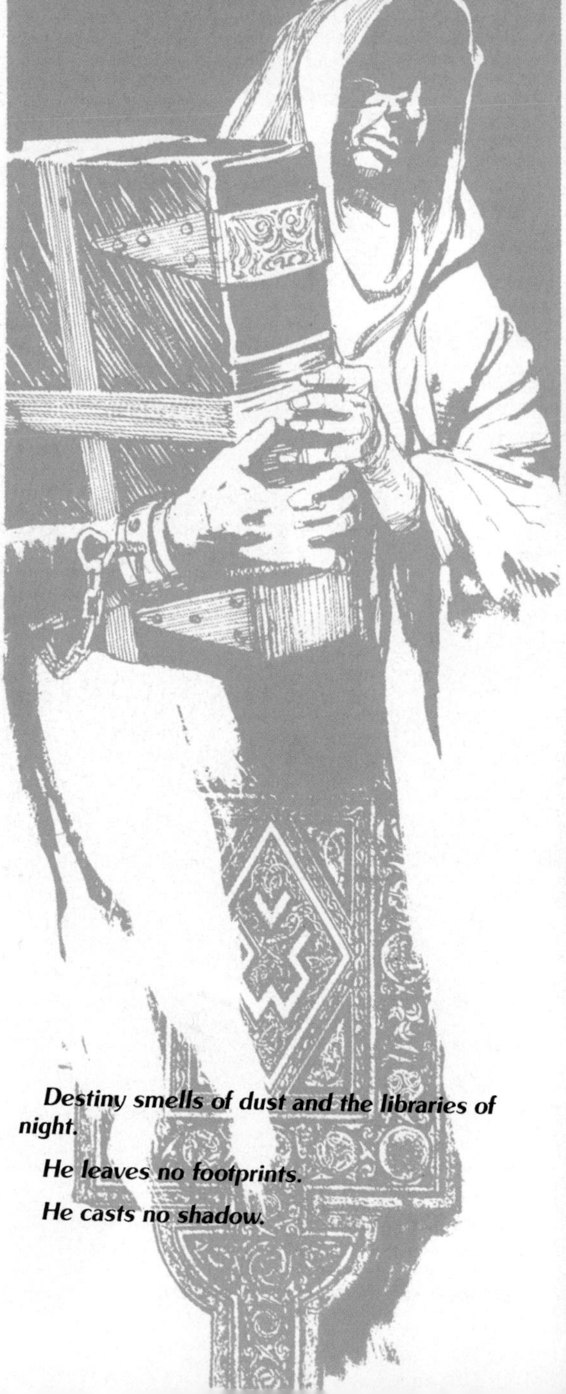

Destiny smells of dust and the libraries of night.

He leaves no footprints.

He casts no shadow.

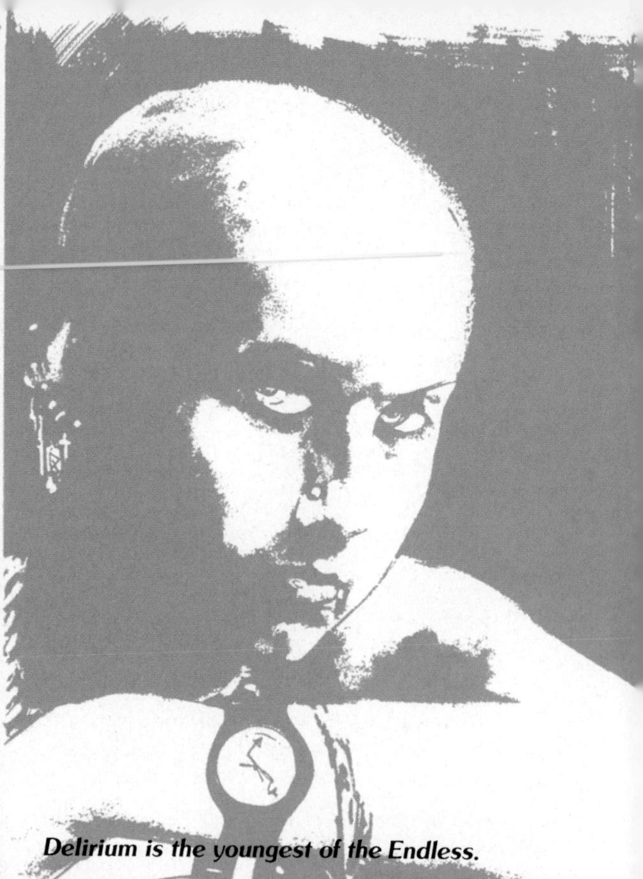

Delirium is the youngest of the Endless.

She smells of sweat, sour wines, late nights, old leather.

Her realm is close, and can be visited; however, human minds were not made to comprehend her domain, and those few who have made the journey have been incapable of reporting back more than the tiniest fragments.

The poet Coleridge claimed to have known her intimately, but the man was an inveterate liar, and in this, as in so much, we must doubt his word.

Her appearance is the most variable of all the Endless, who, at best, are ideas cloaked in the semblance of flesh. Her shadow's shape and outline has no relationship to that of any body she wears, and it is tangible, like old velvet.

Some say the tragedy of Delirium is her knowledge that, despite being older than suns, older than gods, she is forever the youngest of the Endless, who do not measure time as we measure time, or see the worlds through mortal eyes.

Others deny this, and say that Delirium has no tragedy, but here they speak without reflection.

For Delirium was once Delight. And although that was long ago now, even today her eyes are badly matched: one eye is a vivid emerald green, spattered with silver flecks that move; her other eye is vein blue.

Who knows what Delirium sees, through her mismatched eyes?

Dream of the Endless: ah, there's a conundrum.

In this aspect (and we perceive but aspects of the Endless, as we see the light glinting from one tiny facet of some huge and flawlessly cut precious stone), he is rake-thin, with skin the color of falling snow.

Dream accumulates names to himself like others make friends; but he permits himself few friends.

If he is closest to anyone, it is to his elder sister, whom he sees but rarely.

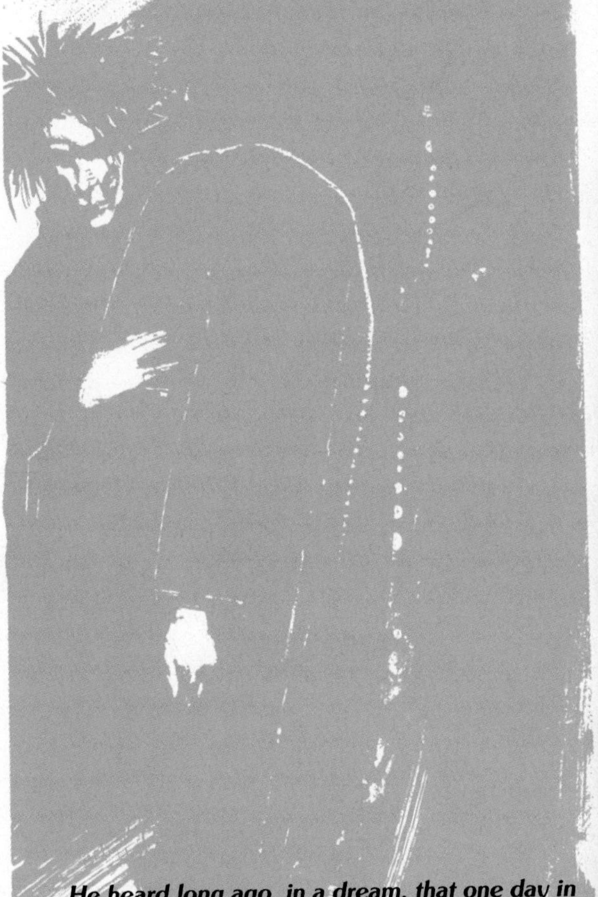

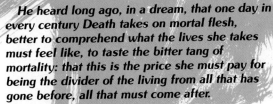

He heard long ago, in a dream, that one day in every century Death takes on mortal flesh, better to comprehend what the lives she takes must feel like, to taste the bitter tang of mortality: that this is the price she must pay for being the divider of the living from all that has gone before, all that must come after.

He broods on this tale, but has never questioned her about its truth. Perhaps he fears that she would answer him.

Of all the Endless, save perhaps Destiny, he is most conscious of his responsibilities, the most meticulous in their execution.

Dream casts a human shadow, when it occurs to him to do so.

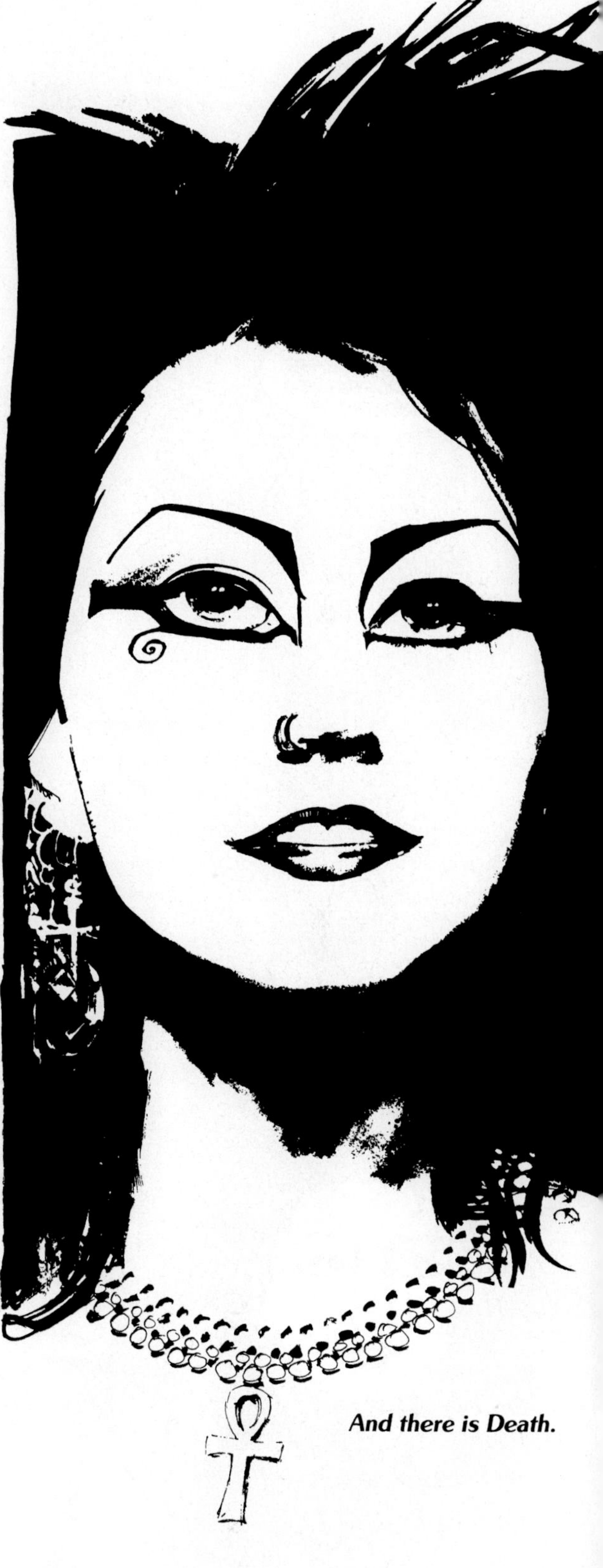

And there is Death.

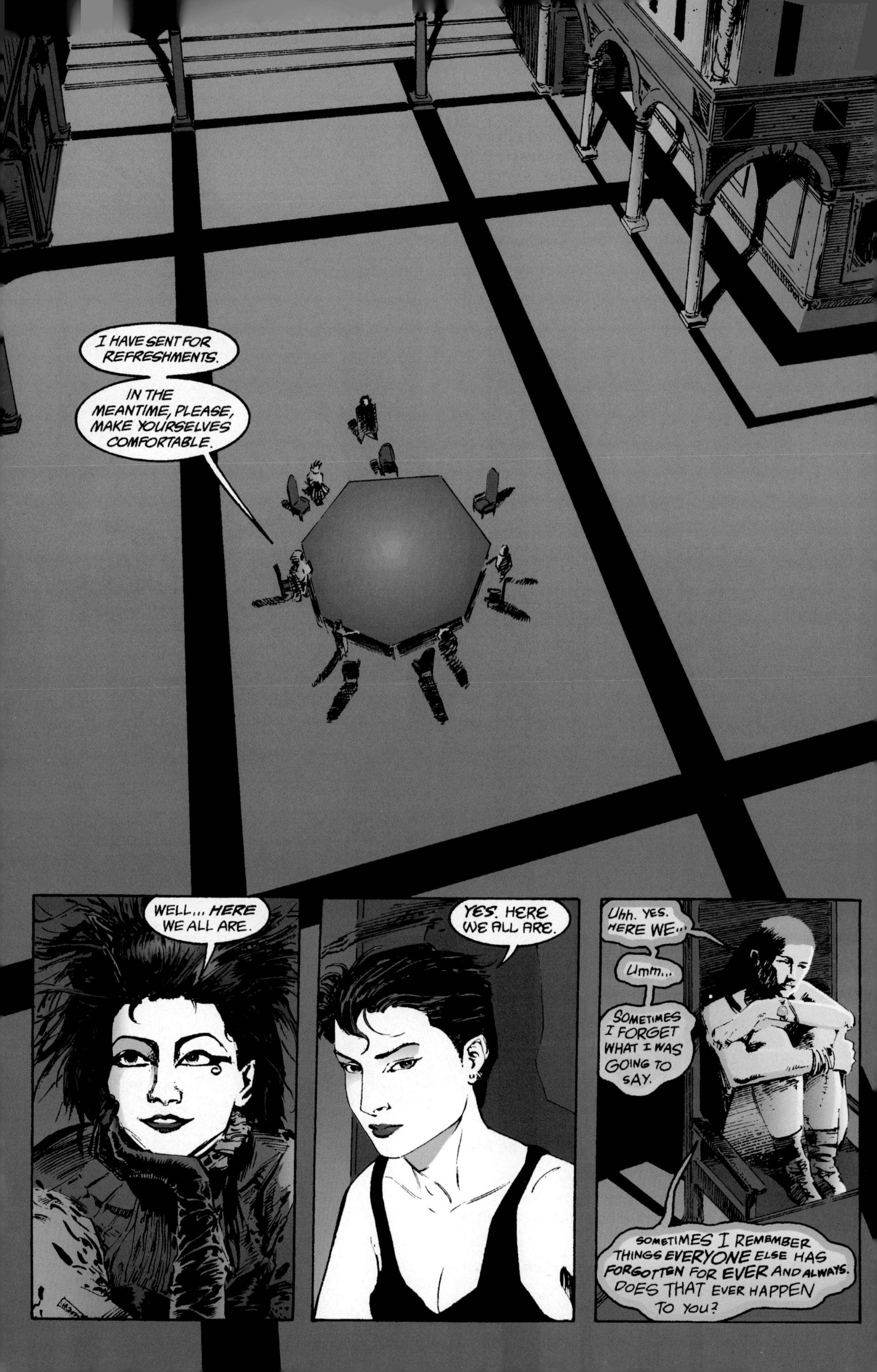
I HAVE SENT FOR REFRESHMENTS.
IN THE MEANTIME, PLEASE, MAKE YOURSELVES COMFORTABLE.
WELL... HERE WE ALL ARE.
YES. HERE WE ALL ARE.
Uhh. YES. HERE WE...
Umm...
SOMETIMES I FORGET WHAT I WAS GOING TO SAY.
SOMETIMES I REMEMBER THINGS EVERYONE ELSE HAS FORGOTTEN FOR EVER AND ALWAYS. DOES THAT EVER HAPPEN TO YOU?

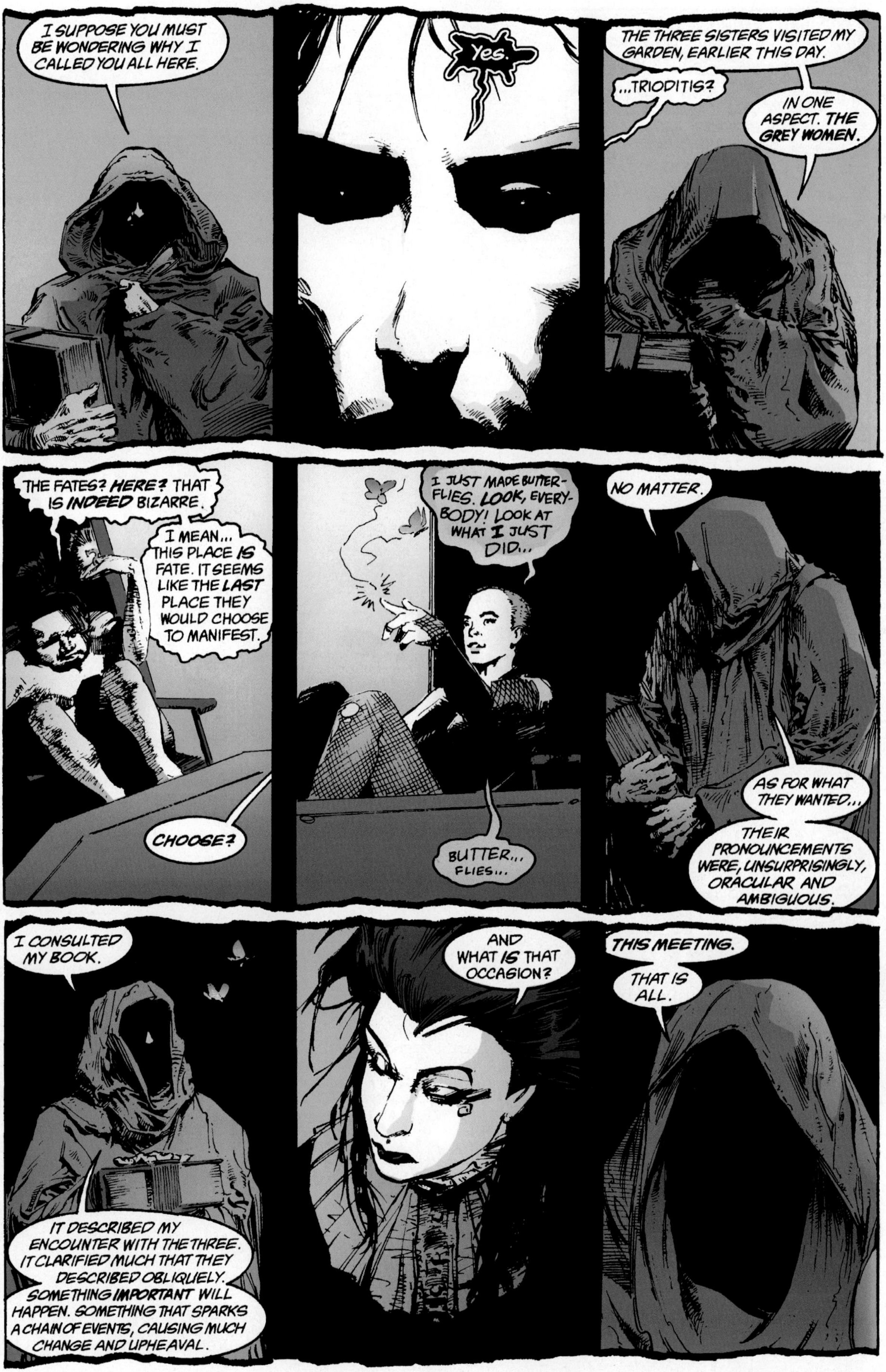
I SUPPOSE YOU MUST BE WONDERING WHY I CALLED YOU ALL HERE.
Yes.
THE THREE SISTERS VISITED MY GARDEN, EARLIER THIS DAY.
...TRIODITIS?
IN ONE ASPECT. THE GREY WOMEN.
THE FATES? HERE? THAT IS INDEED BIZARRE.
I MEAN... THIS PLACE IS FATE. IT SEEMS LIKE THE LAST PLACE THEY WOULD CHOOSE TO MANIFEST.
CHOOSE?
I JUST MADE BUTTER-FLIES. LOOK, EVERY-BODY! LOOK AT WHAT I JUST DID...
BUTTER... FLIES...
NO MATTER.
AS FOR WHAT THEY WANTED...
THEIR PRONOUNCEMENTS WERE, UNSURPRISINGLY, ORACULAR AND AMBIGUOUS.
I CONSULTED MY BOOK.
IT DESCRIBED MY ENCOUNTER WITH THE THREE. IT CLARIFIED MUCH THAT THEY DESCRIBED OBLIQUELY. SOMETHING IMPORTANT WILL HAPPEN. SOMETHING THAT SPARKS A CHAIN OF EVENTS, CAUSING MUCH CHANGE AND UPHEAVAL.
AND WHAT IS THAT OCCASION?
THIS MEETING.
THAT IS ALL.

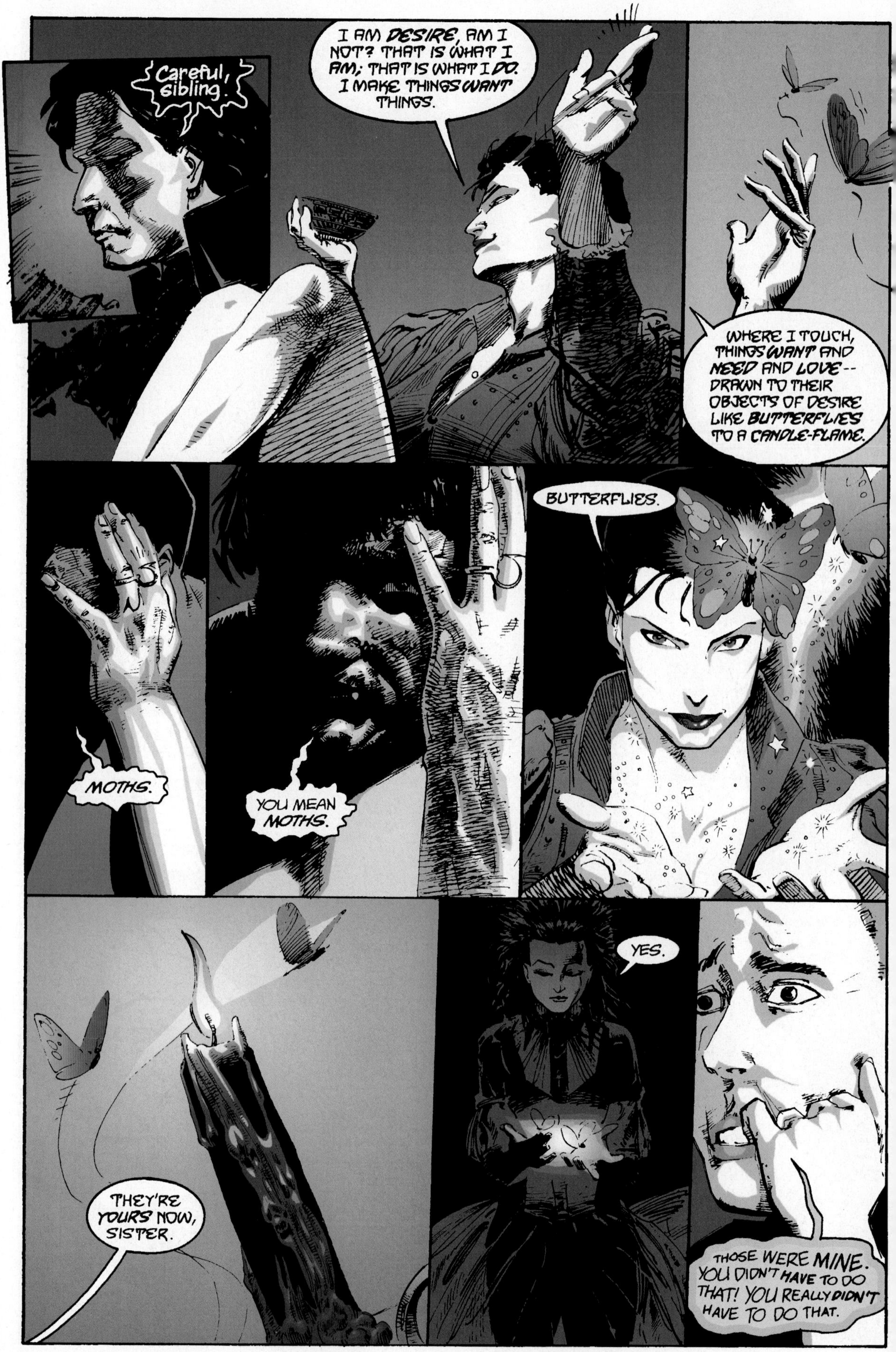
Careful, sibling!
I AM DESIRE, AM I NOT? THAT IS WHAT I AM; THAT IS WHAT I DO. I MAKE THINGS WANT THINGS.
WHERE I TOUCH, THINGS WANT AND NEED AND LOVE -- DRAWN TO THEIR OBJECTS OF DESIRE LIKE BUTTERFLIES TO A CANDLE-FLAME.
MOTHS.
YOU MEAN MOTHS.
BUTTERFLIES.
THEY'RE YOURS NOW, SISTER.
YES.
THOSE WERE MINE. YOU DIDN'T HAVE TO DO THAT! YOU REALLY DIDN'T HAVE TO DO THAT.

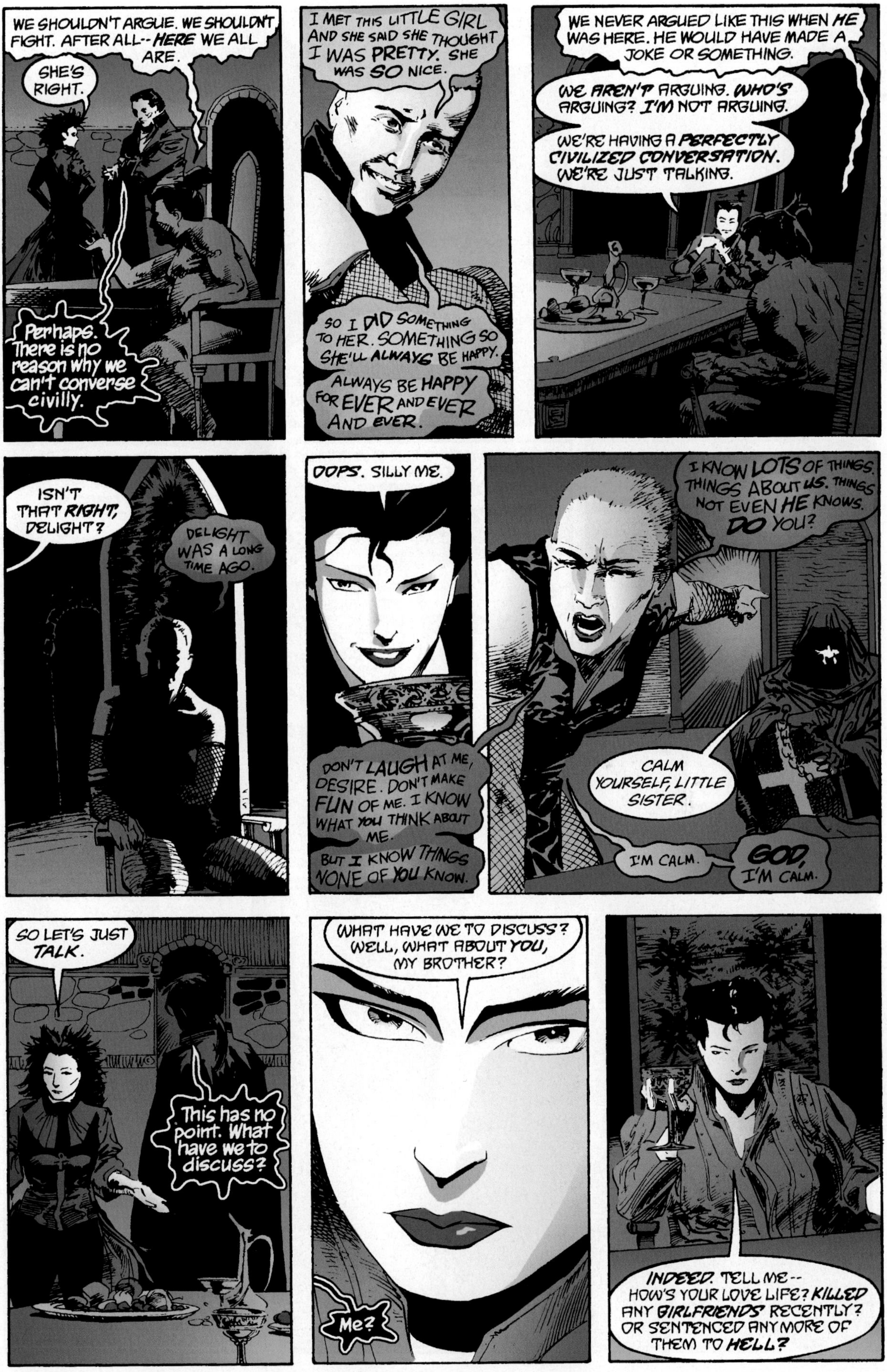
WE SHOULDN'T ARGUE. WE SHOULDN'T FIGHT. AFTER ALL-- HERE WE ALL ARE.
SHE'S RIGHT.
Perhaps. There is no reason why we can't converse civilly.
I MET THIS LITTLE GIRL AND SHE SAID SHE THOUGHT I WAS PRETTY. SHE WAS SO NICE.
SO I DID SOMETHING TO HER. SOMETHING SO SHE'LL ALWAYS BE HAPPY.
ALWAYS BE HAPPY FOR EVER AND EVER AND EVER.
WE NEVER ARGUED LIKE THIS WHEN HE WAS HERE. HE WOULD HAVE MADE A JOKE OR SOMETHING.
WE AREN'T ARGUING. WHO'S ARGUING? I'M NOT ARGUING.
WE'RE HAVING A PERFECTLY CIVILIZED CONVERSATION. WE'RE JUST TALKING.
ISN'T THAT RIGHT, DELIGHT?
DELIGHT WAS A LONG TIME AGO.
OOPS. SILLY ME.
DON'T LAUGH AT ME, DESIRE. DON'T MAKE FUN OF ME. I KNOW WHAT YOU THINK ABOUT ME.
BUT I KNOW THINGS NONE OF YOU KNOW.
I KNOW LOTS OF THINGS. THINGS ABOUT US. THINGS NOT EVEN HE KNOWS. DO YOU?
CALM YOURSELF, LITTLE SISTER.
I'M CALM.
GOD, I'M CALM.
SO LET'S JUST TALK.
This has no point. What have we to discuss?
WHAT HAVE WE TO DISCUSS? WELL, WHAT ABOUT YOU, MY BROTHER?
Me?
INDEED. TELL ME-- HOW'S YOUR LOVE LIFE? KILLED ANY GIRLFRIENDS RECENTLY? OR SENTENCED ANY MORE OF THEM TO HELL?

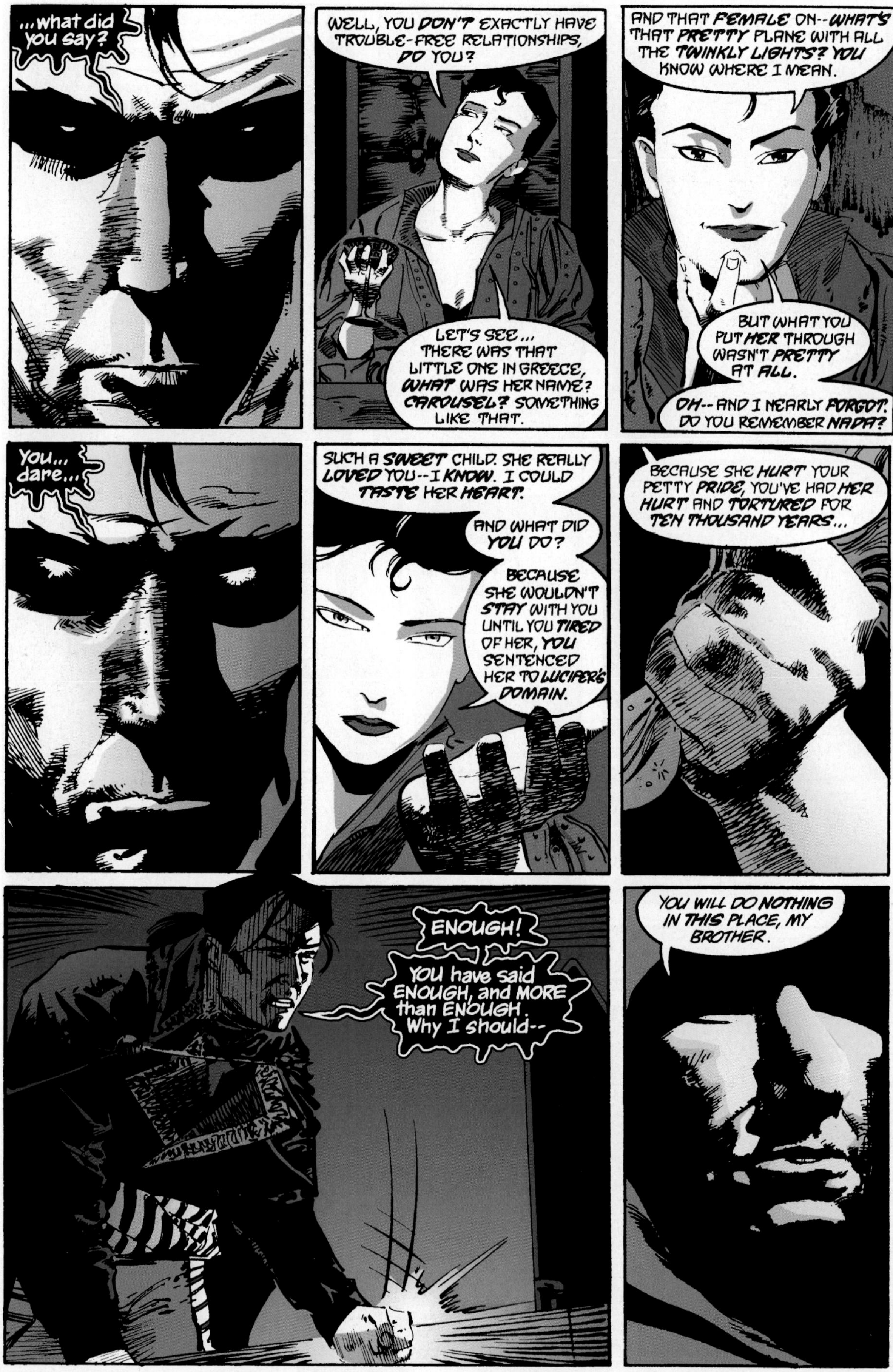

...what did you say?
WELL, YOU DON'T EXACTLY HAVE TROUBLE-FREE RELATIONSHIPS, DO YOU?
LET'S SEE... THERE WAS THAT LITTLE ONE IN GREECE, WHAT WAS HER NAME? CAROUSEL? SOMETHING LIKE THAT.
AND THAT FEMALE ON--WHAT'S THAT PRETTY PLANE WITH ALL THE TWINKLY LIGHTS? YOU KNOW WHERE I MEAN.
BUT WHAT YOU PUT HER THROUGH WASN'T PRETTY AT ALL.
OH--AND I NEARLY FORGOT. DO YOU REMEMBER NADA?
You... dare...
SUCH A SWEET CHILD. SHE REALLY LOVED YOU--I KNOW. I COULD TASTE HER HEART.
AND WHAT DID YOU DO?
BECAUSE SHE WOULDN'T STAY WITH YOU UNTIL YOU TIRED OF HER, YOU SENTENCED HER TO LUCIFER'S DOMAIN.
BECAUSE SHE HURT YOUR PETTY PRIDE, YOU'VE HAD HER HURT AND TORTURED FOR TEN THOUSAND YEARS...
ENOUGH!
YOU have said ENOUGH, and MORE than ENOUGH. Why I should--
YOU WILL DO NOTHING IN THIS PLACE, MY BROTHER.

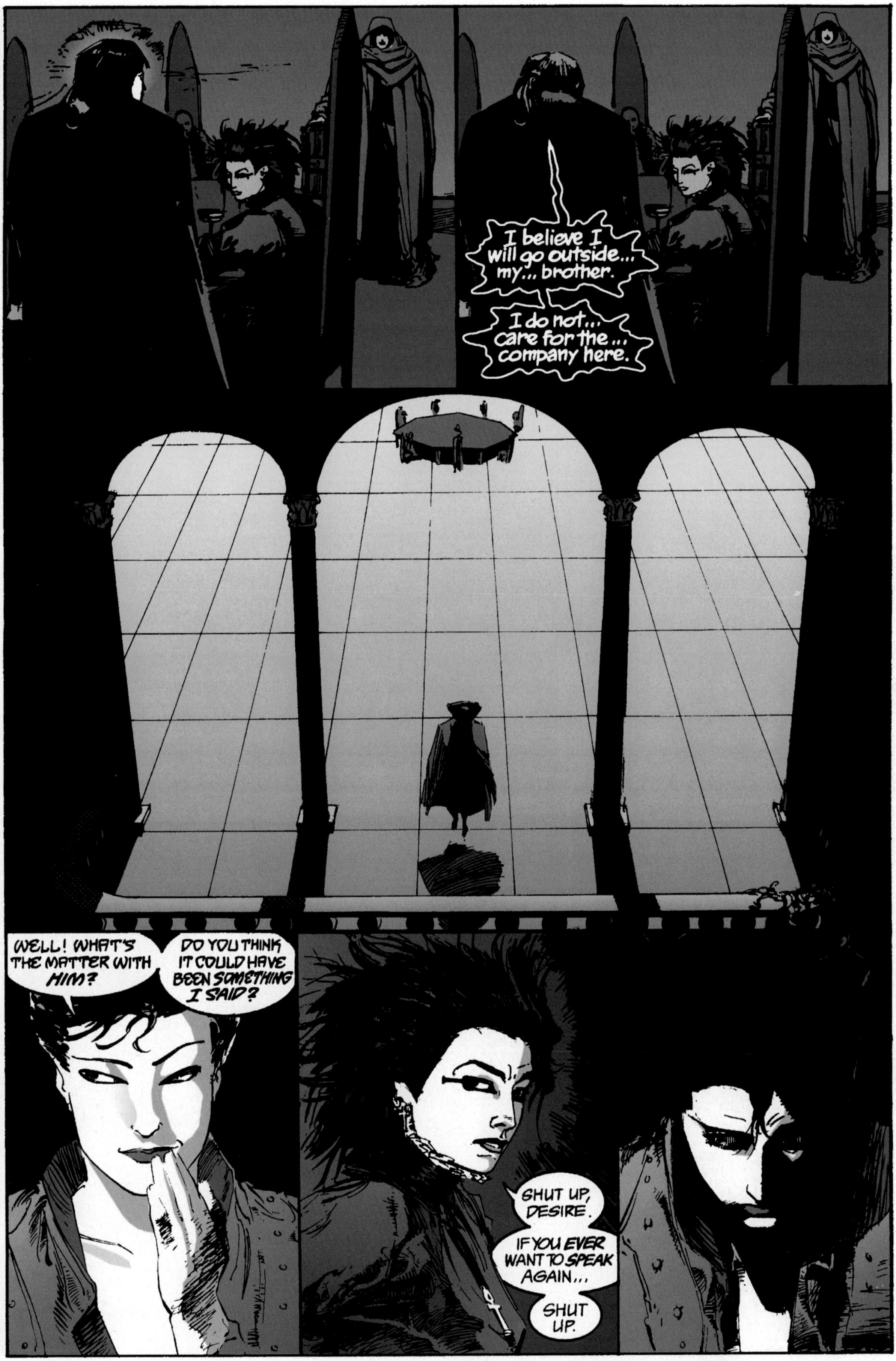

I believe I will go outside... my... brother.
I do not... care for the... company here.
WELL! WHAT'S THE MATTER WITH HIM?
DO YOU THINK IT COULD HAVE BEEN SOMETHING I SAID?
SHUT UP, DESIRE.
IF YOU EVER WANT TO SPEAK AGAIN...
SHUT UP.

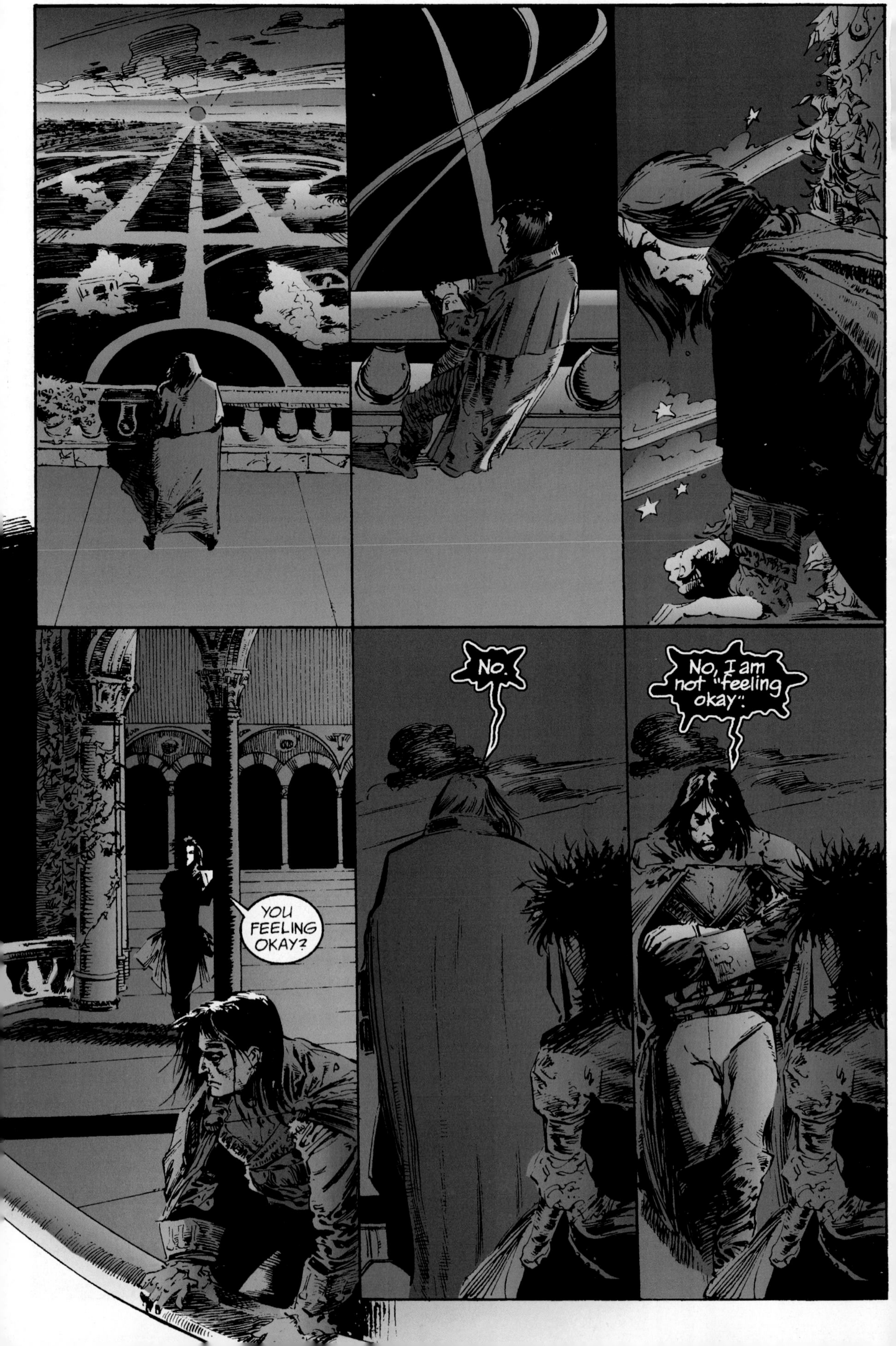
YOU FEELING OKAY?
No.
No, I am not "feeling okay".

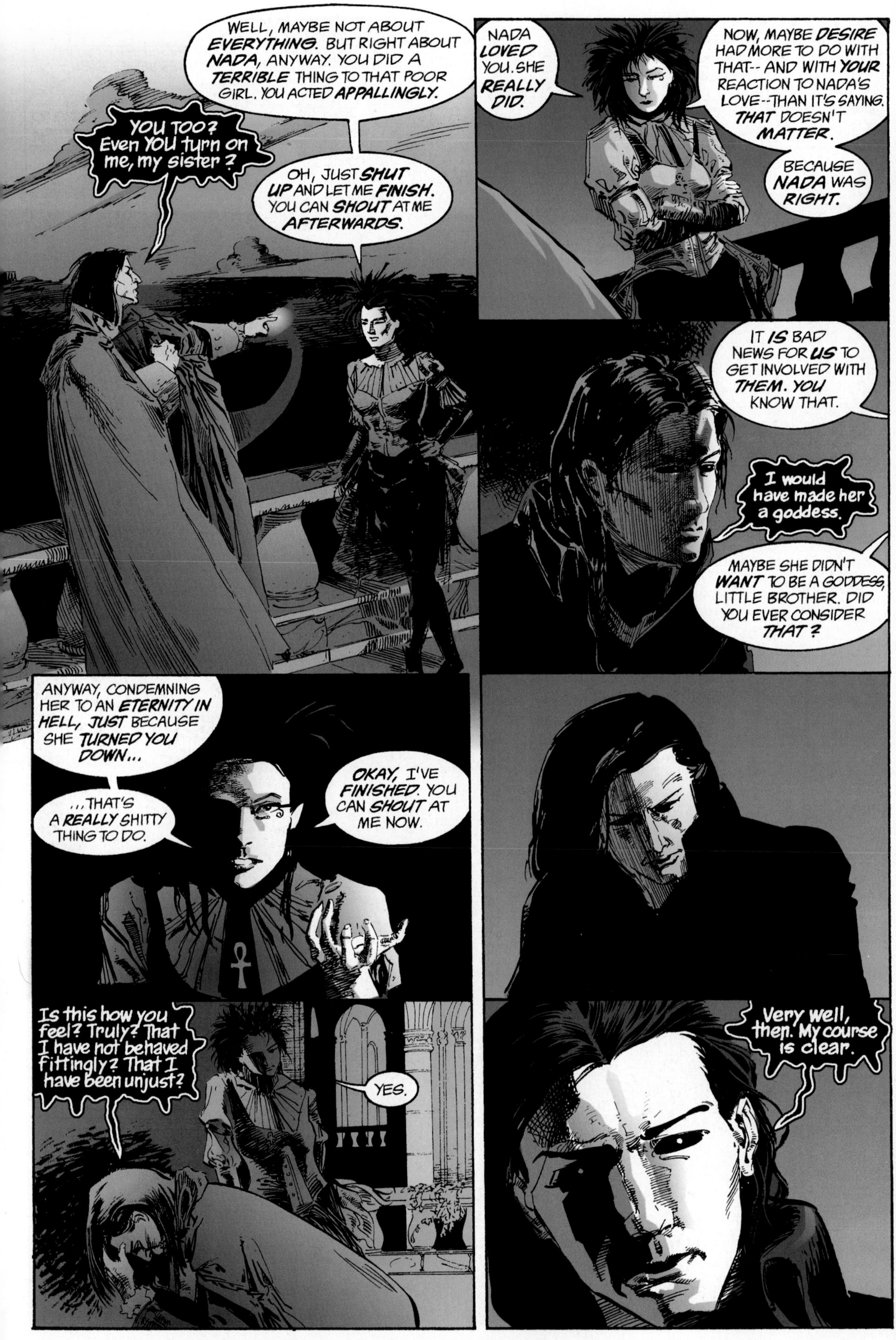
WELL, MAYBE NOT ABOUT EVERYTHING. BUT RIGHT ABOUT NADA, ANYWAY. YOU DID A TERRIBLE THING TO THAT POOR GIRL. YOU ACTED APPALLINGLY.
YOU TOO? Even YOU turn on me, my sister?
OH, JUST SHUT UP AND LET ME FINISH. YOU CAN SHOUT AT ME AFTERWARDS.
NADA LOVED YOU. SHE REALLY DID.
NOW, MAYBE DESIRE HAD MORE TO DO WITH THAT-- AND WITH YOUR REACTION TO NADA'S LOVE--THAN IT'S SAYING. THAT DOESN'T MATTER.
BECAUSE NADA WAS RIGHT.
IT IS BAD NEWS FOR US TO GET INVOLVED WITH THEM. YOU KNOW THAT.
I would have made her a goddess.
MAYBE SHE DIDN'T WANT TO BE A GODDESS, LITTLE BROTHER. DID YOU EVER CONSIDER THAT?
ANYWAY, CONDEMNING HER TO AN ETERNITY IN HELL, JUST BECAUSE SHE TURNED YOU DOWN...
...THAT'S A REALLY SHITTY THING TO DO.
OKAY, I'VE FINISHED. YOU CAN SHOUT AT ME NOW.
Is this how you feel? Truly? That I have not behaved fittingly? That I have been unjust?
YES.
Very well, then. My course is clear.

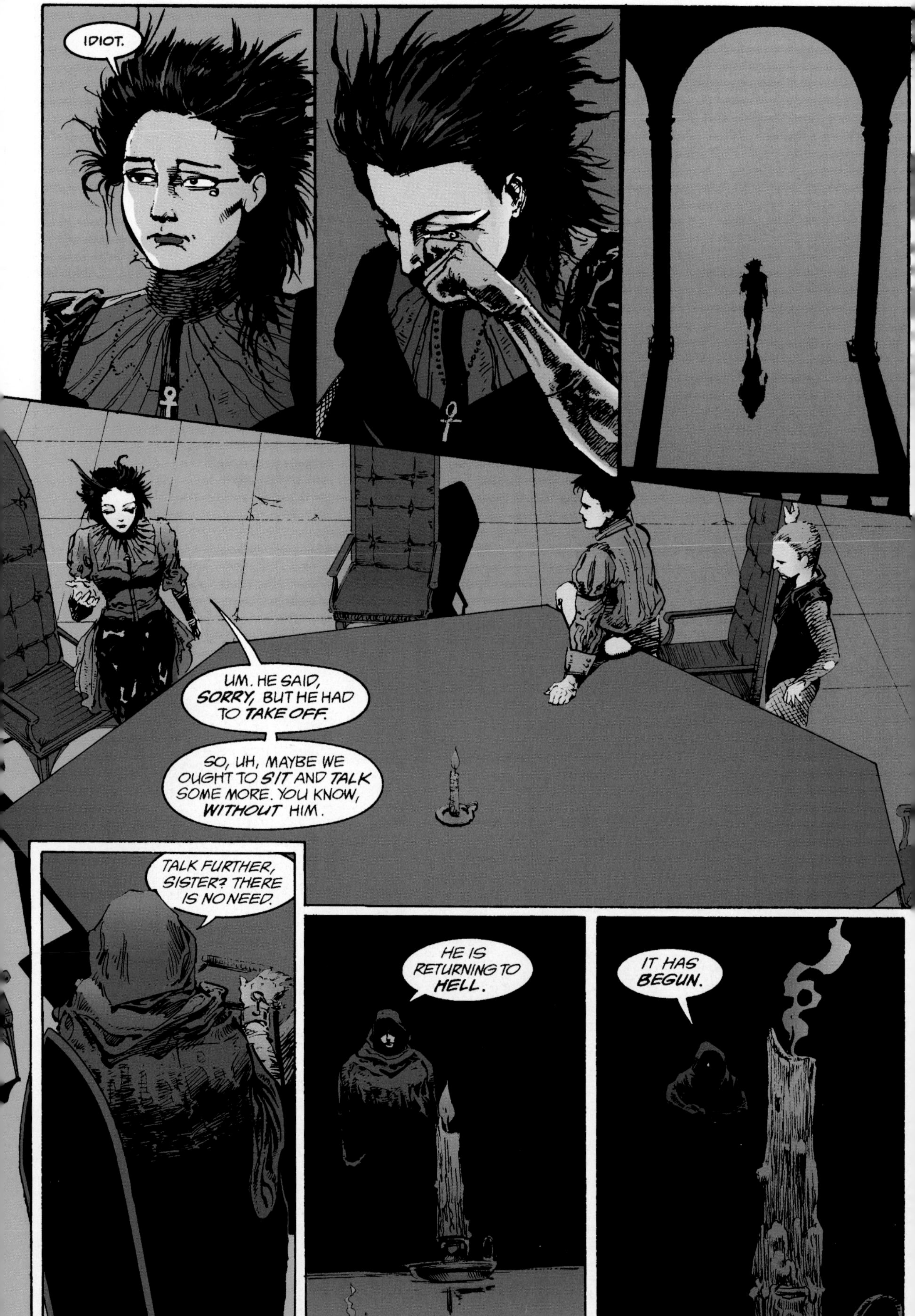
IDIOT.
UM. HE SAID, SORRY, BUT HE HAD TO TAKE OFF.
SO, UH, MAYBE WE OUGHT TO SIT AND TALK SOME MORE. YOU KNOW, WITHOUT HIM.
TALK FURTHER, SISTER? THERE IS NO NEED.
HE IS RETURNING TO HELL.
IT HAS BEGUN.

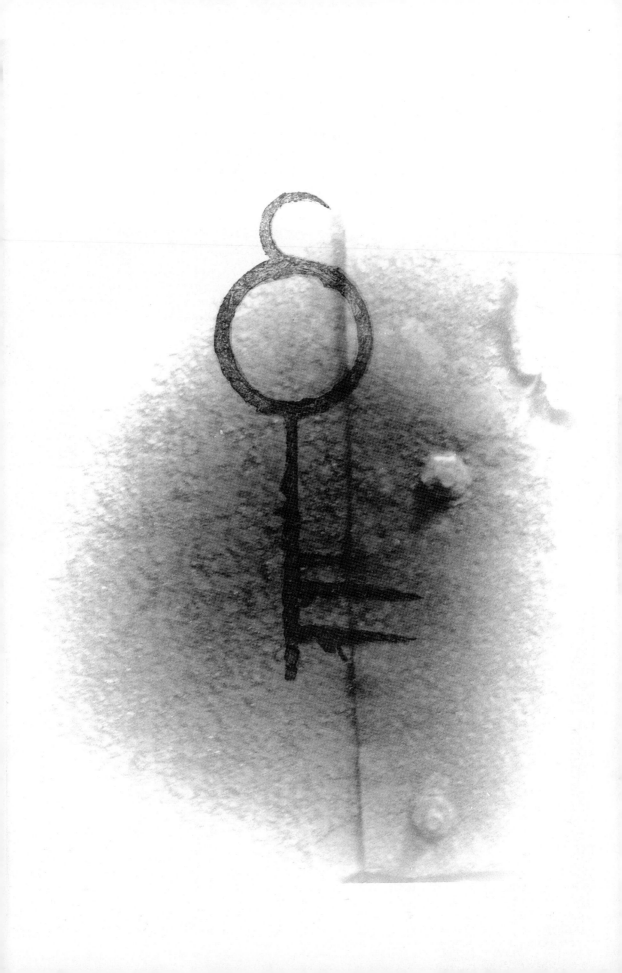

In which the Lord of Dreams makes preparations to visit the realms infernal; farewell's are said; a toast is drunk; and in Hell the Adversary makes certain preparations of his own.

EPISODE 1

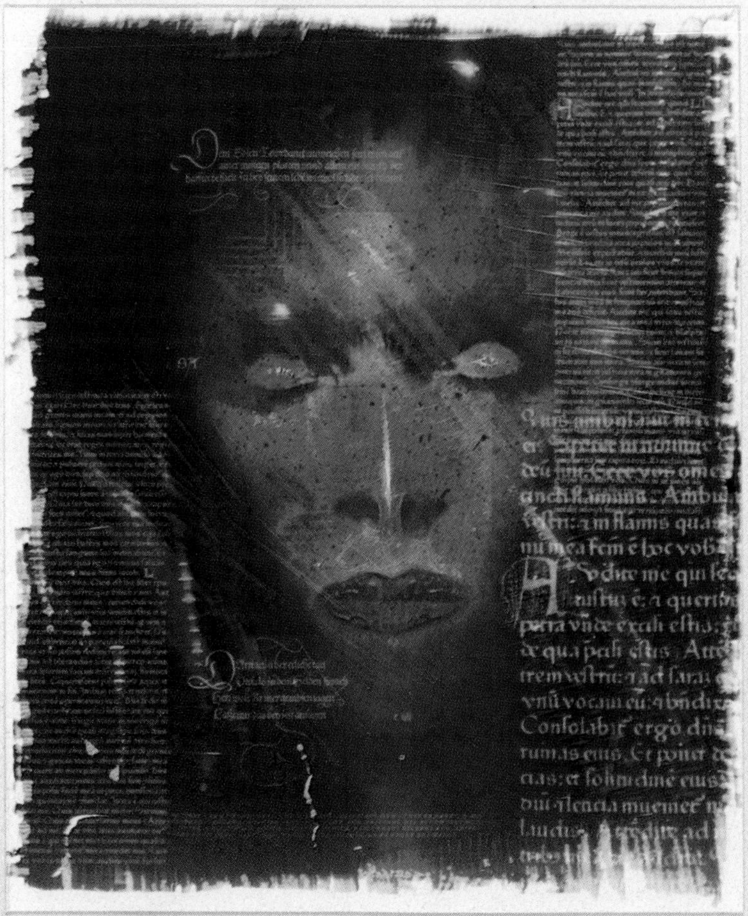

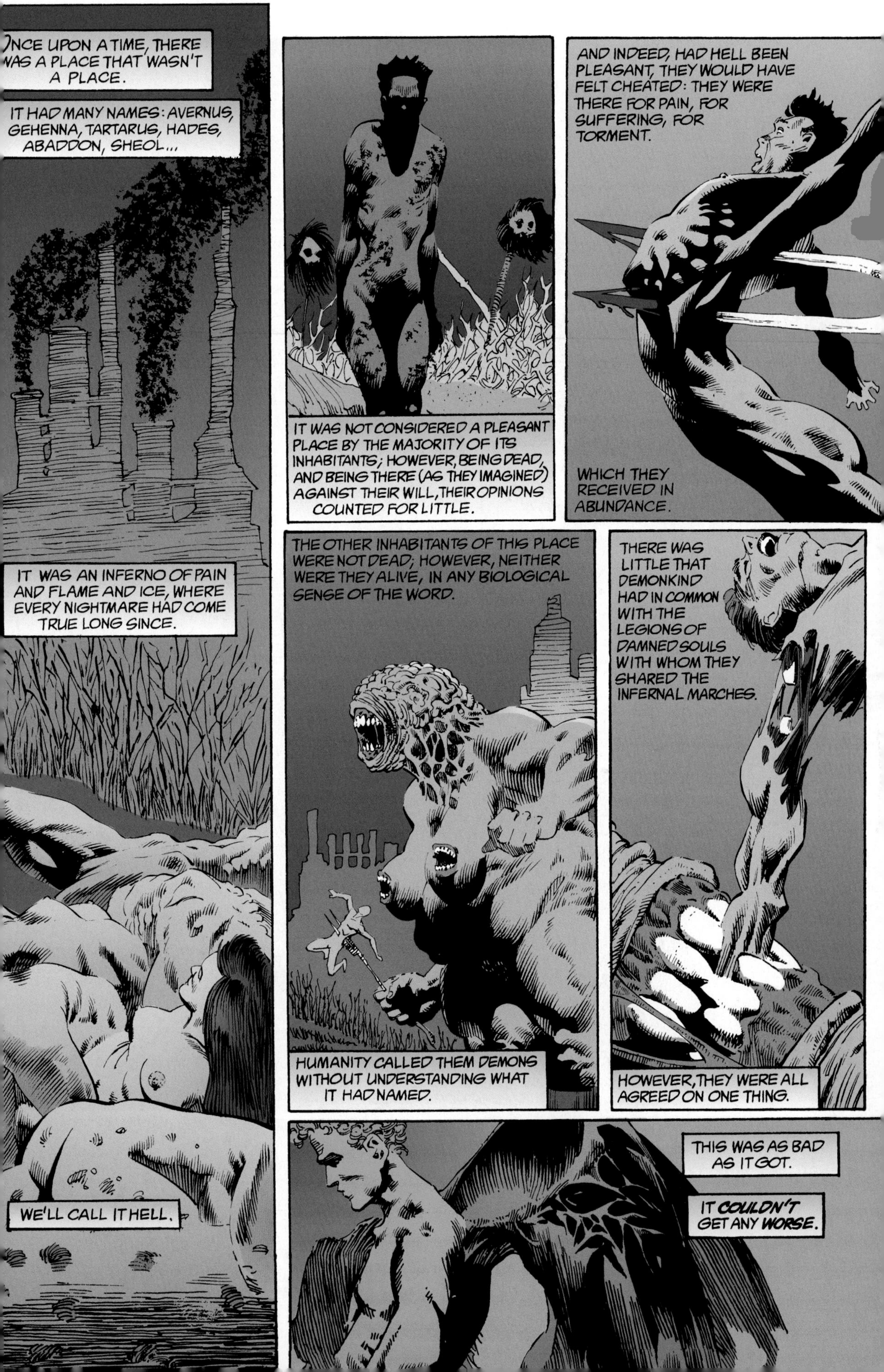
ONCE UPON A TIME, THERE WAS A PLACE THAT WASN'T A PLACE.
IT HAD MANY NAMES: AVERNUS, GEHENNA, TARTARUS, HADES, ABADDON, SHEOL...
IT WAS AN INFERNO OF PAIN AND FLAME AND ICE, WHERE EVERY NIGHTMARE HAD COME TRUE LONG SINCE.
WE'LL CALL IT HELL.
IT WAS NOT CONSIDERED A PLEASANT PLACE BY THE MAJORITY OF ITS INHABITANTS; HOWEVER, BEING DEAD, AND BEING THERE (AS THEY IMAGINED) AGAINST THEIR WILL, THEIR OPINIONS COUNTED FOR LITTLE.
AND INDEED, HAD HELL BEEN PLEASANT, THEY WOULD HAVE FELT CHEATED: THEY WERE THERE FOR PAIN, FOR SUFFERING, FOR TORMENT.
WHICH THEY RECEIVED IN ABUNDANCE.
THE OTHER INHABITANTS OF THIS PLACE WERE NOT DEAD; HOWEVER, NEITHER WERE THEY ALIVE, IN ANY BIOLOGICAL SENSE OF THE WORD.
HUMANITY CALLED THEM DEMONS WITHOUT UNDERSTANDING WHAT IT HAD NAMED.
THERE WAS LITTLE THAT DEMONKIND HAD IN COMMON WITH THE LEGIONS OF DAMNED SOULS WITH WHOM THEY SHARED THE INFERNAL MARCHES.
HOWEVER, THEY WERE ALL AGREED ON ONE THING.
THIS WAS AS BAD AS IT GOT.
IT COULDN'T GET ANY WORSE.

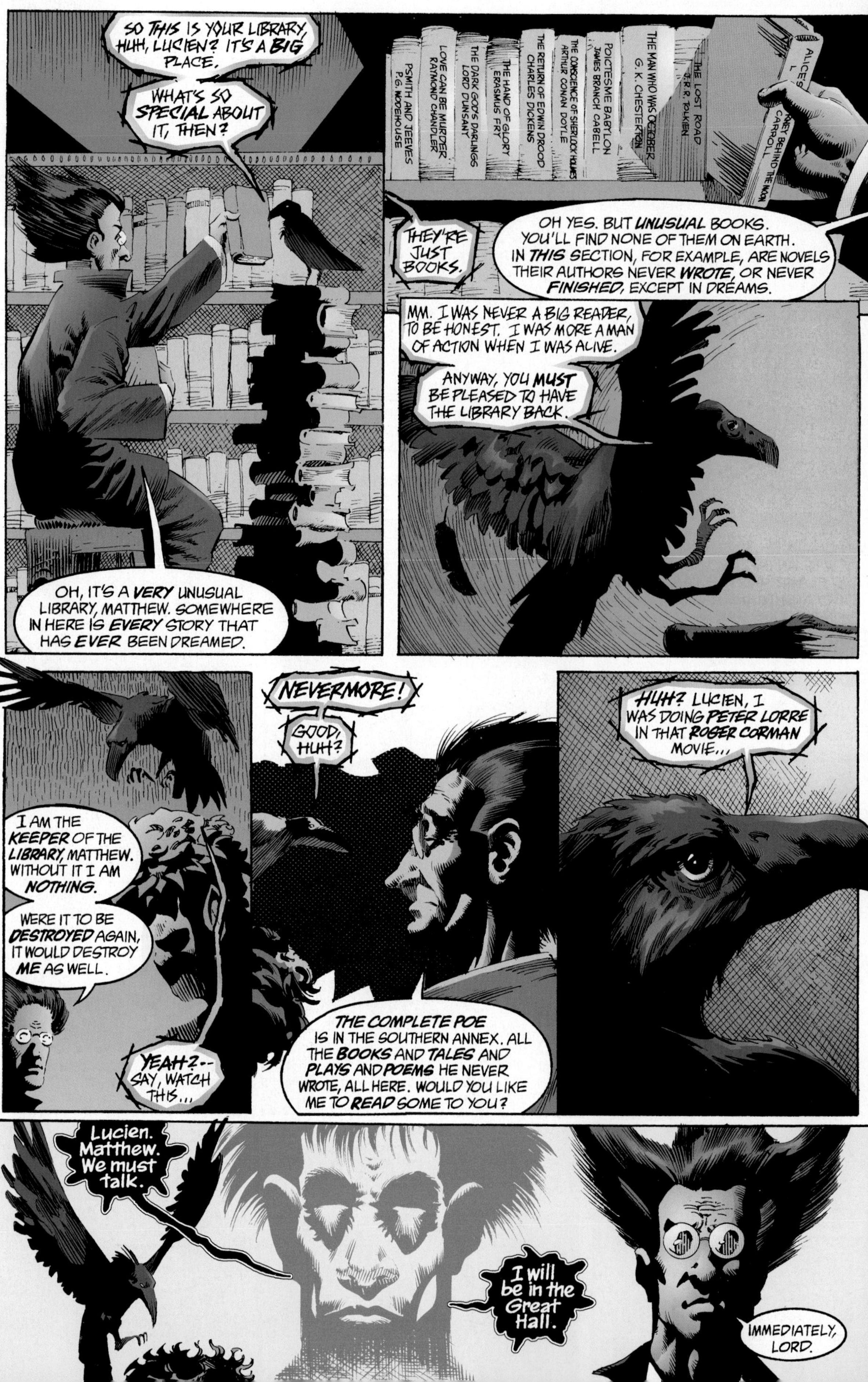
SO THIS IS YOUR LIBRARY, HUH, LUCIEN? IT'S A BIG PLACE.
WHAT'S SO SPECIAL ABOUT IT, THEN?
OH, IT'S A VERY UNUSUAL LIBRARY, MATTHEW. SOMEWHERE IN HERE IS EVERY STORY THAT HAS EVER BEEN DREAMED.
THE LOST ROAD J.R.R. TOLKIEN
THE MAN WHO WAS OCTOBER G.K. CHESTERTON
POICTESME BABYLON JAMES BRANCH CABELL
THE CONSCIENCE OF SHERLOCK HOLMES ARTHUR CONAN DOYLE
THE RETURN OF EDWIN DROOD CHARLES DICKENS
THE HAND OF GLORY ERASMUS FRY
THE DARK GOD'S DARLINGS LORD DUNSANY
LOVE CAN BE MURDER RAYMOND CHANDLER
PSMITH AND JEEVES P.G. WODEHOUSE
THEY'RE JUST BOOKS.
OH YES. BUT UNUSUAL BOOKS. YOU'LL FIND NONE OF THEM ON EARTH. IN THIS SECTION, FOR EXAMPLE, ARE NOVELS THEIR AUTHORS NEVER WROTE, OR NEVER FINISHED, EXCEPT IN DREAMS.
MM. I WAS NEVER A BIG READER, TO BE HONEST. I WAS MORE A MAN OF ACTION WHEN I WAS ALIVE.
ANYWAY, YOU MUST BE PLEASED TO HAVE THE LIBRARY BACK.
I AM THE KEEPER OF THE LIBRARY, MATTHEW. WITHOUT IT I AM NOTHING.
WERE IT TO BE DESTROYED AGAIN, IT WOULD DESTROY ME AS WELL.
YEAH?-- SAY, WATCH THIS...
NEVERMORE!
GOOD, HUH?
THE COMPLETE POE IS IN THE SOUTHERN ANNEX. ALL THE BOOKS AND TALES AND PLAYS AND POEMS HE NEVER WROTE, ALL HERE. WOULD YOU LIKE ME TO READ SOME TO YOU?
HUH? LUCIEN, I WAS DOING PETER LORRE IN THAT ROGER CORMAN MOVIE...
Lucien. Matthew. We must talk.
I will be in the Great Hall.
IMMEDIATELY, LORD.

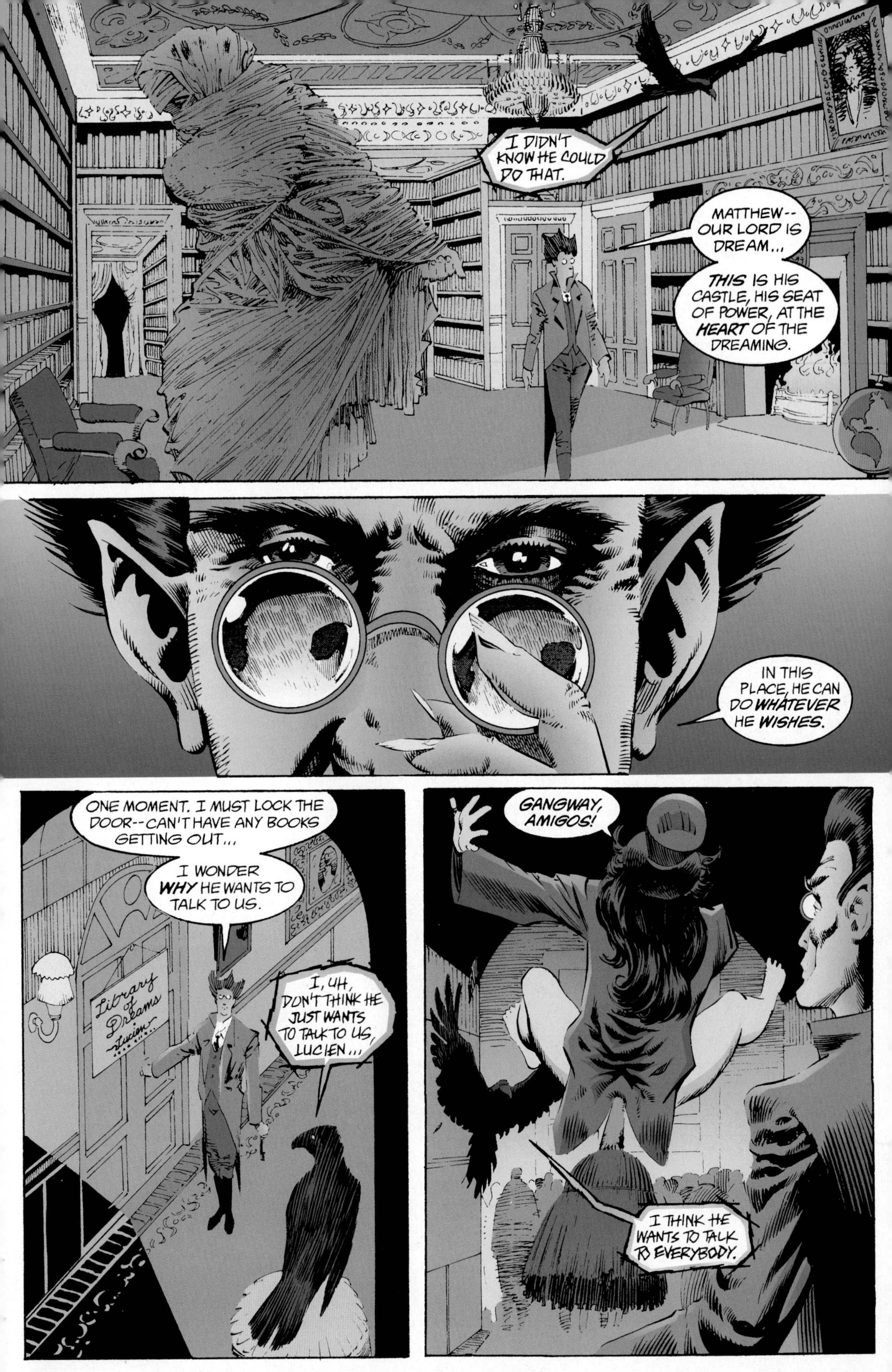
I DIDN'T KNOW HE COULD DO THAT.
MATTHEW-- OUR LORD IS DREAM...,
THIS IS HIS CASTLE, HIS SEAT OF POWER, AT THE HEART OF THE DREAMING.
IN THIS PLACE, HE CAN DO WHATEVER HE WISHES.
ONE MOMENT. I MUST LOCK THE DOOR--CAN'T HAVE ANY BOOKS GETTING OUT...
I WONDER WHY HE WANTS TO TALK TO US.
Library of Dreams
Lucien
I, UH, DON'T THINK HE JUST WANTS TO TALK TO US, LUCIEN...
GANGWAY, AMIGOS!
I THINK HE WANTS TO TALK TO EVERYBODY.

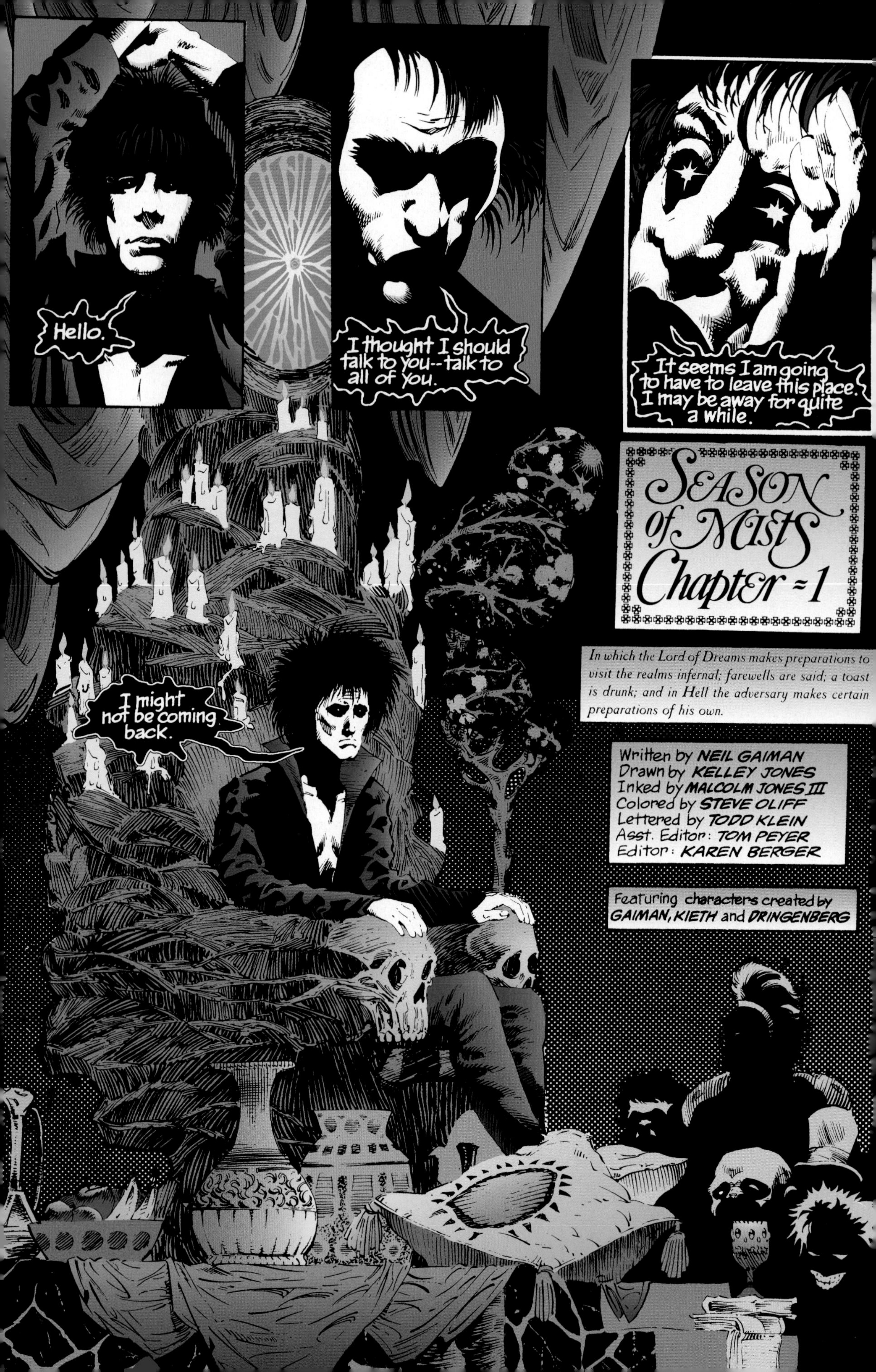
Hello.
I thought I should talk to you--talk to all of you.
It seems I am going to have to leave this place. I may be away for quite a while.
SEASON of MISTS Chapter =1
In which the Lord of Dreams makes preparations to visit the realms infernal; farewells are said; a toast is drunk; and in Hell the adversary makes certain preparations of his own.
I might not be coming back.
Written by NEIL GAIMAN
Drawn by KELLEY JONES
Inked by MALCOLM JONES III
Colored by STEVE OLIFF
Lettered by TODD KLEIN
Asst. Editor: TOM PEYER
Editor: KAREN BERGER
Featuring characters created by GAIMAN, KIETH and DRINGENBERG

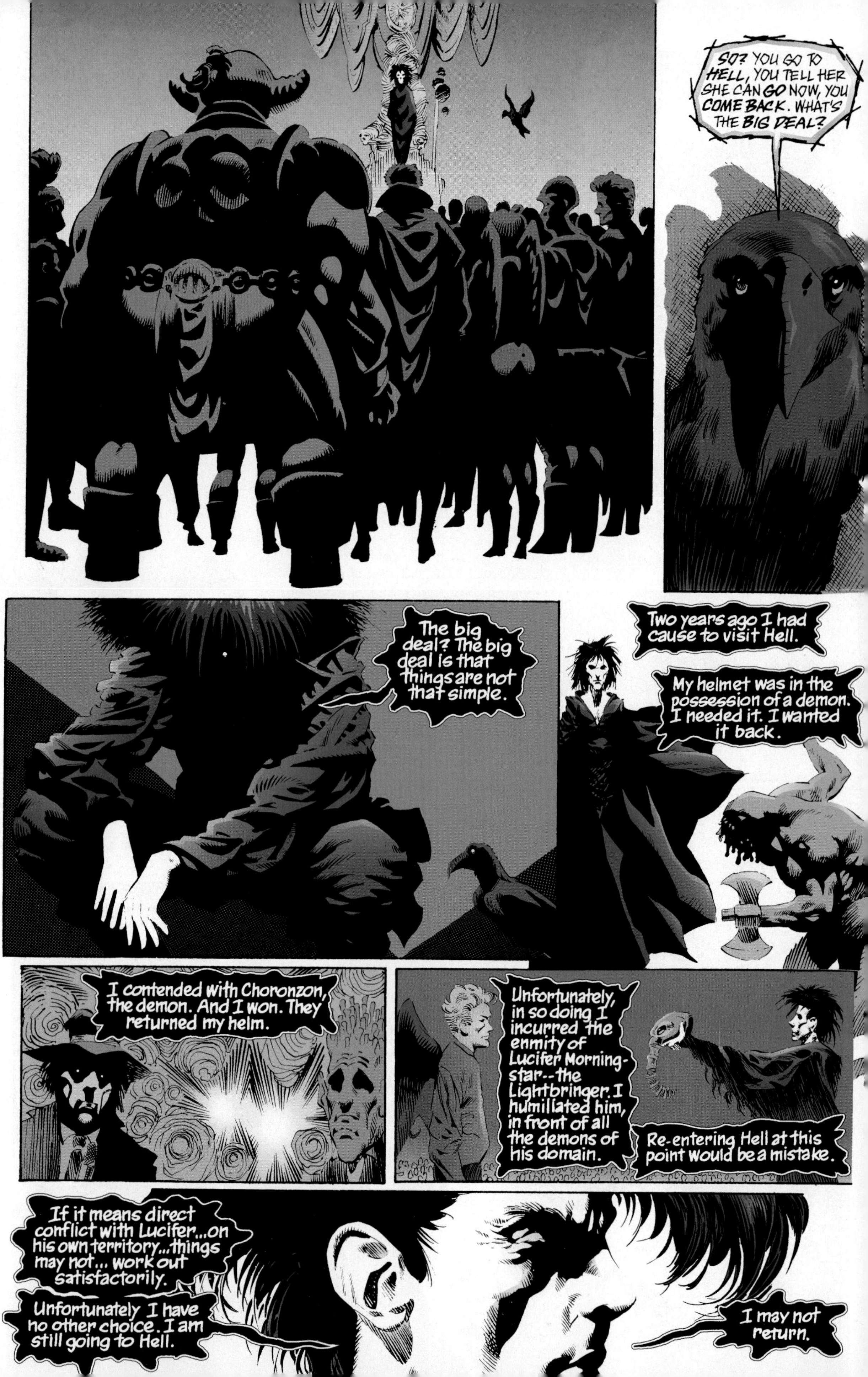
SO? YOU GO TO HELL, YOU TELL HER SHE CAN GO NOW, YOU COME BACK. WHAT'S THE BIG DEAL?
The big deal? The big deal is that things are not that simple.
Two years ago I had cause to visit Hell.
My helmet was in the possession of a demon. I needed it. I wanted it back.
I contended with Choronzon, the demon. And I won. They returned my helm.
Unfortunately, in so doing I incurred the enmity of Lucifer Morningstar--the Lightbringer. I humiliated him, in front of all the demons of his domain.
Re-entering Hell at this point would be a mistake.
If it means direct conflict with Lucifer...on his own territory...things may not... work out satisfactorily.
Unfortunately I have no other choice. I am still going to Hell.
I may not return.

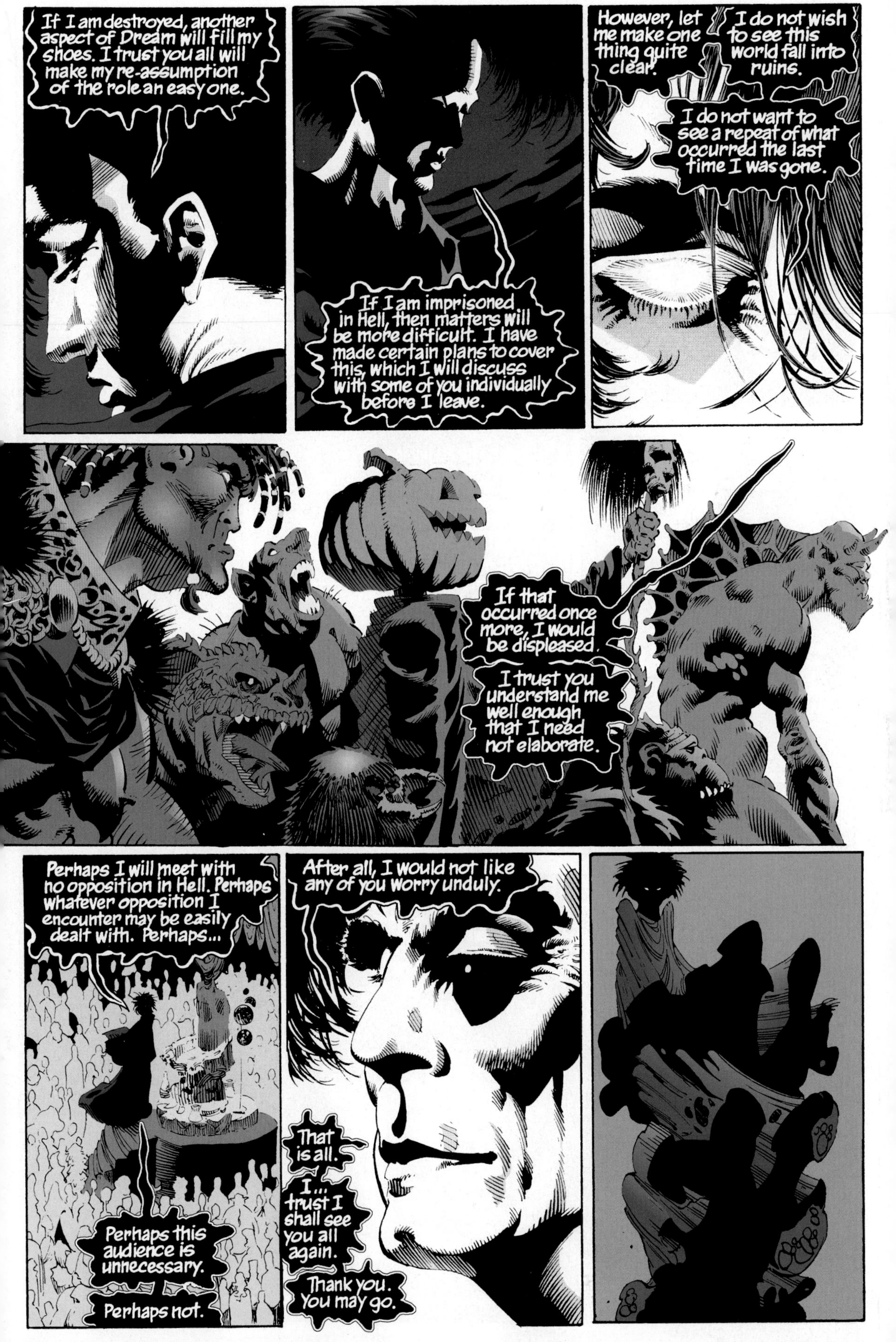

If I am destroyed, another aspect of Dream will fill my shoes. I trust you all will make my re-assumption of the role an easy one.
If I am imprisoned in Hell, then matters will be more difficult. I have made certain plans to cover this, which I will discuss with some of you individually before I leave.
However, let me make one thing quite clear.
I do not wish to see this world fall into ruins.
I do not want to see a repeat of what occurred the last time I was gone.
If that occurred once more, I would be displeased.
I trust you understand me well enough that I need not elaborate.
Perhaps I will meet with no opposition in Hell. Perhaps whatever opposition I encounter may be easily dealt with. Perhaps...
Perhaps this audience is unnecessary.
Perhaps not.
After all, I would not like any of you worry unduly.
That is all.
I... trust I shall see you all again.
Thank you. You may go.

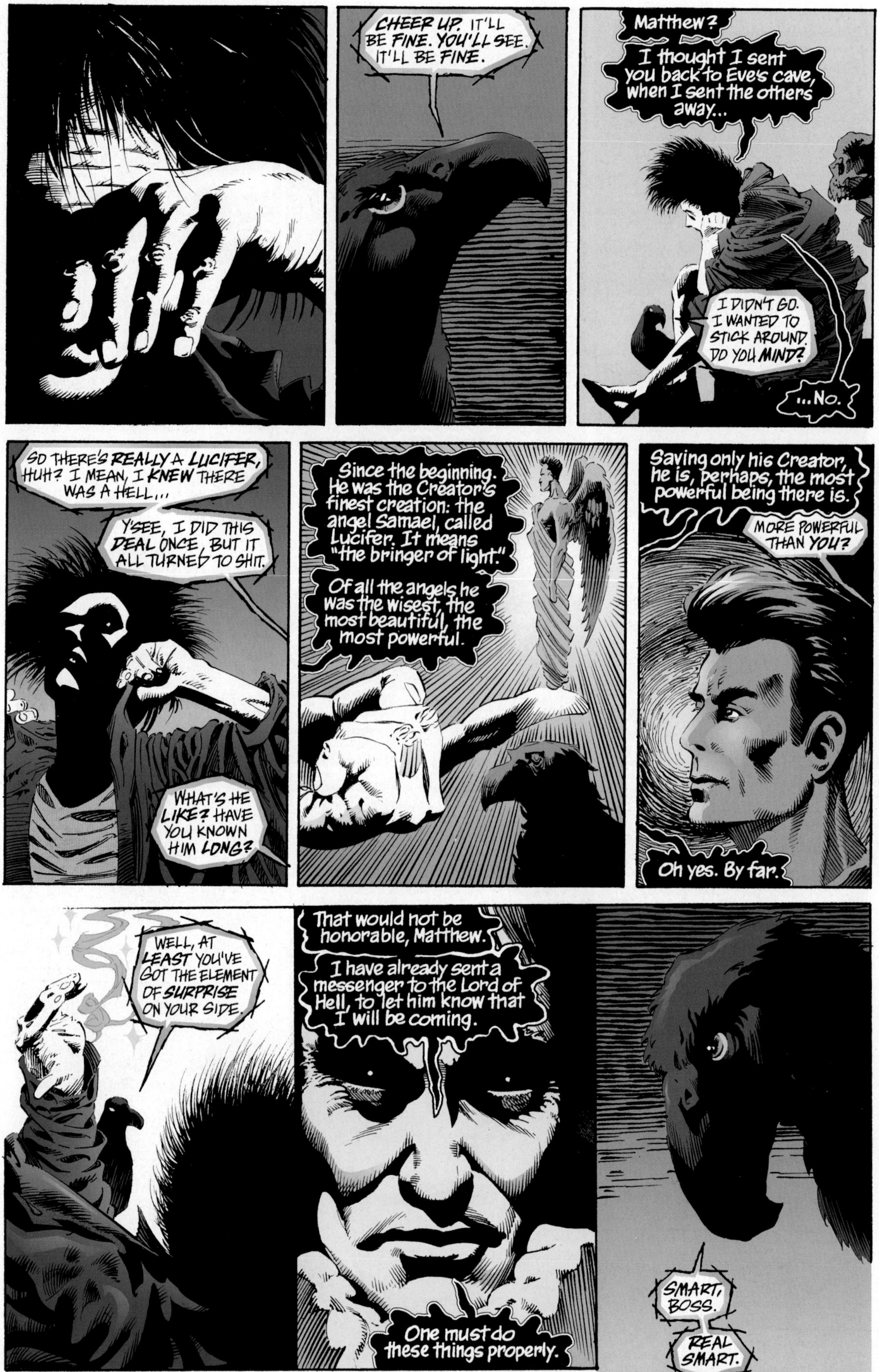

CHEER UP. IT'LL BE FINE. YOU'LL SEE. IT'LL BE FINE.
Matthew?
I thought I sent you back to Eve's cave, when I sent the others away...
I DIDN'T GO. I WANTED TO STICK AROUND. DO YOU MIND?
...No.
SO THERE'S REALLY A LUCIFER, HUH? I MEAN, I KNEW THERE WAS A HELL...
Y'SEE, I DID THIS DEAL ONCE, BUT IT ALL TURNED TO SHIT.
WHAT'S HE LIKE? HAVE YOU KNOWN HIM LONG?
Since the beginning. He was the Creator's finest creation: the angel Samael, called Lucifer. It means "the bringer of light."
Of all the angels he was the wisest, the most beautiful, the most powerful.
Saving only his Creator, he is, perhaps, the most powerful being there is.
MORE POWERFUL THAN YOU?
Oh yes. By far.
WELL, AT LEAST YOU'VE GOT THE ELEMENT OF SURPRISE ON YOUR SIDE.
That would not be honorable, Matthew.
I have already sent a messenger to the Lord of Hell, to let him know that I will be coming.
One must do these things properly.
SMART, BOSS.
REAL SMART.

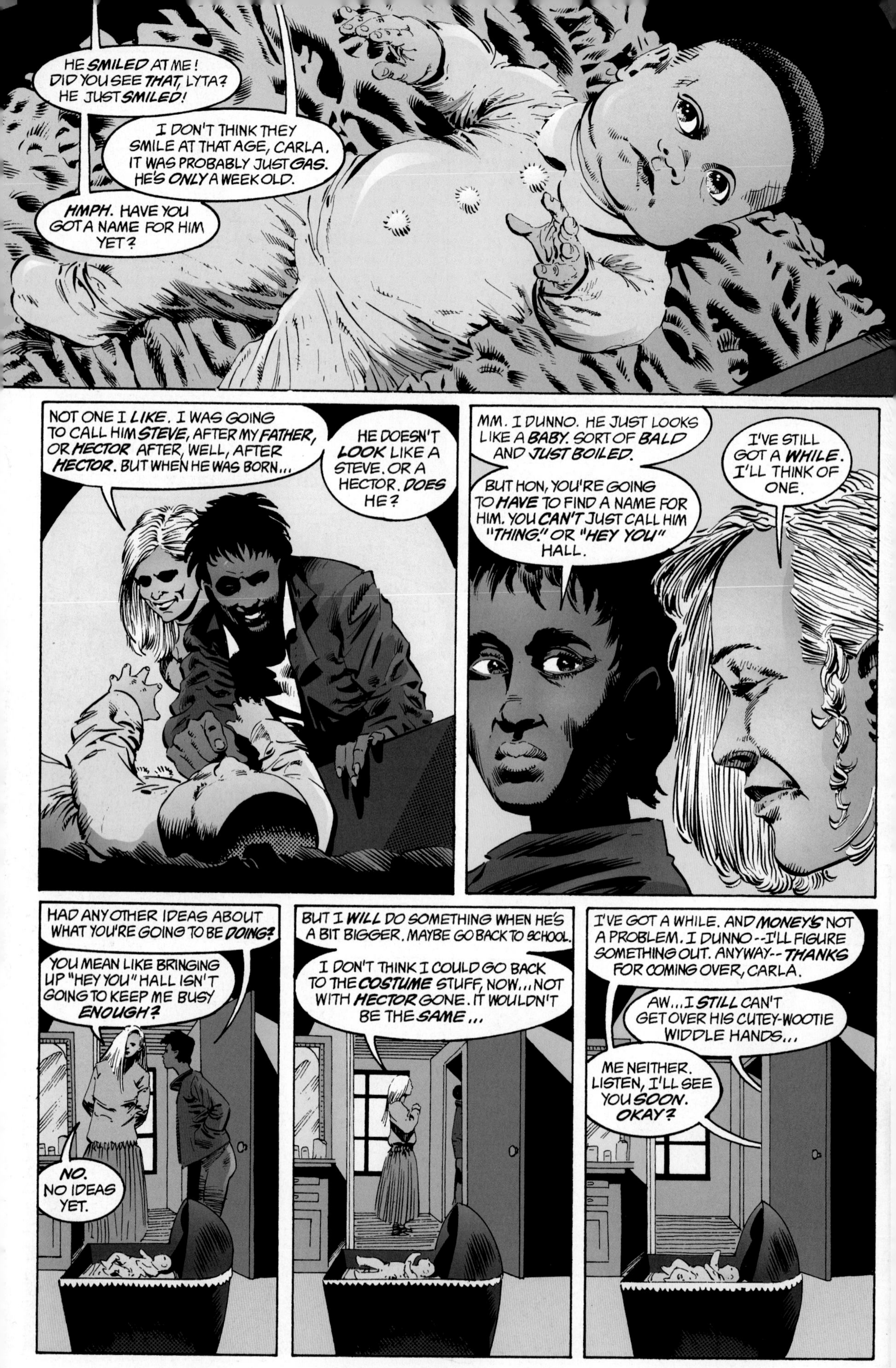
HE SMILED AT ME! DID YOU SEE THAT, LYTA? HE JUST SMILED!
I DON'T THINK THEY SMILE AT THAT AGE, CARLA. IT WAS PROBABLY JUST GAS. HE'S ONLY A WEEK OLD.
HMPH. HAVE YOU GOT A NAME FOR HIM YET?
NOT ONE I LIKE. I WAS GOING TO CALL HIM STEVE, AFTER MY FATHER, OR HECTOR AFTER, WELL, AFTER HECTOR. BUT WHEN HE WAS BORN...
HE DOESN'T LOOK LIKE A STEVE. OR A HECTOR. DOES HE?
MM. I DUNNO. HE JUST LOOKS LIKE A BABY. SORT OF BALD AND JUST BOILED.
BUT HON, YOU'RE GOING TO HAVE TO FIND A NAME FOR HIM. YOU CAN'T JUST CALL HIM "THING." OR "HEY YOU" HALL.
I'VE STILL GOT A WHILE. I'LL THINK OF ONE.
HAD ANY OTHER IDEAS ABOUT WHAT YOU'RE GOING TO BE DOING?
YOU MEAN LIKE BRINGING UP "HEY YOU" HALL ISN'T GOING TO KEEP ME BUSY ENOUGH?
NO. NO IDEAS YET.
BUT I WILL DO SOMETHING WHEN HE'S A BIT BIGGER. MAYBE GO BACK TO SCHOOL.
I DON'T THINK I COULD GO BACK TO THE COSTUME STUFF, NOW... NOT WITH HECTOR GONE. IT WOULDN'T BE THE SAME...
I'VE GOT A WHILE. AND MONEY'S NOT A PROBLEM. I DUNNO--I'LL FIGURE SOMETHING OUT. ANYWAY--THANKS FOR COMING OVER, CARLA.
AW... I STILL CAN'T GET OVER HIS CUTEY-WOOTIE WIDDLE HANDS...
ME NEITHER. LISTEN, I'LL SEE YOU SOON. OKAY?

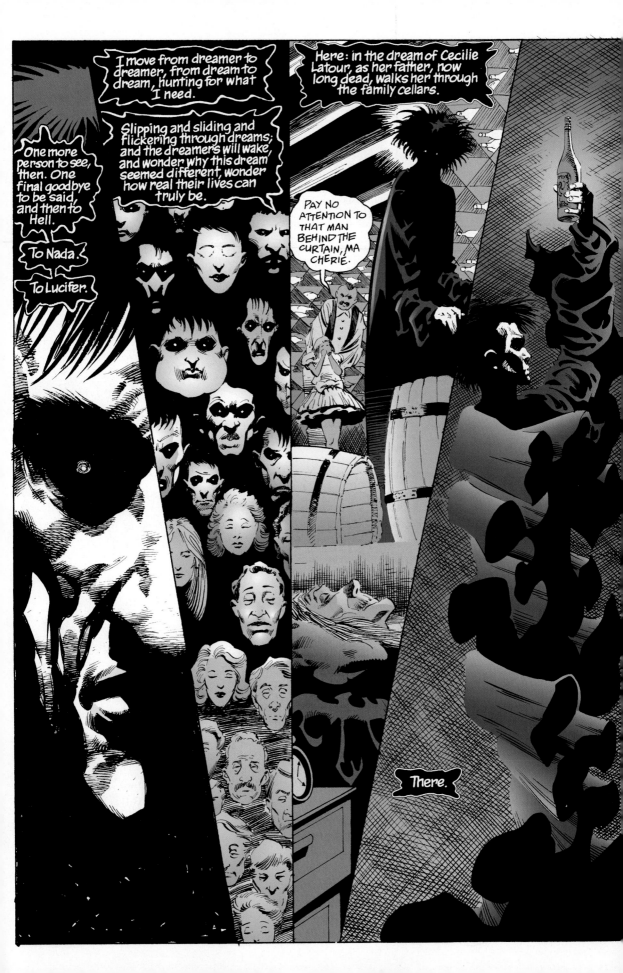

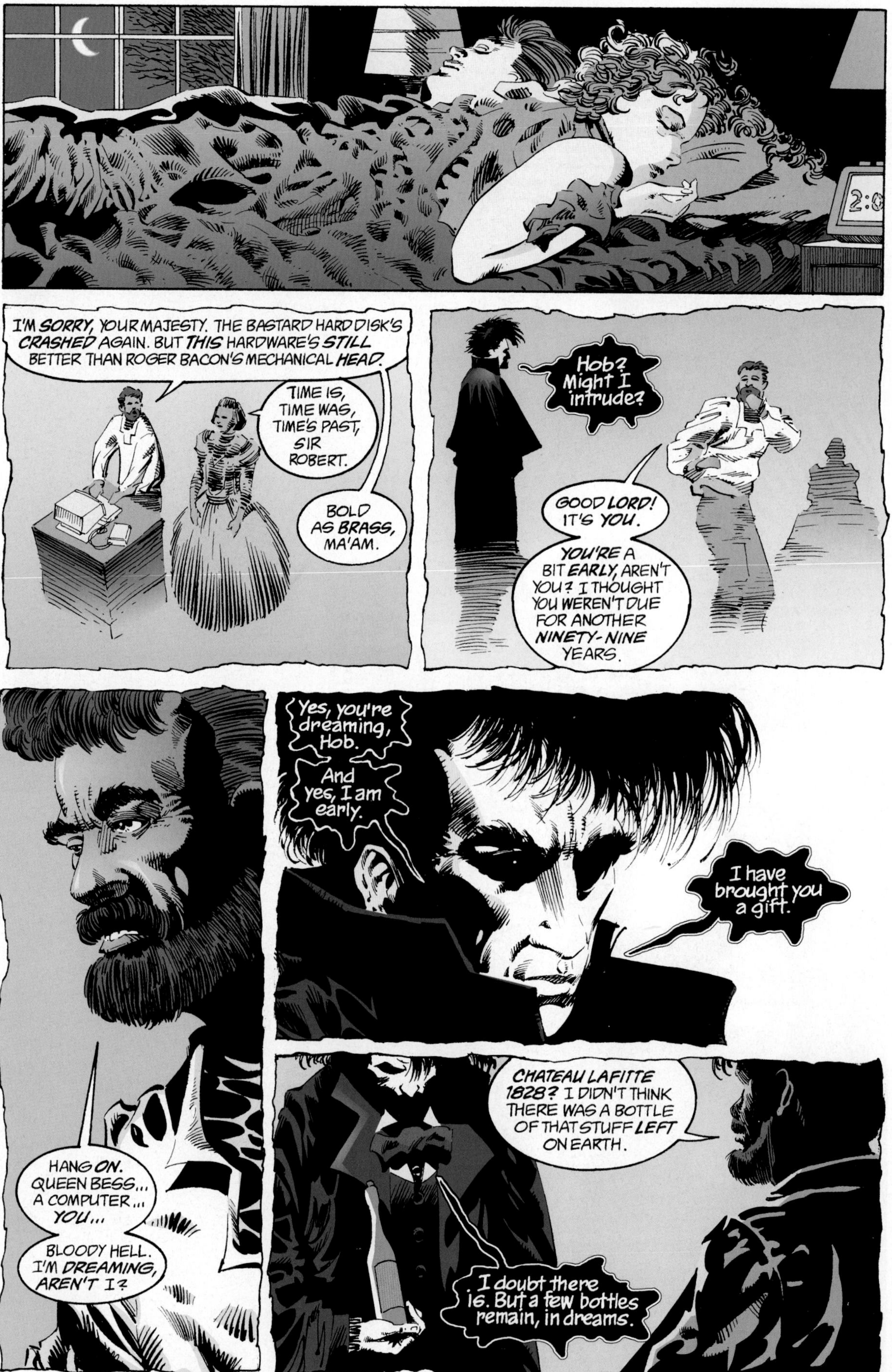

2:0
I'M SORRY, YOUR MAJESTY. THE BASTARD HARD DISK'S CRASHED AGAIN. BUT THIS HARDWARE'S STILL BETTER THAN ROGER BACON'S MECHANICAL HEAD.
TIME IS, TIME WAS, TIME'S PAST, SIR ROBERT.
BOLD AS BRASS, MA'AM.
Hob? Might I intrude?
GOOD LORD! IT'S YOU.
YOU'RE A BIT EARLY, AREN'T YOU? I THOUGHT YOU WEREN'T DUE FOR ANOTHER NINETY-NINE YEARS.
HANG ON. QUEEN BESS... A COMPUTER... YOU...
BLOODY HELL. I'M DREAMING, AREN'T I?
Yes, you're dreaming, Hob.
And yes, I am early.
I have brought you a gift.
CHATEAU LAFITTE 1828? I DIDN'T THINK THERE WAS A BOTTLE OF THAT STUFF LEFT ON EARTH.
I doubt there is. But a few bottles remain, in dreams.

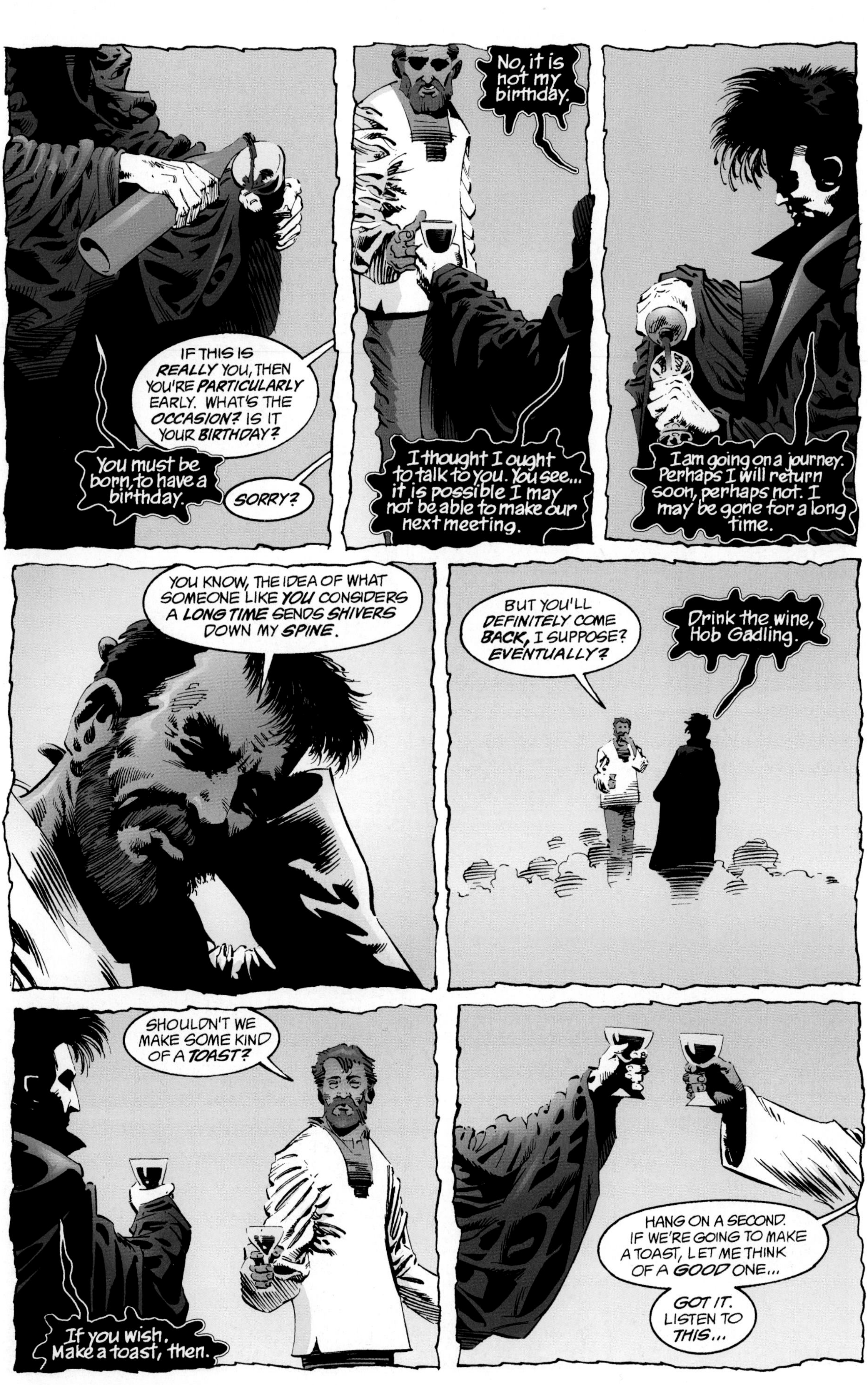
IF THIS IS REALLY YOU, THEN YOU'RE PARTICULARLY EARLY. WHAT'S THE OCCASION? IS IT YOUR BIRTHDAY?
You must be born, to have a birthday.
SORRY?
No, it is not my birthday.
I thought I ought to talk to you. You see... it is possible I may not be able to make our next meeting.
I am going on a journey. Perhaps I will return soon, perhaps not. I may be gone for a long time.
YOU KNOW, THE IDEA OF WHAT SOMEONE LIKE YOU CONSIDERS A LONG TIME SENDS SHIVERS DOWN MY SPINE.
BUT YOU'LL DEFINITELY COME BACK, I SUPPOSE? EVENTUALLY?
Drink the wine, Hob Gadling.
SHOULDN'T WE MAKE SOME KIND OF A TOAST?
If you wish. Make a toast, then.
HANG ON A SECOND. IF WE'RE GOING TO MAKE A TOAST, LET ME THINK OF A GOOD ONE...
GOT IT. LISTEN TO THIS...

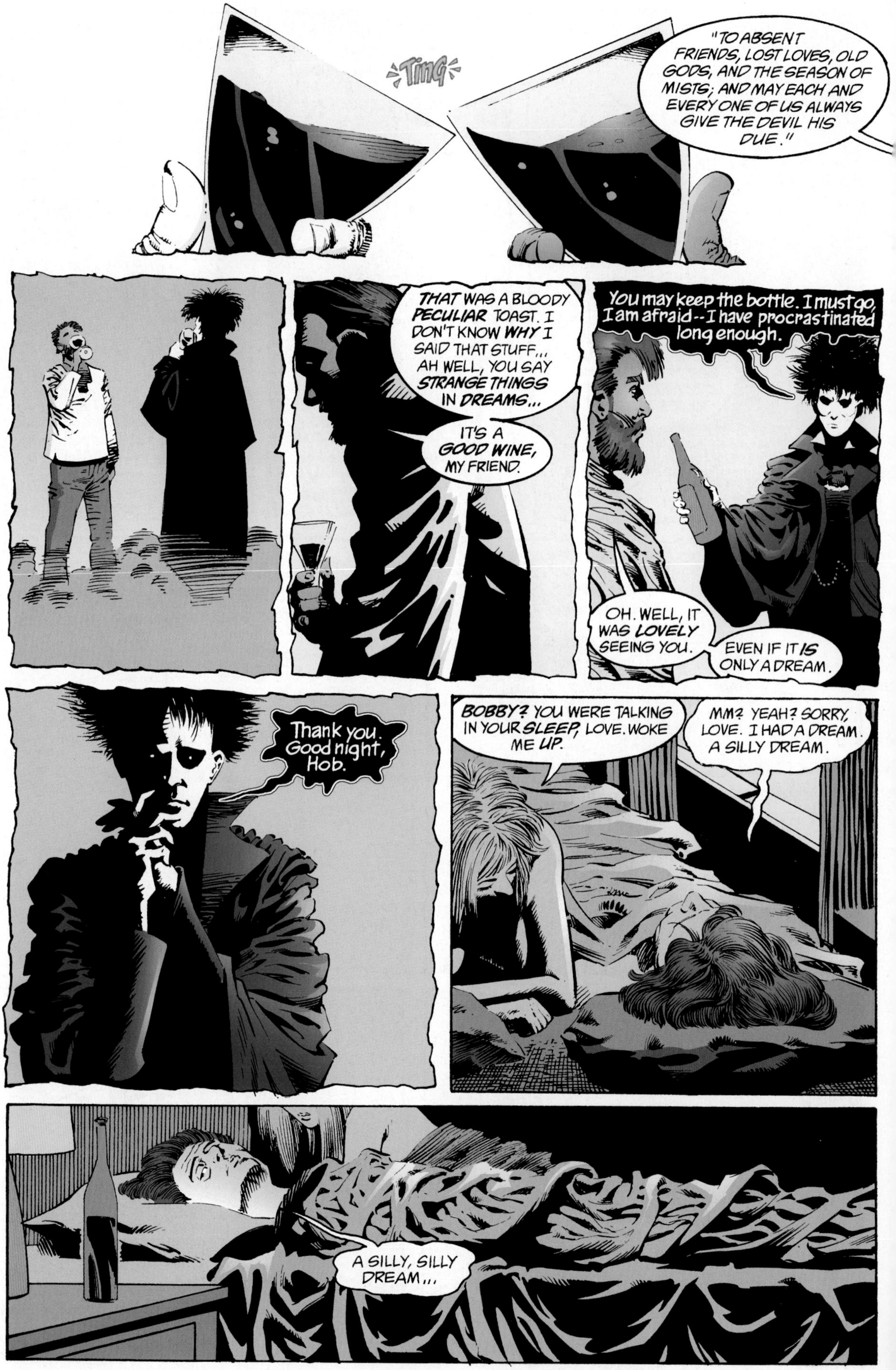
TING
"TO ABSENT FRIENDS, LOST LOVES, OLD GODS, AND THE SEASON OF MISTS; AND MAY EACH AND EVERY ONE OF US ALWAYS GIVE THE DEVIL HIS DUE."
THAT WAS A BLOODY PECULIAR TOAST. I DON'T KNOW WHY I SAID THAT STUFF... AH WELL, YOU SAY STRANGE THINGS IN DREAMS...
IT'S A GOOD WINE, MY FRIEND.
You may keep the bottle. I must go, I am afraid--I have procrastinated long enough.
OH. WELL, IT WAS LOVELY SEEING YOU.
EVEN IF IT IS ONLY A DREAM.
Thank you. Good night, Hob.
BOBBY? YOU WERE TALKING IN YOUR SLEEP, LOVE. WOKE ME UP.
MM? YEAH? SORRY, LOVE. I HAD A DREAM. A SILLY DREAM.
A SILLY, SILLY DREAM...

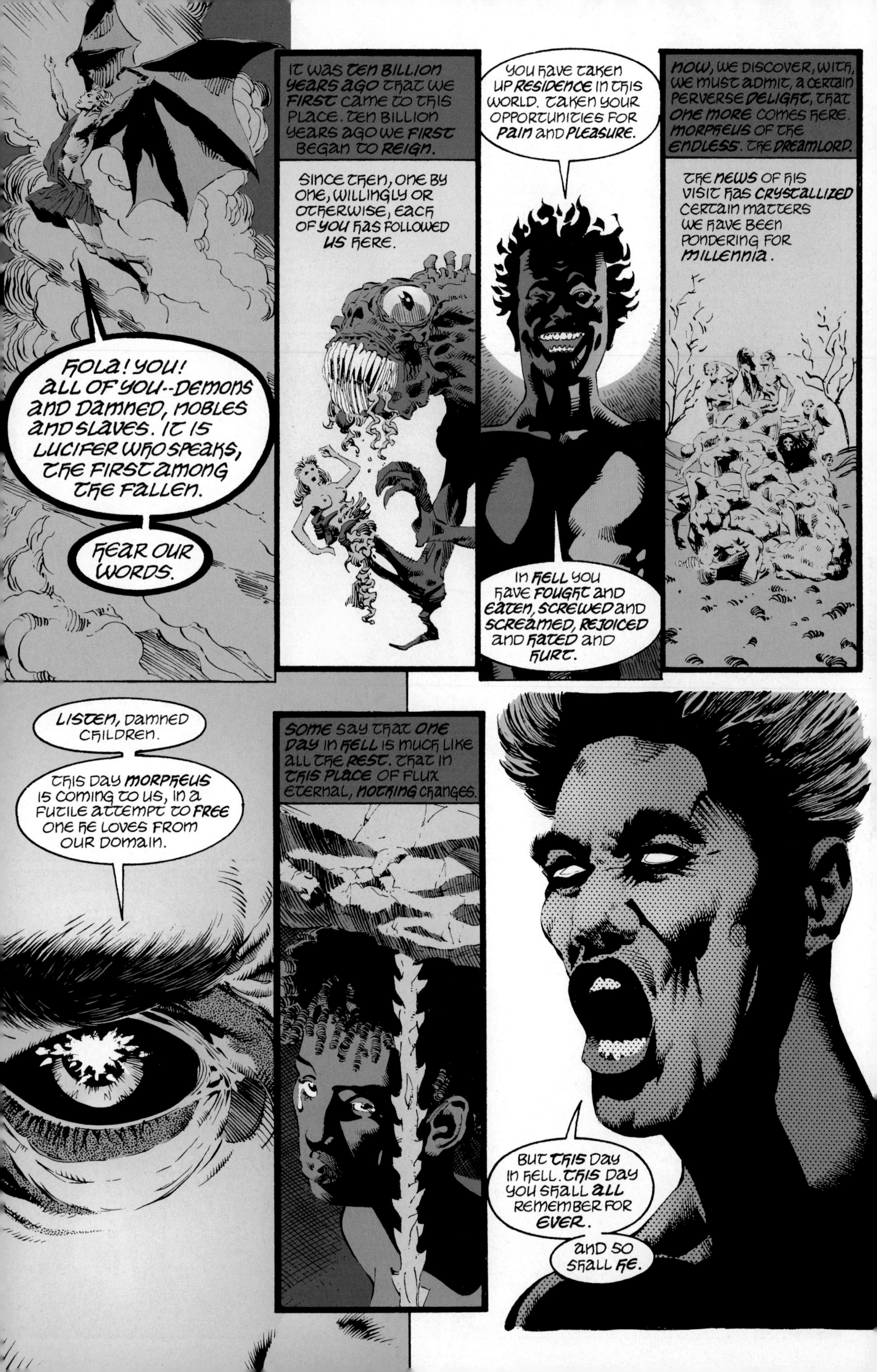
HOLA! YOU! ALL OF YOU--DEMONS AND DAMNED, NOBLES AND SLAVES. IT IS LUCIFER WHO SPEAKS, THE FIRST AMONG THE FALLEN.
HEAR OUR WORDS.
IT WAS TEN BILLION YEARS AGO THAT WE FIRST CAME TO THIS PLACE. TEN BILLION YEARS AGO WE FIRST BEGAN TO REIGN.
SINCE THEN, ONE BY ONE, WILLINGLY OR OTHERWISE, EACH OF YOU HAS FOLLOWED US HERE.
YOU HAVE TAKEN UP RESIDENCE IN THIS WORLD. TAKEN YOUR OPPORTUNITIES FOR PAIN AND PLEASURE.
IN HELL YOU HAVE FOUGHT AND EATEN, SCREWED AND SCREAMED, REJOICED AND HATED AND HURT.
NOW, WE DISCOVER, WITH, WE MUST ADMIT, A CERTAIN PERVERSE DELIGHT, THAT ONE MORE COMES HERE. MORPHEUS OF THE ENDLESS. THE DREAMLORD.
THE NEWS OF HIS VISIT HAS CRYSTALLIZED CERTAIN MATTERS WE HAVE BEEN PONDERING FOR MILLENNIA.
LISTEN, DAMNED CHILDREN.
THIS DAY MORPHEUS IS COMING TO US, IN A FUTILE ATTEMPT TO FREE ONE HE LOVES FROM OUR DOMAIN.
SOME SAY THAT ONE DAY IN HELL IS MUCH LIKE ALL THE REST. THAT IN THIS PLACE OF FLUX ETERNAL, NOTHING CHANGES.
BUT THIS DAY IN HELL. THIS DAY YOU SHALL ALL REMEMBER FOR EVER.
AND SO SHALL HE.

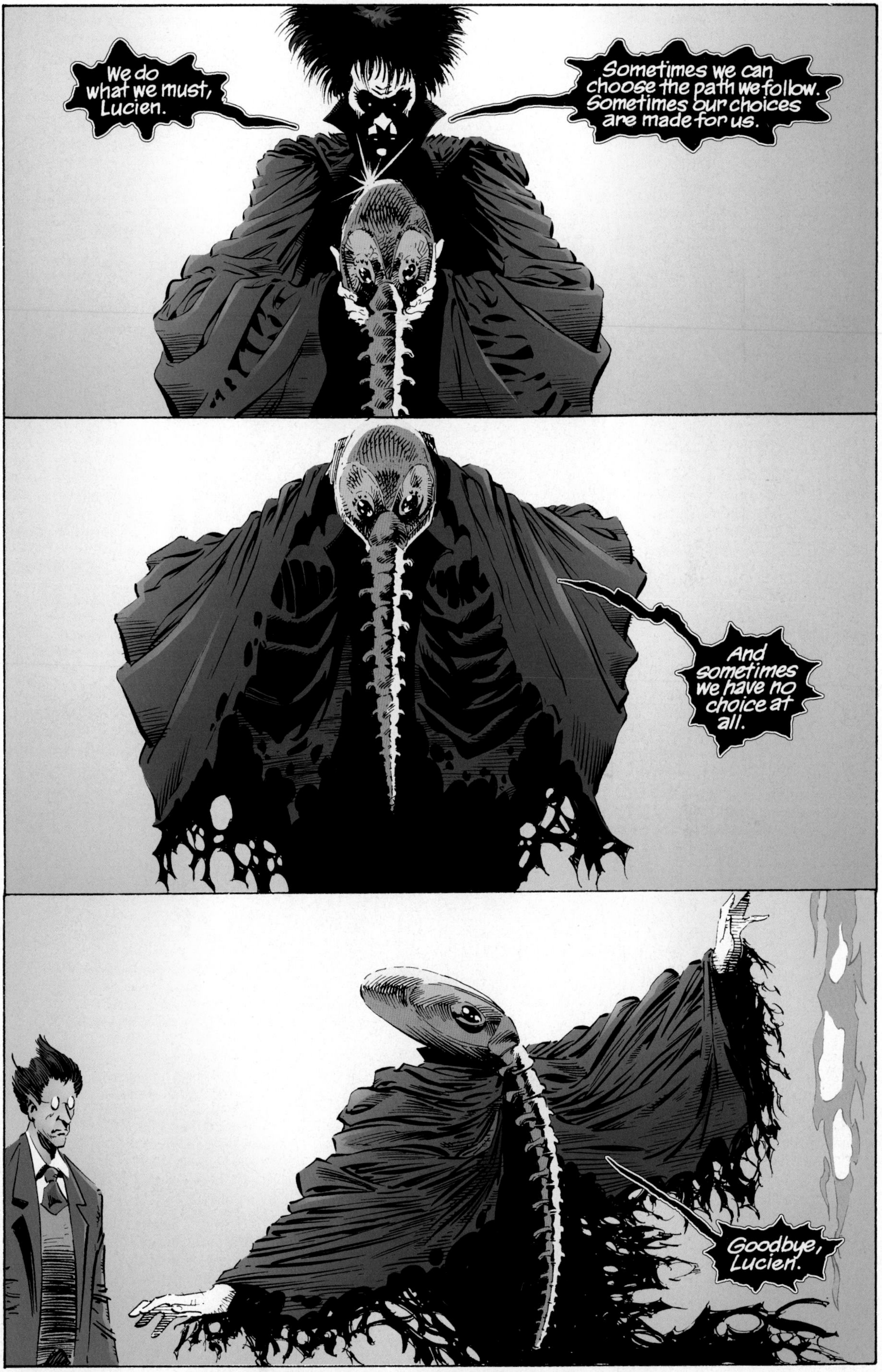
We do what we must, Lucien.
Sometimes we can choose the path we follow. Sometimes our choices are made for us.
And sometimes we have no choice at all.
Goodbye, Lucien.

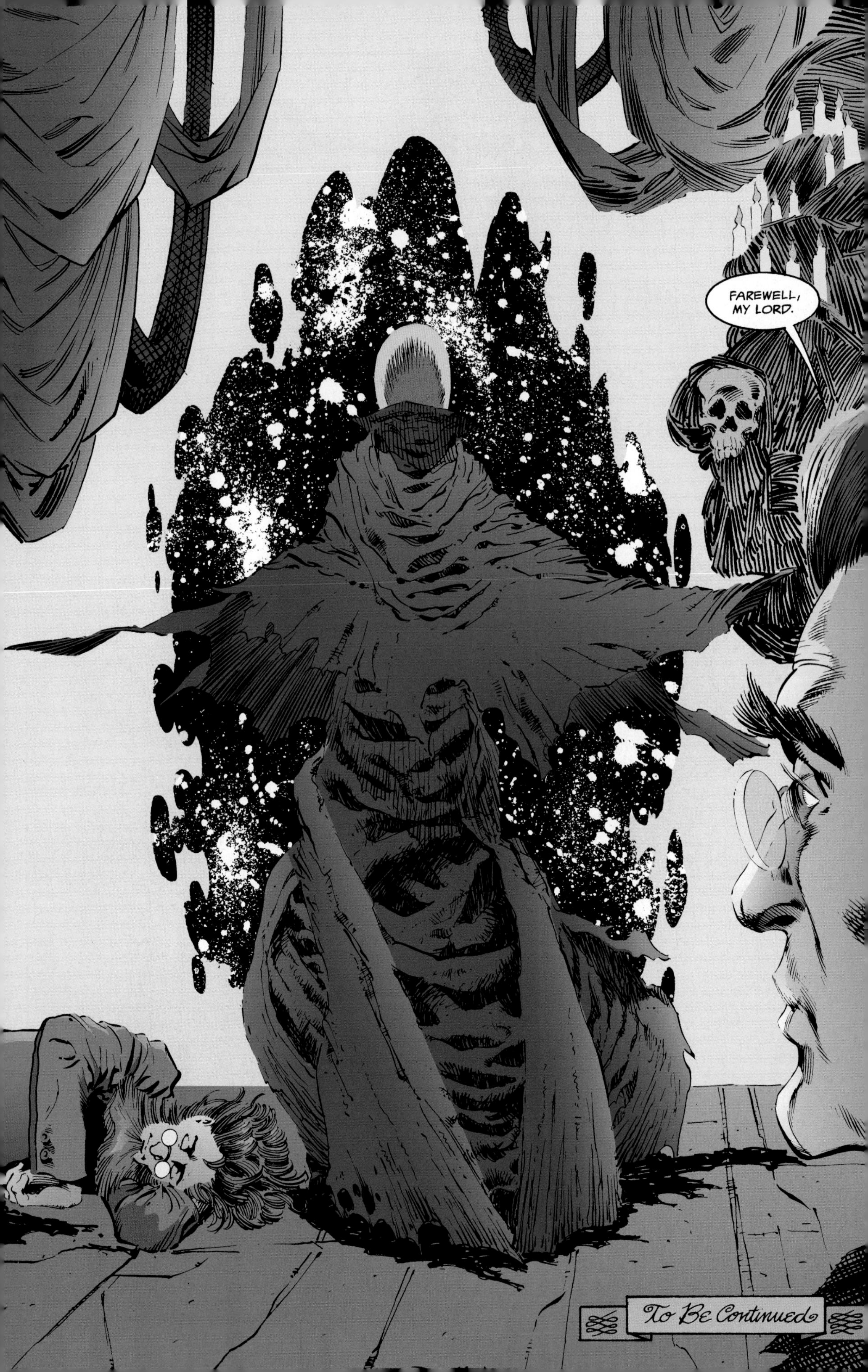
FAREWELL, MY LORD.
To Be Continued

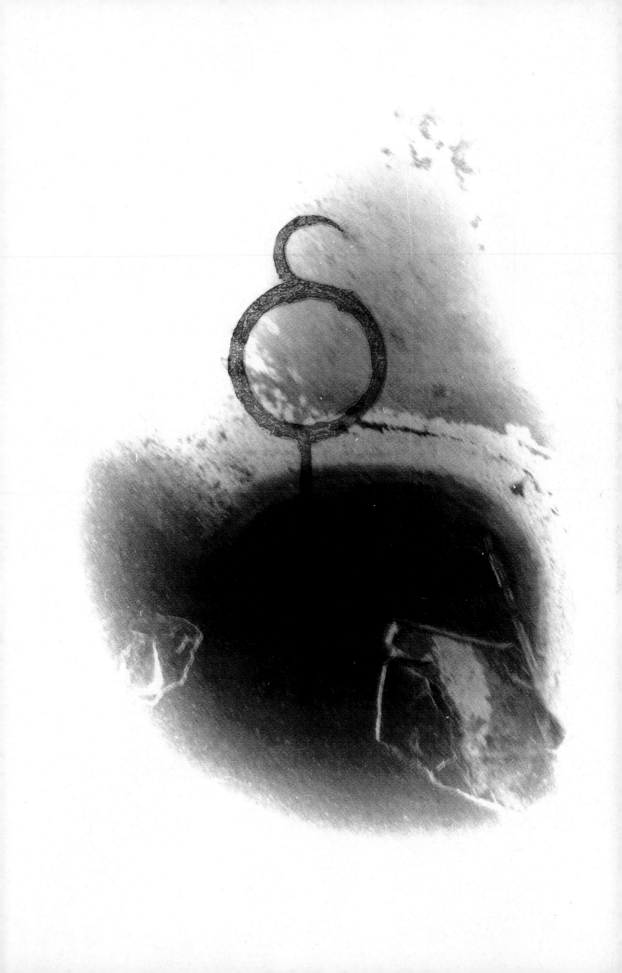

In which the Lord of Dreams returns to Hell, and his confrontation with the Lord of that realm; in which a number of doors are closed for the last time; and concerning the strange disposition of a knife and a key.

EPISODE 2

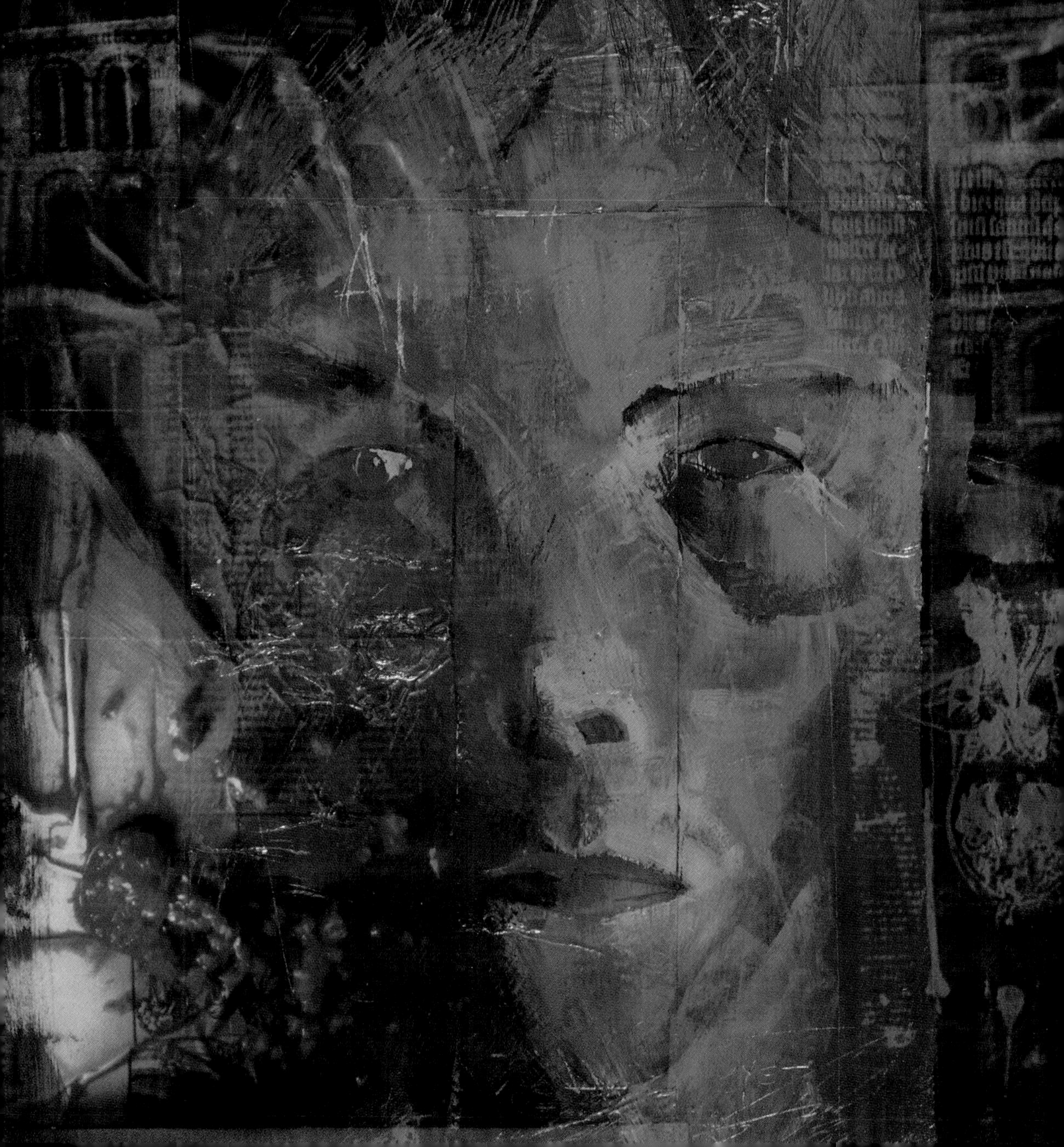

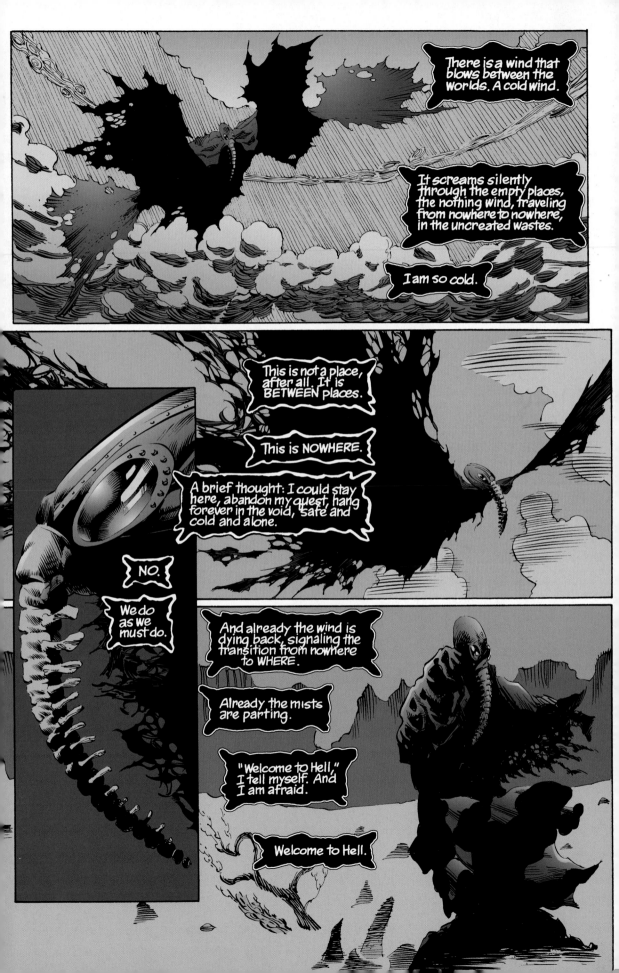

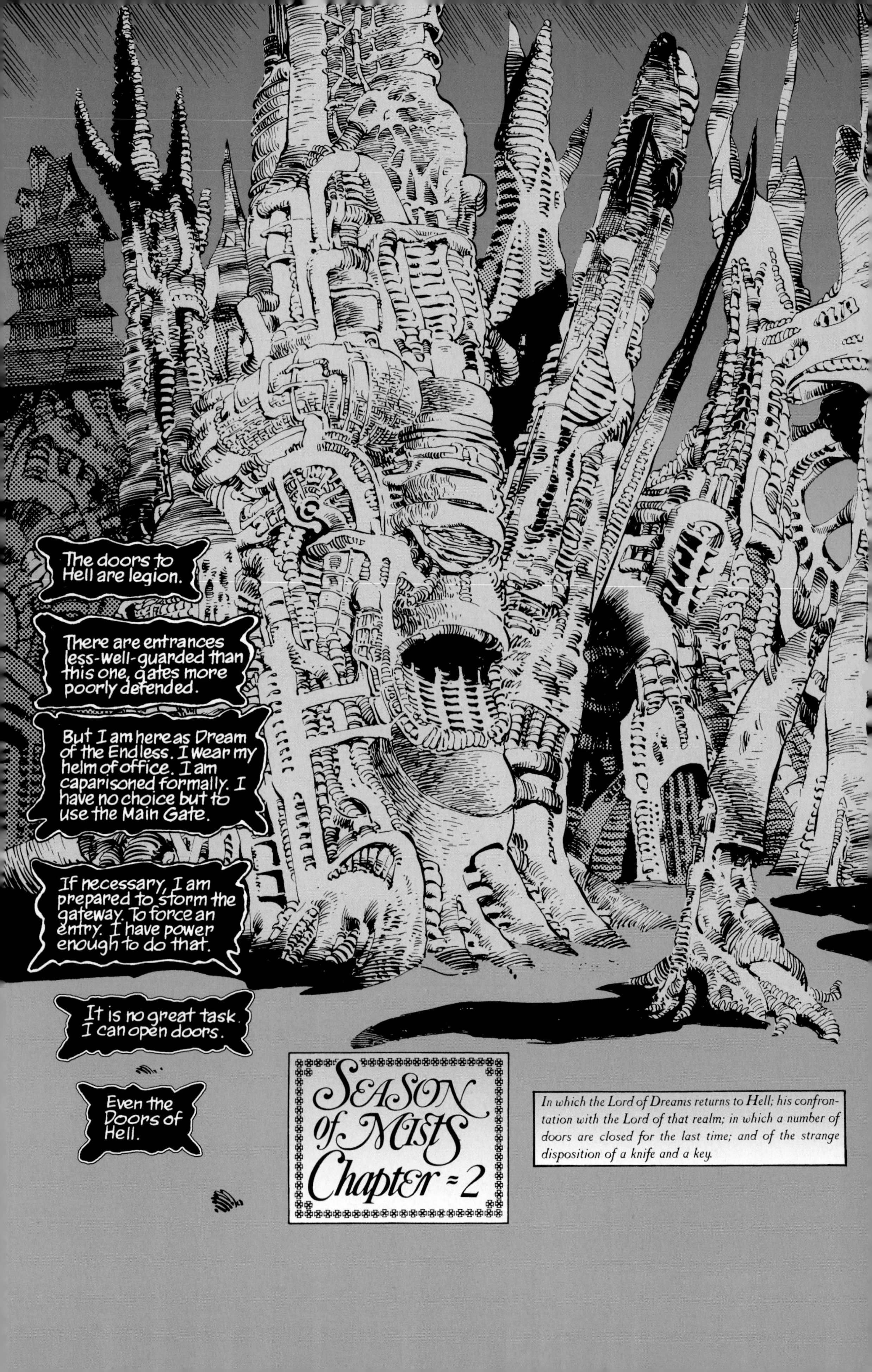
The doors to Hell are legion.
There are entrances less-well-guarded than this one, gates more poorly defended.
But I am here as Dream of the Endless. I wear my helm of office. I am caparisoned formally. I have no choice but to use the Main Gate.
If necessary, I am prepared to storm the gateway. To force an entry. I have power enough to do that.
It is no great task. I can open doors.
Even the Doors of Hell.
Season of Mists Chapter 2
In which the Lord of Dreams returns to Hell; his confrontation with the Lord of that realm; in which a number of doors are closed for the last time; and of the strange disposition of a knife and a key.

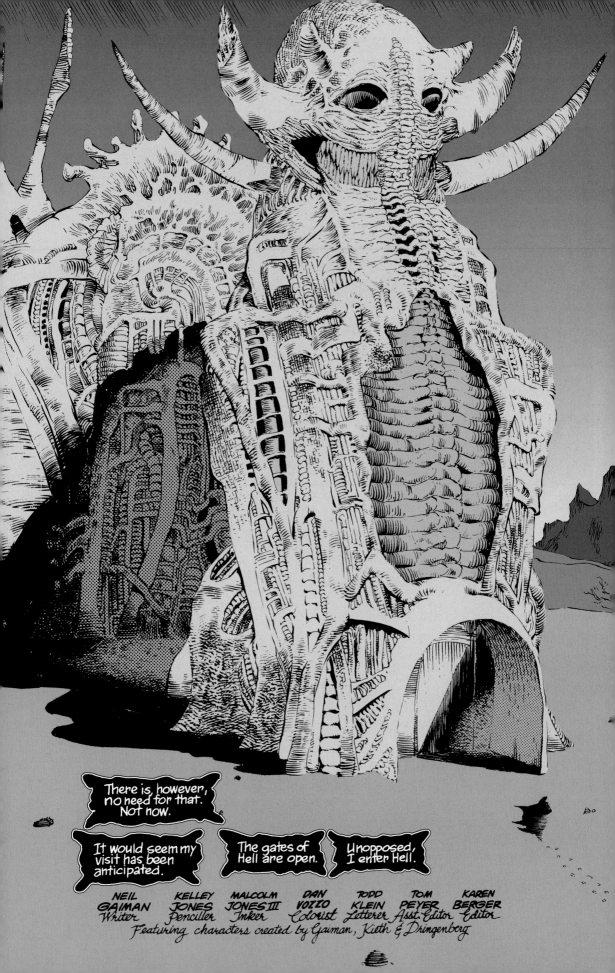

There is, however, no need for that. Not now.

It would seem my visit has been anticipated.

The gates of Hell are open.

Unopposed, I enter Hell.

NEIL GAIMAN
Writer

KELLEY JONES
Penciller

MALCOLM JONES III
Inker

DAN VOZZO
Colorist

TODD KLEIN
Letterer

TOM PEYER
Asst. Editor

KAREN BERGER
Editor

Featuring characters created by Gaiman, Kieth & Dringenberg

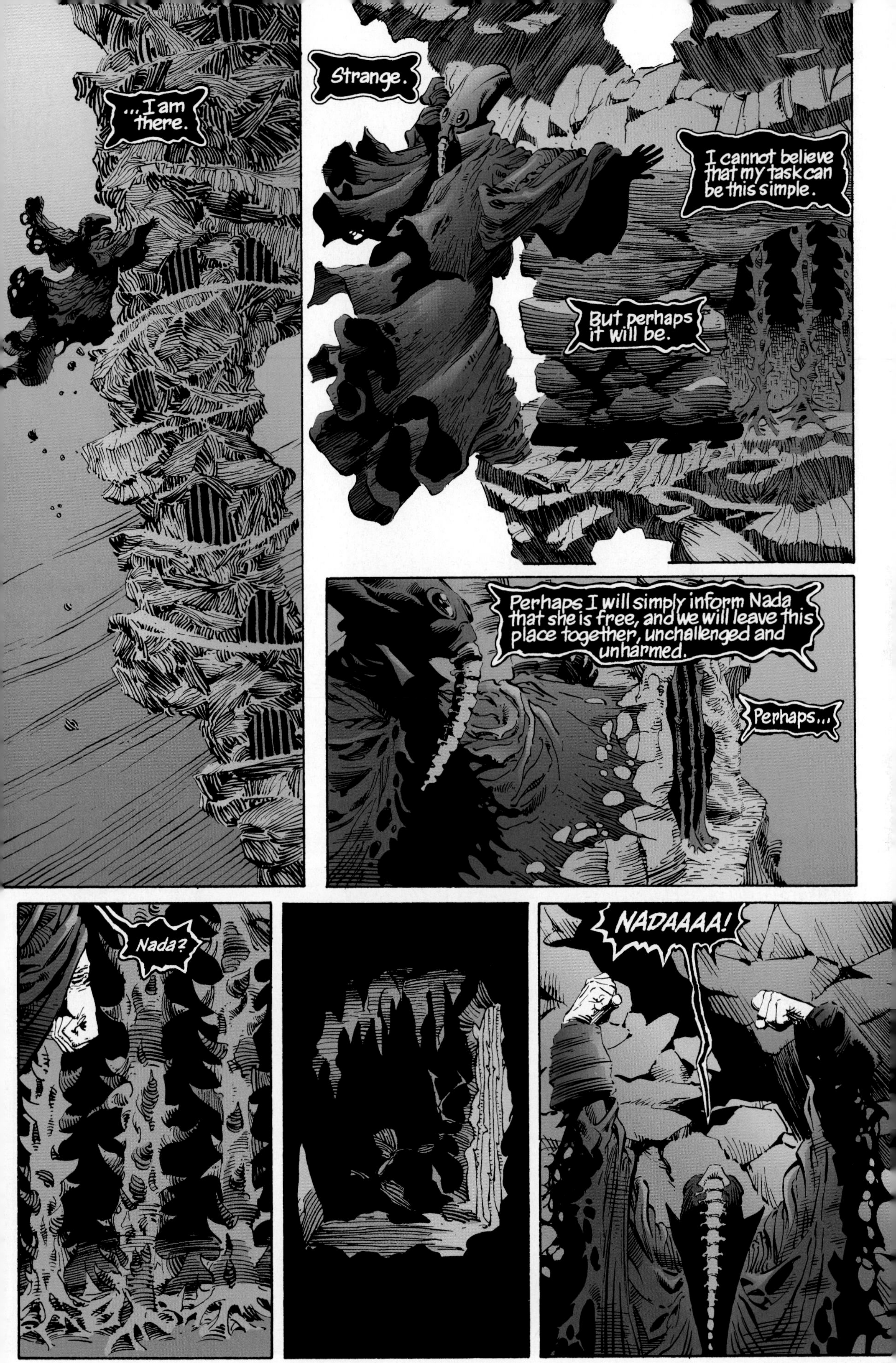
...I am there.
Strange.
I cannot believe that my task can be this simple.
But perhaps it will be.
Perhaps I will simply inform Nada that she is free, and we will leave this place together, unchallenged and unharmed.
Perhaps...
Nada?
NADAAAA!

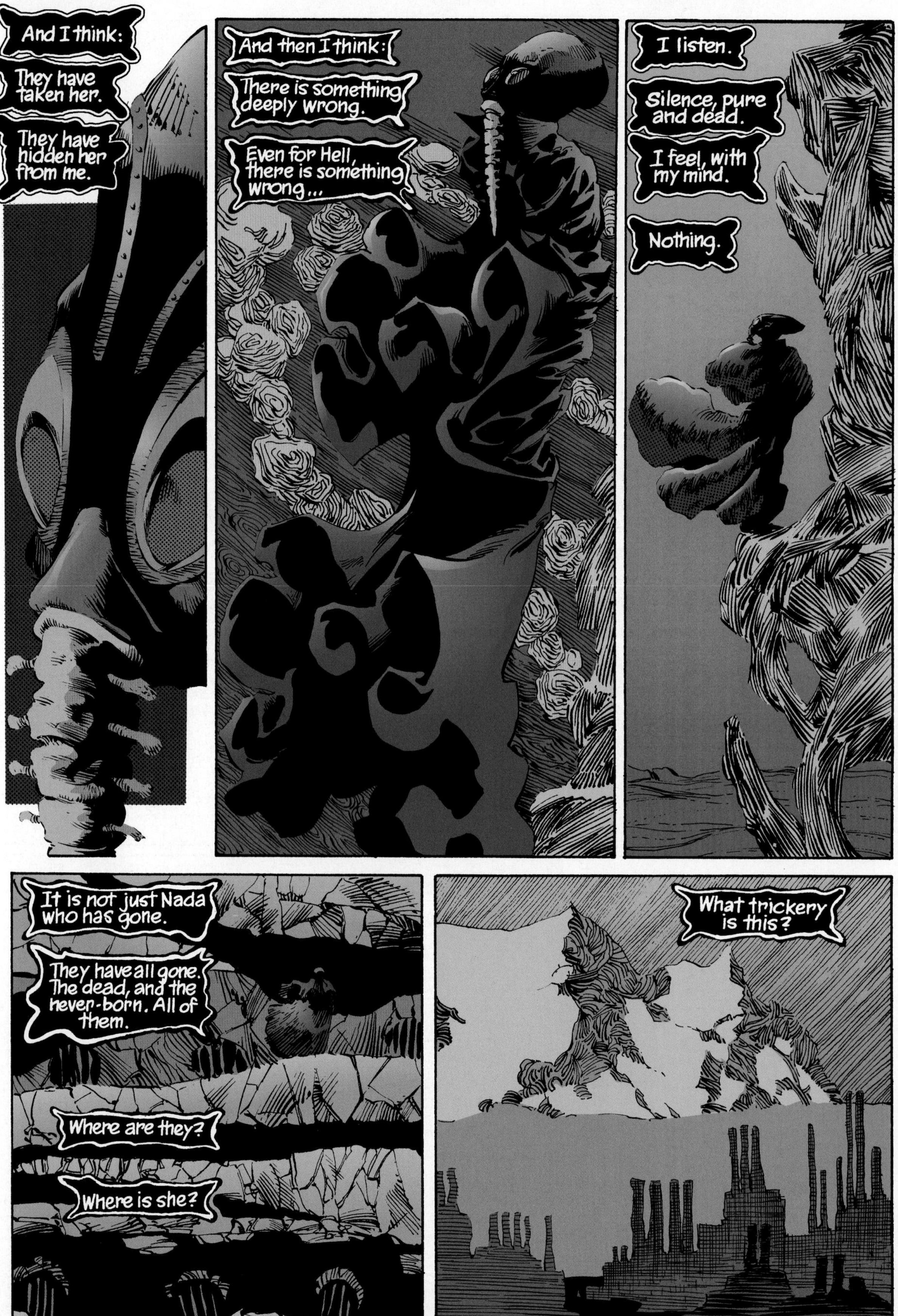
And I think:
They have taken her.
They have hidden her from me.
And then I think:
There is something deeply wrong.
Even for Hell, there is something wrong...
I listen.
Silence, pure and dead.
I feel, with my mind.
Nothing.
It is not just Nada who has gone.
They have all gone. The dead, and the never-born. All of them.
Where are they?
Where is she?
What trickery is this?

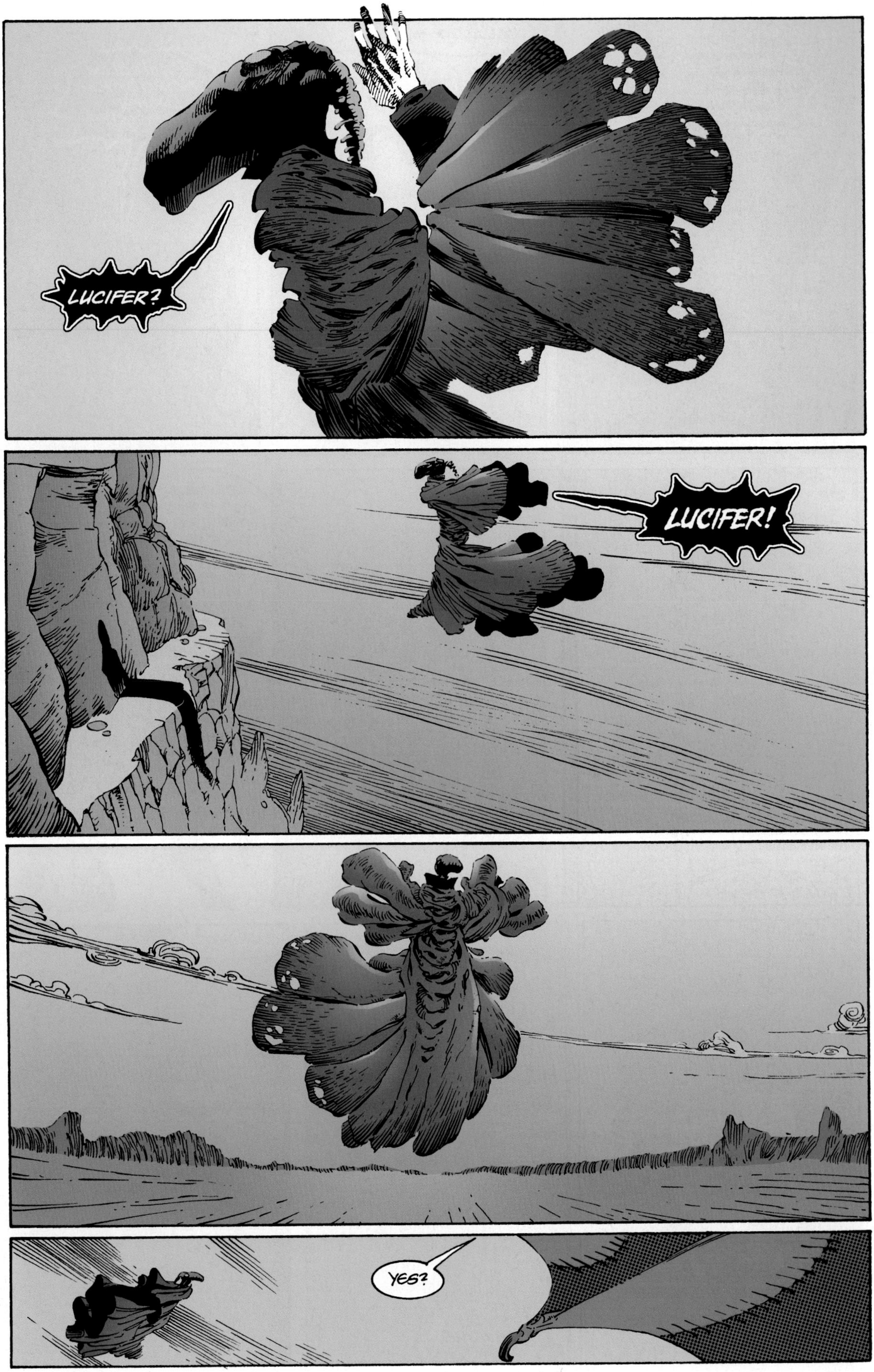
LUCIFER?
LUCIFER!
YES?

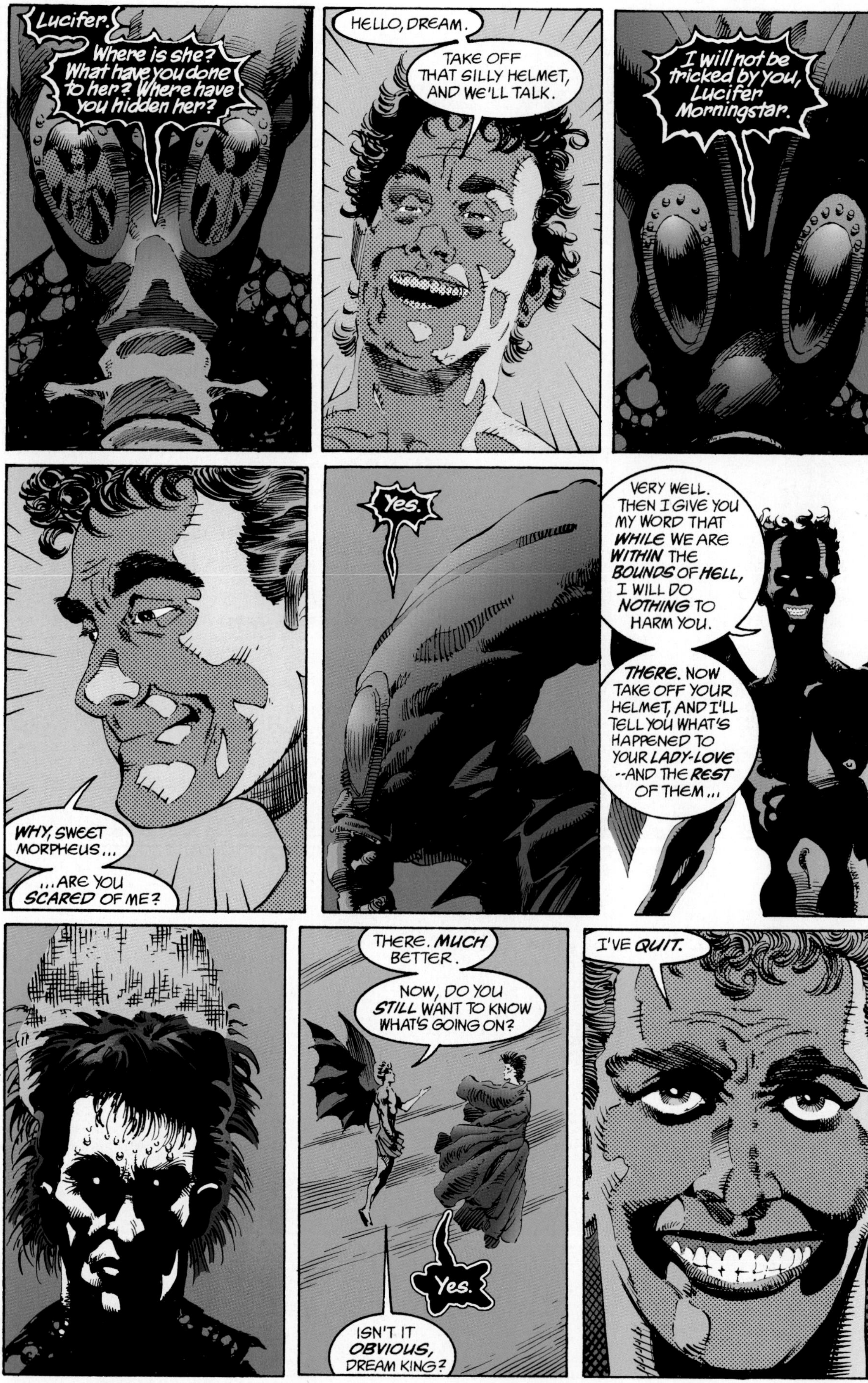
Lucifer.
Where is she? What have you done to her? Where have you hidden her?
HELLO, DREAM.
TAKE OFF THAT SILLY HELMET, AND WE'LL TALK.
I will not be tricked by you, Lucifer Morningstar.
WHY, SWEET MORPHEUS...
...ARE YOU SCARED OF ME?
Yes.
VERY WELL. THEN I GIVE YOU MY WORD THAT WHILE WE ARE WITHIN THE BOUNDS OF HELL, I WILL DO NOTHING TO HARM YOU.
THERE. NOW TAKE OFF YOUR HELMET, AND I'LL TELL YOU WHAT'S HAPPENED TO YOUR LADY-LOVE --AND THE REST OF THEM...
THERE. MUCH BETTER.
NOW, DO YOU STILL WANT TO KNOW WHAT'S GOING ON?
Yes.
ISN'T IT OBVIOUS, DREAM KING?
I'VE QUIT.

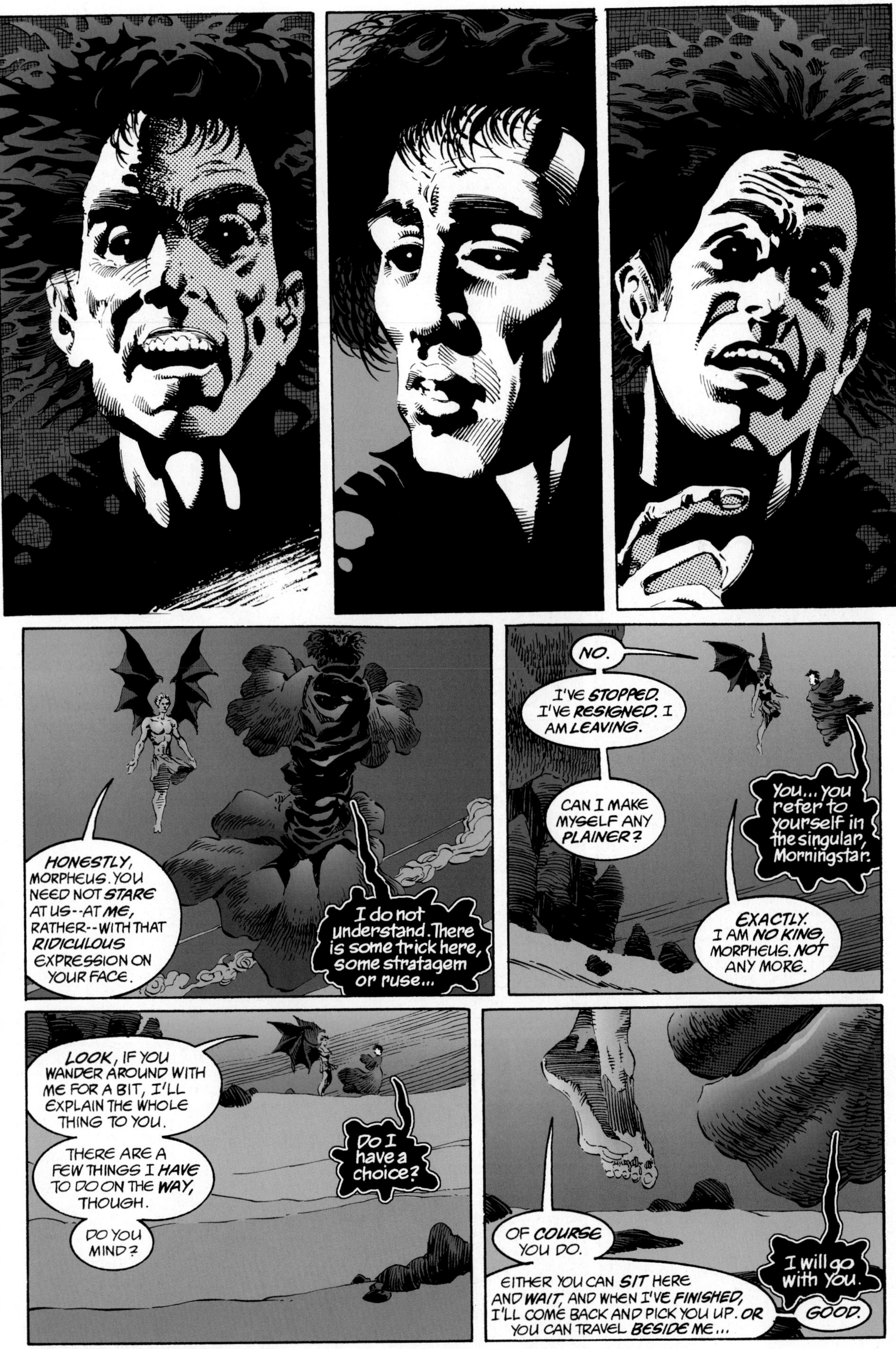
HONESTLY, MORPHEUS. YOU NEED NOT STARE AT US--AT ME, RATHER--WITH THAT RIDICULOUS EXPRESSION ON YOUR FACE.
I do not understand. There is some trick here, some stratagem or ruse...
NO.
I'VE STOPPED. I'VE RESIGNED. I AM LEAVING.
CAN I MAKE MYSELF ANY PLAINER?
You... you refer to yourself in the singular, Morningstar.
EXACTLY. I AM NO KING, MORPHEUS. NOT ANY MORE.
LOOK, IF YOU WANDER AROUND WITH ME FOR A BIT, I'LL EXPLAIN THE WHOLE THING TO YOU.
THERE ARE A FEW THINGS I HAVE TO DO ON THE WAY, THOUGH.
DO YOU MIND?
Do I have a choice?
OF COURSE YOU DO.
EITHER YOU CAN SIT HERE AND WAIT, AND WHEN I'VE FINISHED, I'LL COME BACK AND PICK YOU UP. OR YOU CAN TRAVEL BESIDE ME...
I will go with You.
GOOD.

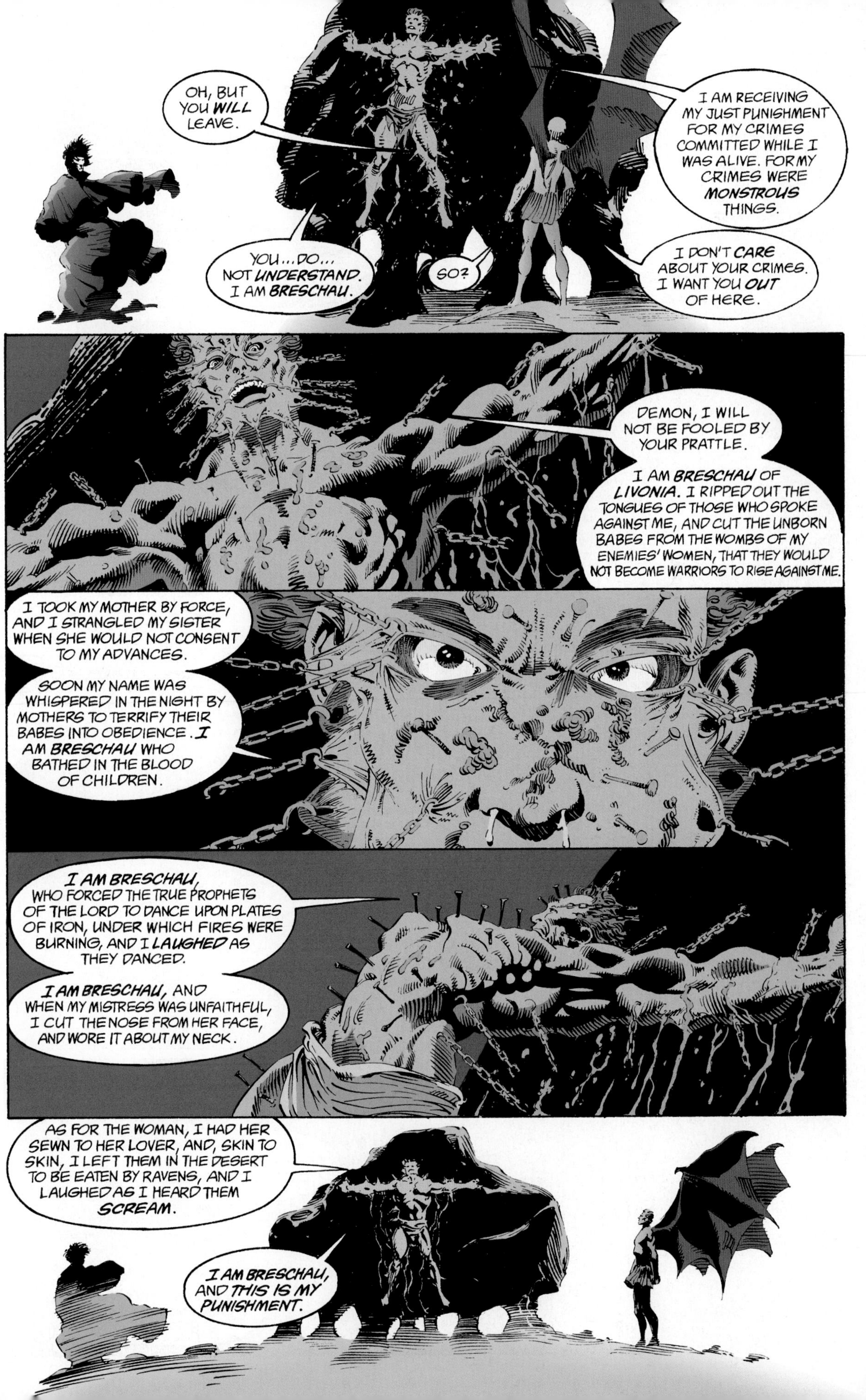

OH, BUT YOU WILL LEAVE.
I AM RECEIVING MY JUST PUNISHMENT FOR MY CRIMES COMMITTED WHILE I WAS ALIVE. FOR MY CRIMES WERE MONSTROUS THINGS.
YOU...DO... NOT UNDERSTAND. I AM BRESCHAU.
SO?
I DON'T CARE ABOUT YOUR CRIMES. I WANT YOU OUT OF HERE.
DEMON, I WILL NOT BE FOOLED BY YOUR PRATTLE.
I AM BRESCHAU OF LIVONIA. I RIPPED OUT THE TONGUES OF THOSE WHO SPOKE AGAINST ME, AND CUT THE UNBORN BABES FROM THE WOMBS OF MY ENEMIES' WOMEN, THAT THEY WOULD NOT BECOME WARRIORS TO RISE AGAINST ME.
I TOOK MY MOTHER BY FORCE, AND I STRANGLED MY SISTER WHEN SHE WOULD NOT CONSENT TO MY ADVANCES.
SOON MY NAME WAS WHISPERED IN THE NIGHT BY MOTHERS TO TERRIFY THEIR BABES INTO OBEDIENCE. I AM BRESCHAU WHO BATHED IN THE BLOOD OF CHILDREN.
I AM BRESCHAU, WHO FORCED THE TRUE PROPHETS OF THE LORD TO DANCE UPON PLATES OF IRON, UNDER WHICH FIRES WERE BURNING, AND I LAUGHED AS THEY DANCED.
I AM BRESCHAU, AND WHEN MY MISTRESS WAS UNFAITHFUL, I CUT THE NOSE FROM HER FACE, AND WORE IT ABOUT MY NECK.
AS FOR THE WOMAN, I HAD HER SEWN TO HER LOVER, AND, SKIN TO SKIN, I LEFT THEM IN THE DESERT TO BE EATEN BY RAVENS, AND I LAUGHED AS I HEARD THEM SCREAM.
I AM BRESCHAU, AND THIS IS MY PUNISHMENT.

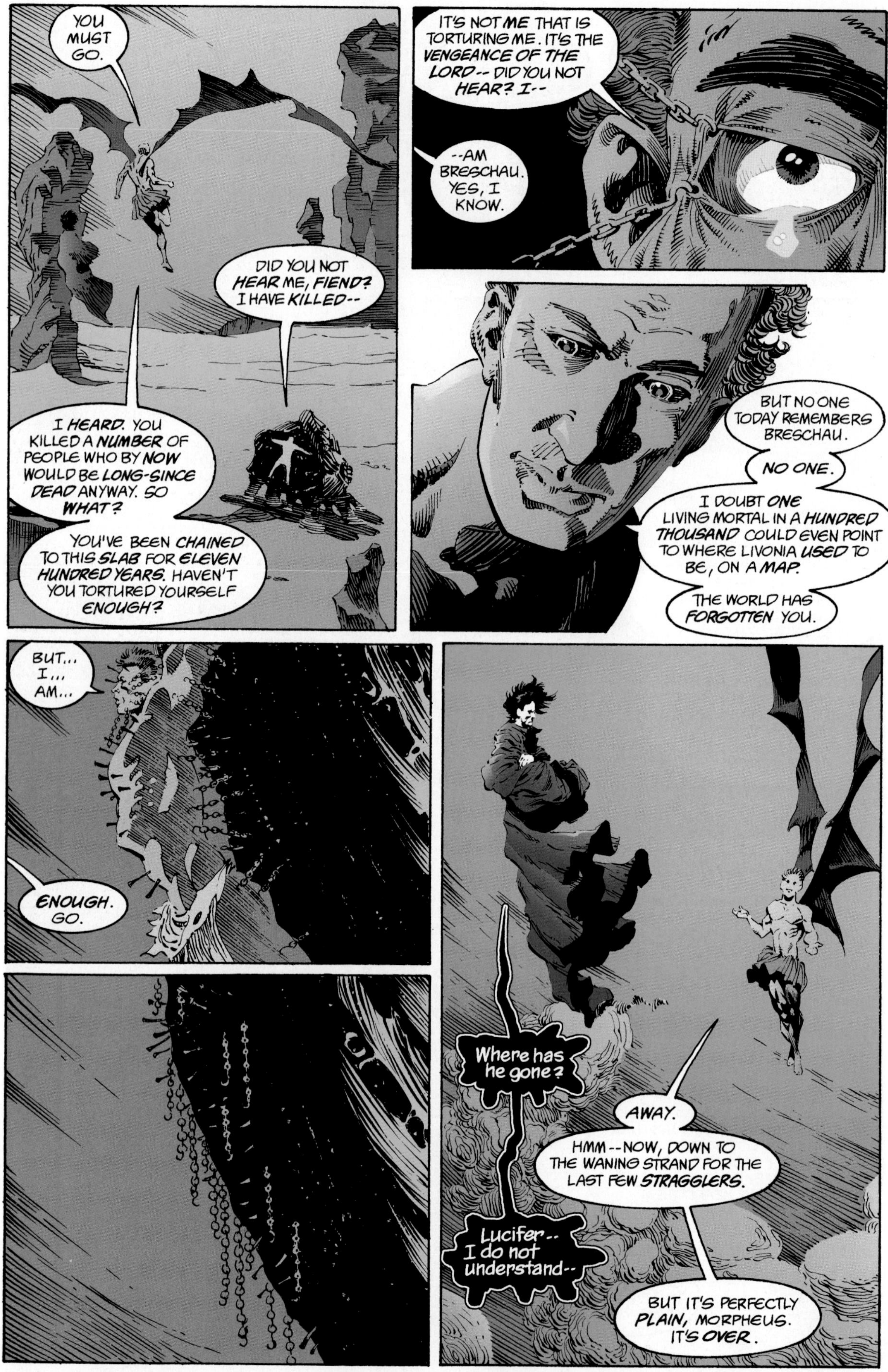
YOU MUST GO.
IT'S NOT ME THAT IS TORTURING ME. IT'S THE VENGEANCE OF THE LORD-- DID YOU NOT HEAR? I--
--AM BRESCHAU. YES, I KNOW.
DID YOU NOT HEAR ME, FIEND? I HAVE KILLED--
I HEARD. YOU KILLED A NUMBER OF PEOPLE WHO BY NOW WOULD BE LONG-SINCE DEAD ANYWAY. SO WHAT?
YOU'VE BEEN CHAINED TO THIS SLAB FOR ELEVEN HUNDRED YEARS. HAVEN'T YOU TORTURED YOURSELF ENOUGH?
BUT NO ONE TODAY REMEMBERS BRESCHAU.
NO ONE.
I DOUBT ONE LIVING MORTAL IN A HUNDRED THOUSAND COULD EVEN POINT TO WHERE LIVONIA USED TO BE, ON A MAP.
THE WORLD HAS FORGOTTEN YOU.
BUT... I... AM...
ENOUGH. GO.
Where has he gone?
AWAY.
HMM --NOW, DOWN TO THE WANING STRAND FOR THE LAST FEW STRAGGLERS.
Lucifer-- I do not understand--
BUT IT'S PERFECTLY PLAIN, MORPHEUS. IT'S OVER.

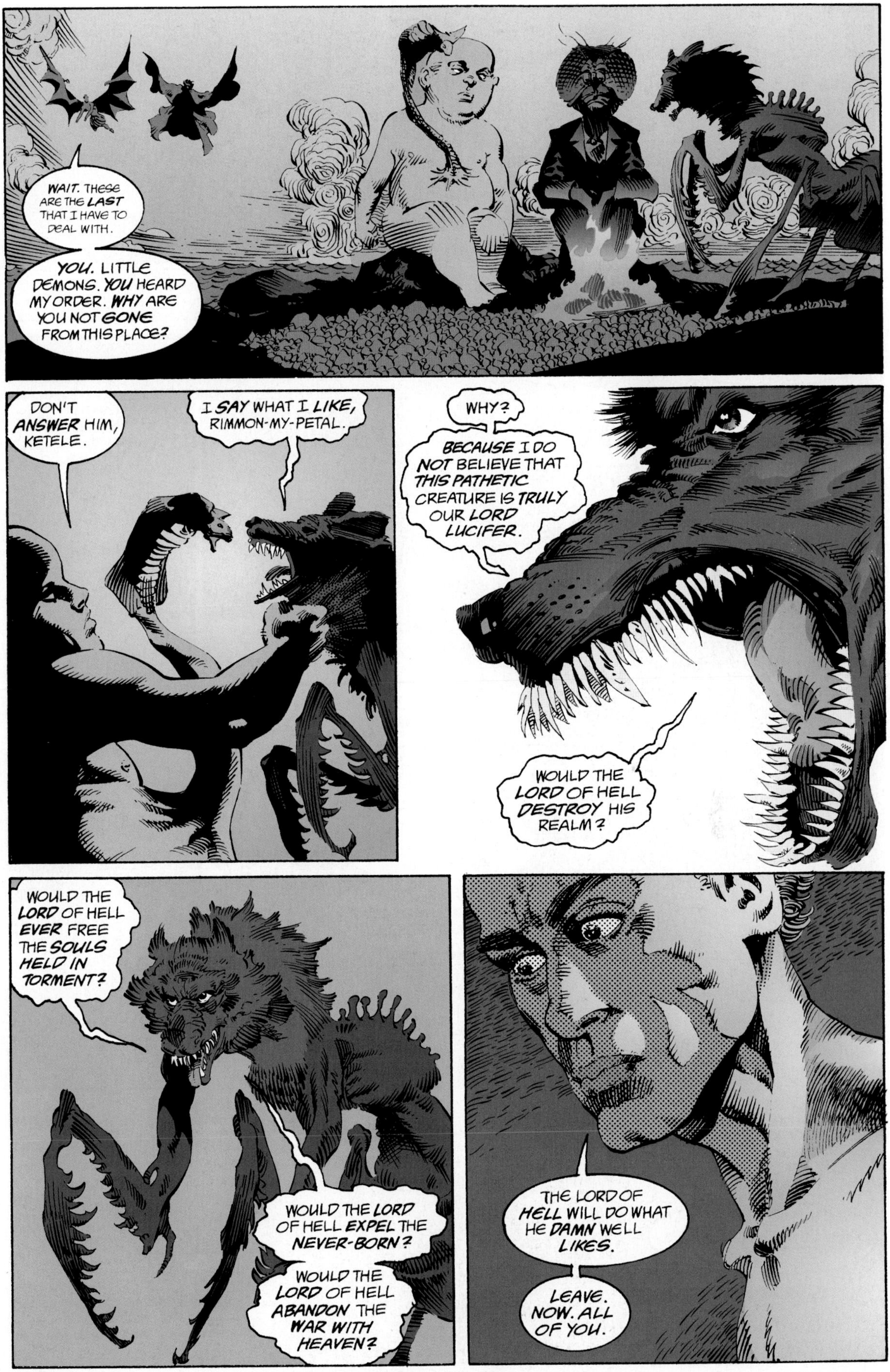
WAIT. THESE ARE THE LAST THAT I HAVE TO DEAL WITH.
YOU. LITTLE DEMONS. YOU HEARD MY ORDER. WHY ARE YOU NOT GONE FROM THIS PLACE?
DON'T ANSWER HIM, KETELE.
I SAY WHAT I LIKE, RIMMON-MY-PETAL.
WHY?
BECAUSE I DO NOT BELIEVE THAT THIS PATHETIC CREATURE IS TRULY OUR LORD LUCIFER.
WOULD THE LORD OF HELL DESTROY HIS REALM?
WOULD THE LORD OF HELL EVER FREE THE SOULS HELD IN TORMENT?
WOULD THE LORD OF HELL EXPEL THE NEVER-BORN?
WOULD THE LORD OF HELL ABANDON THE WAR WITH HEAVEN?
THE LORD OF HELL WILL DO WHAT HE DAMN WELL LIKES.
LEAVE. NOW. ALL OF YOU.

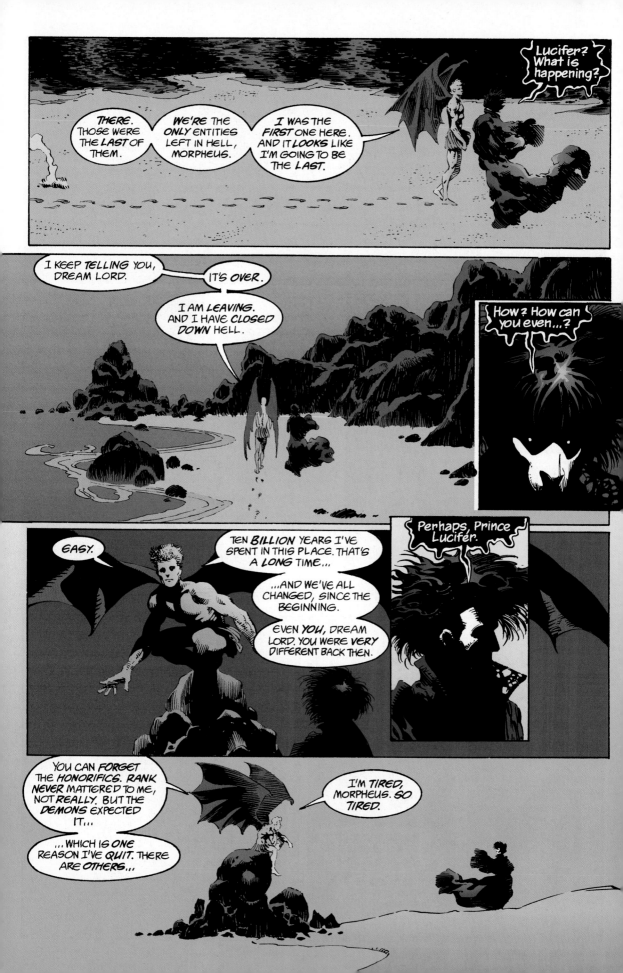

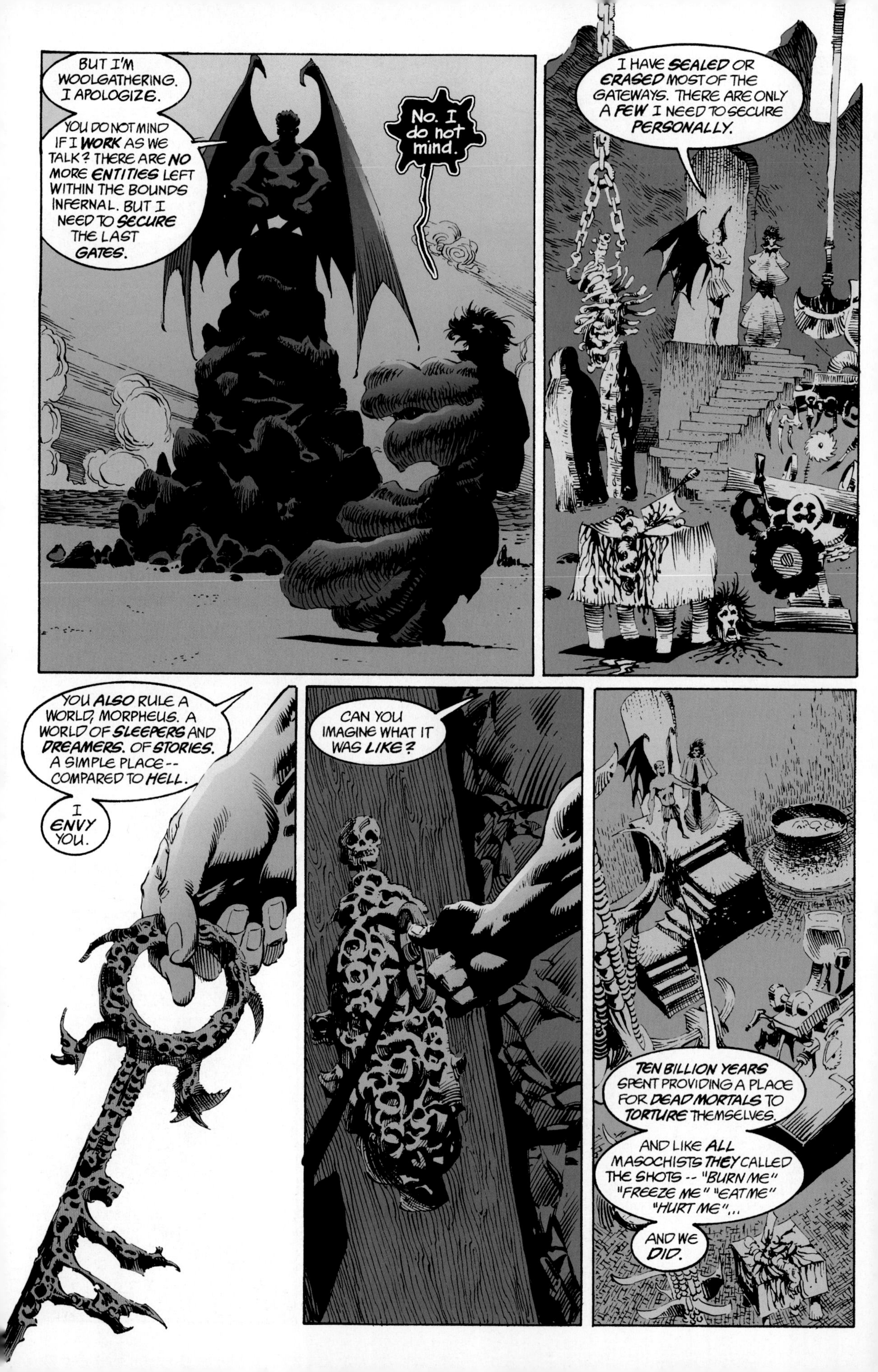
BUT I'M WOOLGATHERING. I APOLOGIZE.
YOU DO NOT MIND IF I WORK AS WE TALK? THERE ARE NO MORE ENTITIES LEFT WITHIN THE BOUNDS INFERNAL. BUT I NEED TO SECURE THE LAST GATES.
No. I do not mind.
I HAVE SEALED OR ERASED MOST OF THE GATEWAYS. THERE ARE ONLY A FEW I NEED TO SECURE PERSONALLY.
YOU ALSO RULE A WORLD, MORPHEUS. A WORLD OF SLEEPERS AND DREAMERS. OF STORIES. A SIMPLE PLACE-- COMPARED TO HELL.
I ENVY YOU.
CAN YOU IMAGINE WHAT IT WAS LIKE?
TEN BILLION YEARS SPENT PROVIDING A PLACE FOR DEAD MORTALS TO TORTURE THEMSELVES.
AND LIKE ALL MASOCHISTS THEY CALLED THE SHOTS -- "BURN ME" "FREEZE ME" "EAT ME" "HURT ME",..
AND WE DID.

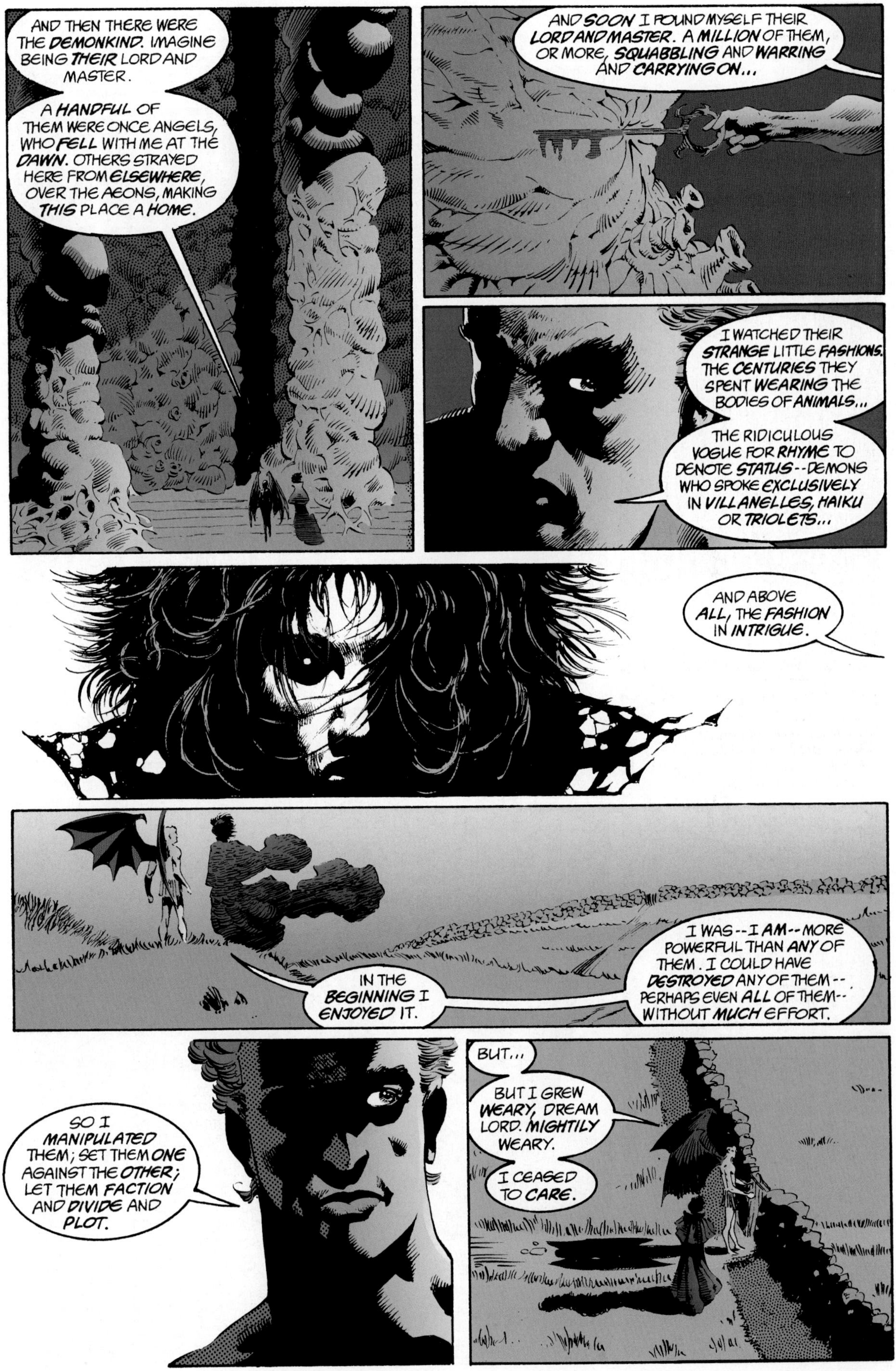
AND THEN THERE WERE THE DEMONKIND. IMAGINE BEING THEIR LORD AND MASTER.
A HANDFUL OF THEM WERE ONCE ANGELS, WHO FELL WITH ME AT THE DAWN. OTHERS STRAYED HERE FROM ELSEWHERE, OVER THE AEONS, MAKING THIS PLACE A HOME.
AND SOON I FOUND MYSELF THEIR LORD AND MASTER. A MILLION OF THEM, OR MORE, SQUABBLING AND WARRING AND CARRYING ON...
I WATCHED THEIR STRANGE LITTLE FASHIONS. THE CENTURIES THEY SPENT WEARING THE BODIES OF ANIMALS...
THE RIDICULOUS VOGUE FOR RHYME TO DENOTE STATUS--DEMONS WHO SPOKE EXCLUSIVELY IN VILLANELLES, HAIKU OR TRIOLETS...
AND ABOVE ALL, THE FASHION IN INTRIGUE.
IN THE BEGINNING I ENJOYED IT.
I WAS--I AM--MORE POWERFUL THAN ANY OF THEM. I COULD HAVE DESTROYED ANY OF THEM--PERHAPS EVEN ALL OF THEM--WITHOUT MUCH EFFORT.
SO I MANIPULATED THEM; SET THEM ONE AGAINST THE OTHER; LET THEM FACTION AND DIVIDE AND PLOT.
BUT...
BUT I GREW WEARY, DREAM LORD. MIGHTILY WEARY.
I CEASED TO CARE.

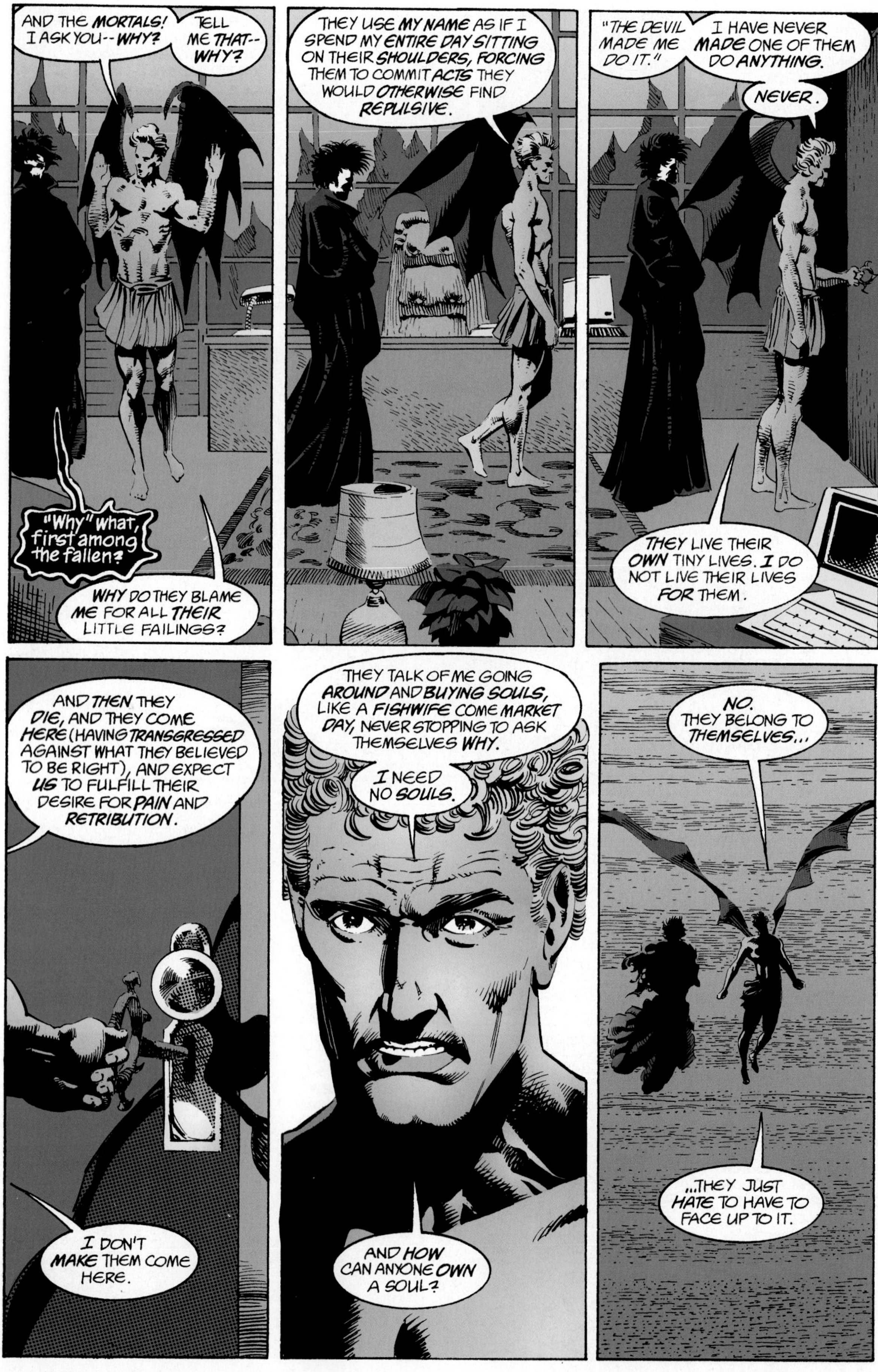
AND THE MORTALS! I ASK YOU-- WHY?
TELL ME THAT-- WHY?
"Why" what, first among the fallen?
WHY DO THEY BLAME ME FOR ALL THEIR LITTLE FAILINGS?
THEY USE MY NAME AS IF I SPEND MY ENTIRE DAY SITTING ON THEIR SHOULDERS, FORCING THEM TO COMMIT ACTS THEY WOULD OTHERWISE FIND REPULSIVE.
"THE DEVIL MADE ME DO IT."
I HAVE NEVER MADE ONE OF THEM DO ANYTHING.
NEVER.
THEY LIVE THEIR OWN TINY LIVES. I DO NOT LIVE THEIR LIVES FOR THEM.
AND THEN THEY DIE, AND THEY COME HERE (HAVING TRANSGRESSED AGAINST WHAT THEY BELIEVED TO BE RIGHT), AND EXPECT US TO FULFILL THEIR DESIRE FOR PAIN AND RETRIBUTION.
I DON'T MAKE THEM COME HERE.
THEY TALK OF ME GOING AROUND AND BUYING SOULS, LIKE A FISHWIFE COME MARKET DAY, NEVER STOPPING TO ASK THEMSELVES WHY.
I NEED NO SOULS.
AND HOW CAN ANYONE OWN A SOUL?
NO. THEY BELONG TO THEMSELVES...
...THEY JUST HATE TO HAVE TO FACE UP TO IT.

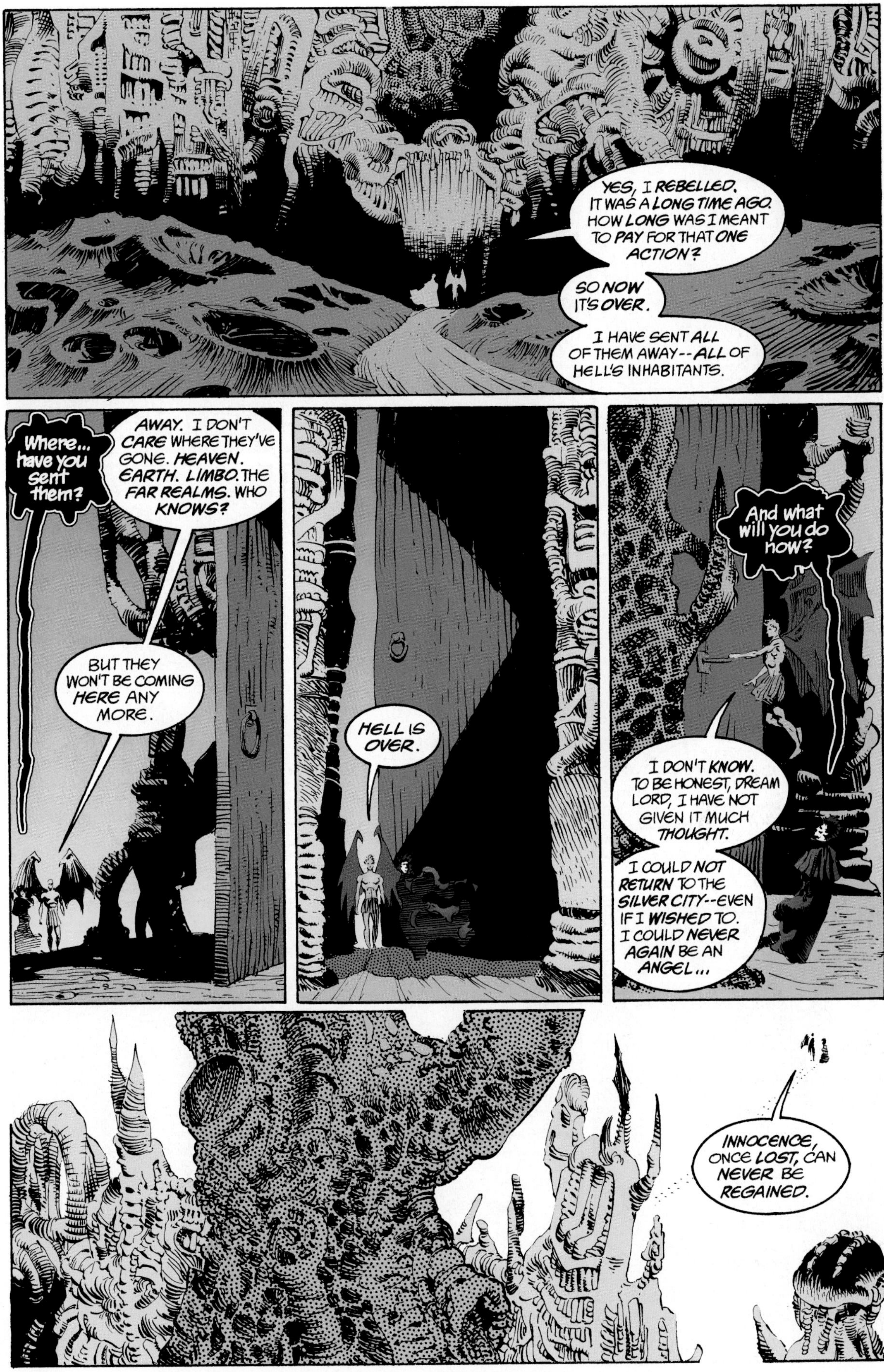
YES, I REBELLED. IT WAS A LONG TIME AGO. HOW LONG WAS I MEANT TO PAY FOR THAT ONE ACTION?
SO NOW IT'S OVER.
I HAVE SENT ALL OF THEM AWAY--ALL OF HELL'S INHABITANTS.
Where... have you sent them?
AWAY. I DON'T CARE WHERE THEY'VE GONE. HEAVEN. EARTH. LIMBO. THE FAR REALMS. WHO KNOWS?
BUT THEY WON'T BE COMING HERE ANY MORE.
HELL IS OVER.
And what will you do now?
I DON'T KNOW. TO BE HONEST, DREAM LORD, I HAVE NOT GIVEN IT MUCH THOUGHT.
I COULD NOT RETURN TO THE SILVER CITY--EVEN IF I WISHED TO. I COULD NEVER AGAIN BE AN ANGEL...
INNOCENCE, ONCE LOST, CAN NEVER BE REGAINED.

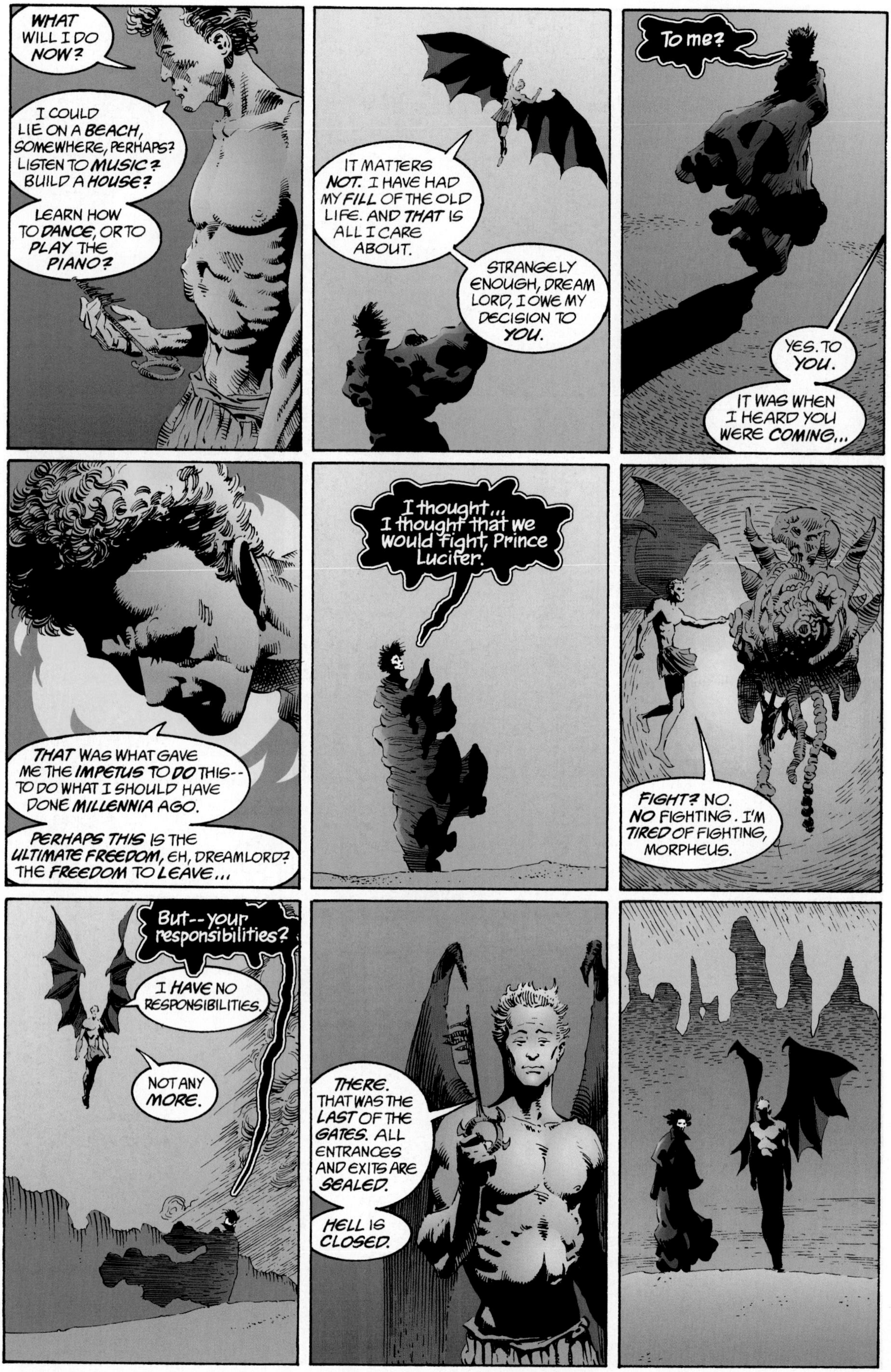
WHAT WILL I DO NOW?
I COULD LIE ON A BEACH, SOMEWHERE, PERHAPS? LISTEN TO MUSIC? BUILD A HOUSE?
LEARN HOW TO DANCE, OR TO PLAY THE PIANO?
IT MATTERS NOT. I HAVE HAD MY FILL OF THE OLD LIFE. AND THAT IS ALL I CARE ABOUT.
STRANGELY ENOUGH, DREAM LORD, I OWE MY DECISION TO YOU.
To me?
YES. TO YOU.
IT WAS WHEN I HEARD YOU WERE COMING...
THAT WAS WHAT GAVE ME THE IMPETUS TO DO THIS-- TO DO WHAT I SHOULD HAVE DONE MILLENNIA AGO.
PERHAPS THIS IS THE ULTIMATE FREEDOM, EH, DREAMLORD? THE FREEDOM TO LEAVE...
I thought... I thought that we would fight, Prince Lucifer.
FIGHT? NO. NO FIGHTING. I'M TIRED OF FIGHTING, MORPHEUS.
But--your responsibilities?
I HAVE NO RESPONSIBILITIES.
NOT ANY MORE.
THERE. THAT WAS THE LAST OF THE GATES. ALL ENTRANCES AND EXITS ARE SEALED.
HELL IS CLOSED.

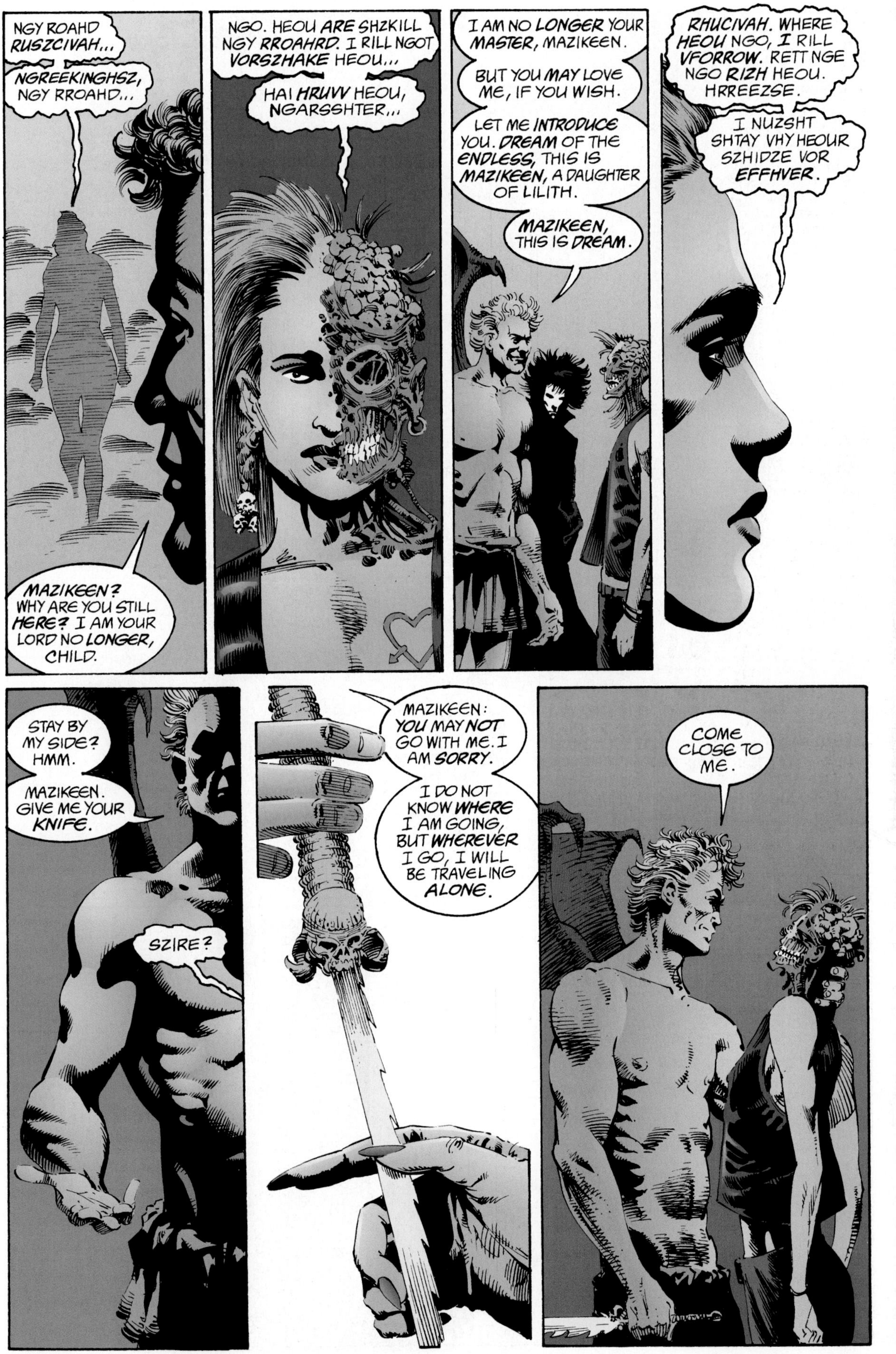
NGY ROAHD RUSZCIVAH...
NGREEKINGHSZ, NGY RROAHD...
MAZIKEEN? WHY ARE YOU STILL HERE? I AM YOUR LORD NO LONGER, CHILD.
NGO. HEOU ARE SHZKILL NGY RROAHRD. I RILL NGOT VORSZHAKE HEOU...
HAI HRUVV HEOU, NGARSSHTER...
I AM NO LONGER YOUR MASTER, MAZIKEEN.
BUT YOU MAY LOVE ME, IF YOU WISH.
LET ME INTRODUCE YOU. DREAM OF THE ENDLESS, THIS IS MAZIKEEN, A DAUGHTER OF LILITH.
MAZIKEEN, THIS IS DREAM.
RHUCIVAH. WHERE HEOU NGO, I RILL VFORROW. RETT NGE NGO RIZH HEOU. HRREEZSE.
I NUZSHT SHTAY VHY HEOUR SZHIDZE VOR EFFHVER.
STAY BY MY SIDE? HMM.
MAZIKEEN. GIVE ME YOUR KNIFE.
SZIRE?
MAZIKEEN: YOU MAY NOT GO WITH ME. I AM SORRY.
I DO NOT KNOW WHERE I AM GOING, BUT WHEREVER I GO, I WILL BE TRAVELING ALONE.
COME CLOSE TO ME.

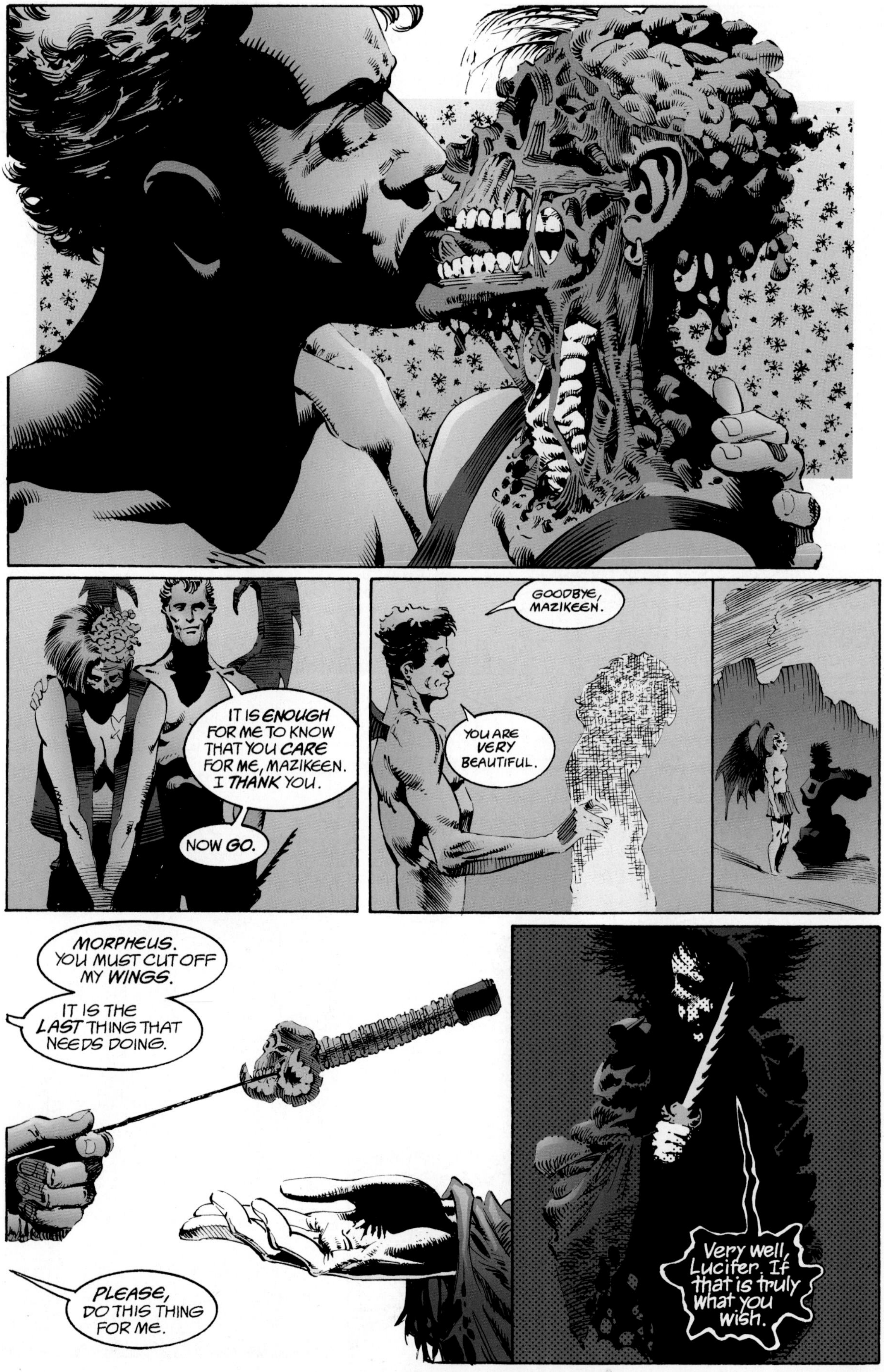
IT IS ENOUGH FOR ME TO KNOW THAT YOU CARE FOR ME, MAZIKEEN. I THANK YOU.
NOW GO.
GOODBYE, MAZIKEEN.
YOU ARE VERY BEAUTIFUL.
MORPHEUS. YOU MUST CUT OFF MY WINGS.
IT IS THE LAST THING THAT NEEDS DOING.
PLEASE, DO THIS THING FOR ME.
Very well, Lucifer. If that is truly what you wish.

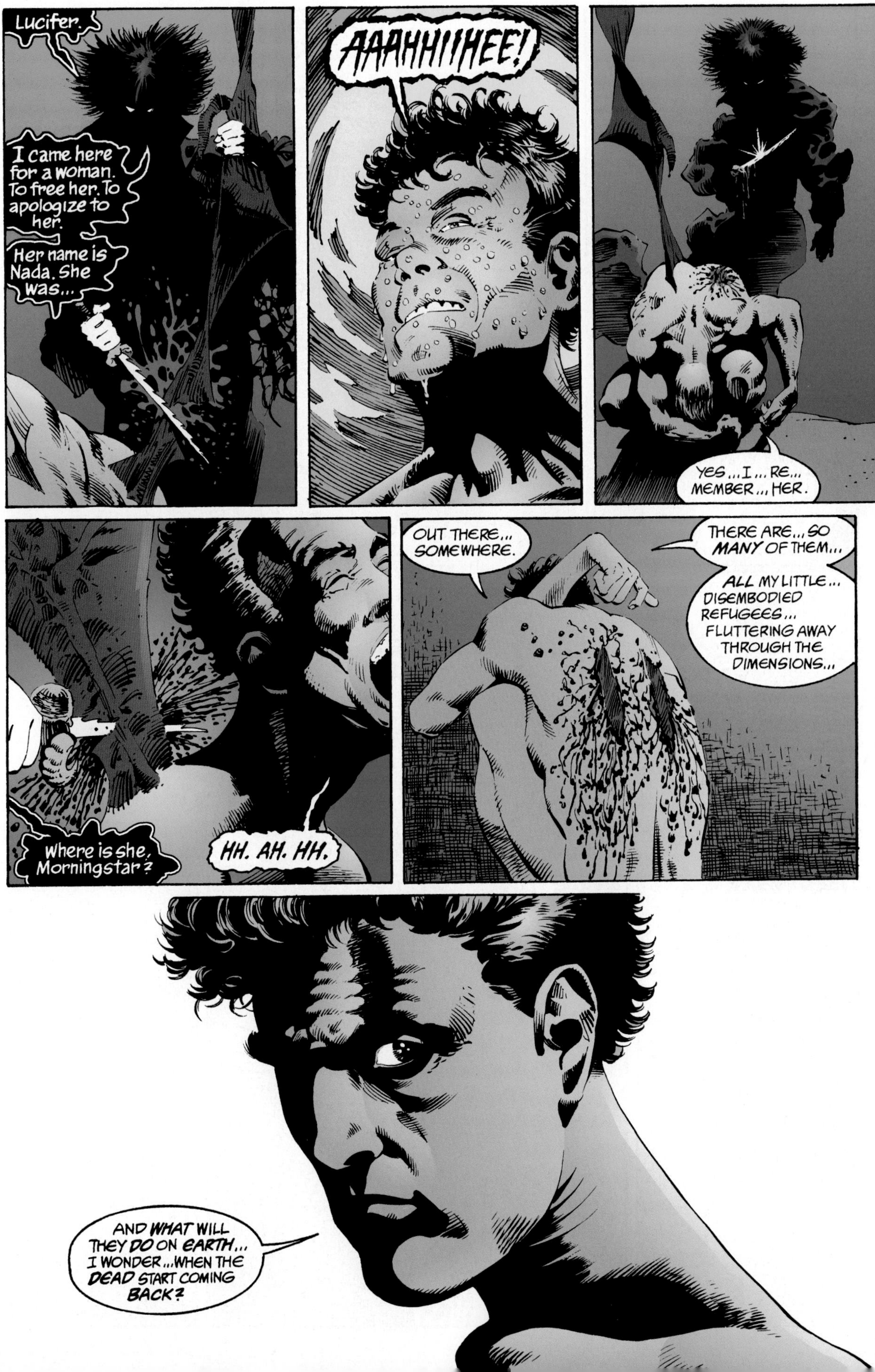
Lucifer.
I came here for a woman. To free her. To apologize to her.
Her name is Nada. She was...
AAAHHIIHEE!
YES... I... RE... MEMBER... HER.
Where is she, Morningstar?
HH. AH. HH.
OUT THERE... SOMEWHERE.
THERE ARE... SO MANY OF THEM...
ALL MY LITTLE... DISEMBODIED REFUGEES... FLUTTERING AWAY THROUGH THE DIMENSIONS...
AND WHAT WILL THEY DO ON EARTH... I WONDER... WHEN THE DEAD START COMING BACK?

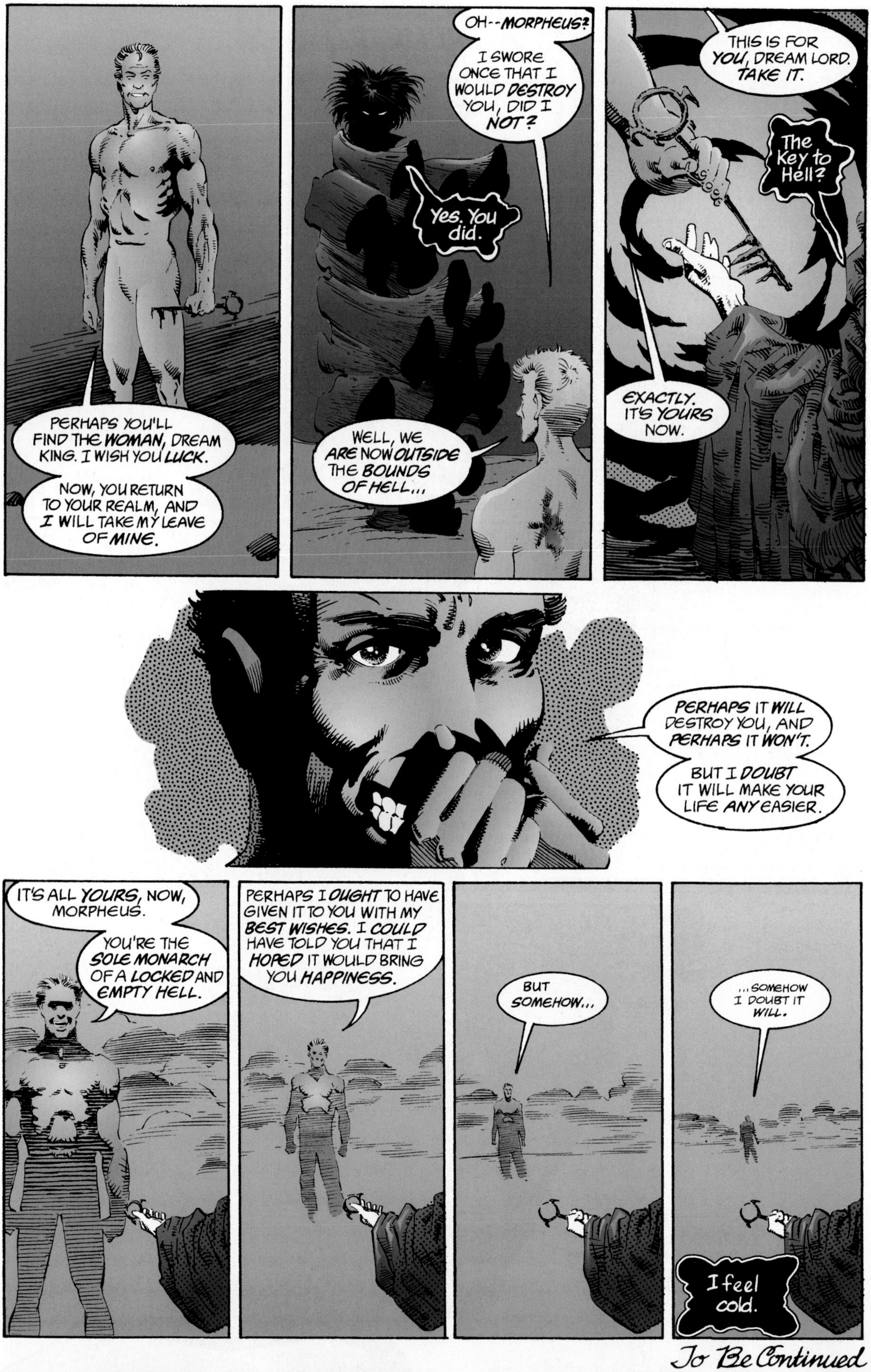
PERHAPS YOU'LL FIND THE WOMAN, DREAM KING. I WISH YOU LUCK.
NOW, YOU RETURN TO YOUR REALM, AND I WILL TAKE MY LEAVE OF MINE.
OH--MORPHEUS?
I SWORE ONCE THAT I WOULD DESTROY YOU, DID I NOT?
Yes. You did.
WELL, WE ARE NOW OUTSIDE THE BOUNDS OF HELL...
THIS IS FOR YOU, DREAM LORD. TAKE IT.
The Key to Hell?
EXACTLY. IT'S YOURS NOW.
PERHAPS IT WILL DESTROY YOU, AND PERHAPS IT WON'T.
BUT I DOUBT IT WILL MAKE YOUR LIFE ANY EASIER.
IT'S ALL YOURS, NOW, MORPHEUS.
YOU'RE THE SOLE MONARCH OF A LOCKED AND EMPTY HELL.
PERHAPS I OUGHT TO HAVE GIVEN IT TO YOU WITH MY BEST WISHES. I COULD HAVE TOLD YOU THAT I HOPED IT WOULD BRING YOU HAPPINESS.
BUT SOMEHOW...
...SOMEHOW I DOUBT IT WILL.
I feel cold.
To Be Continued

In which Lucifer's parting gift attracts unwanted attention; and the Dream Lord receives unwelcome visitors.

EPISODE 3

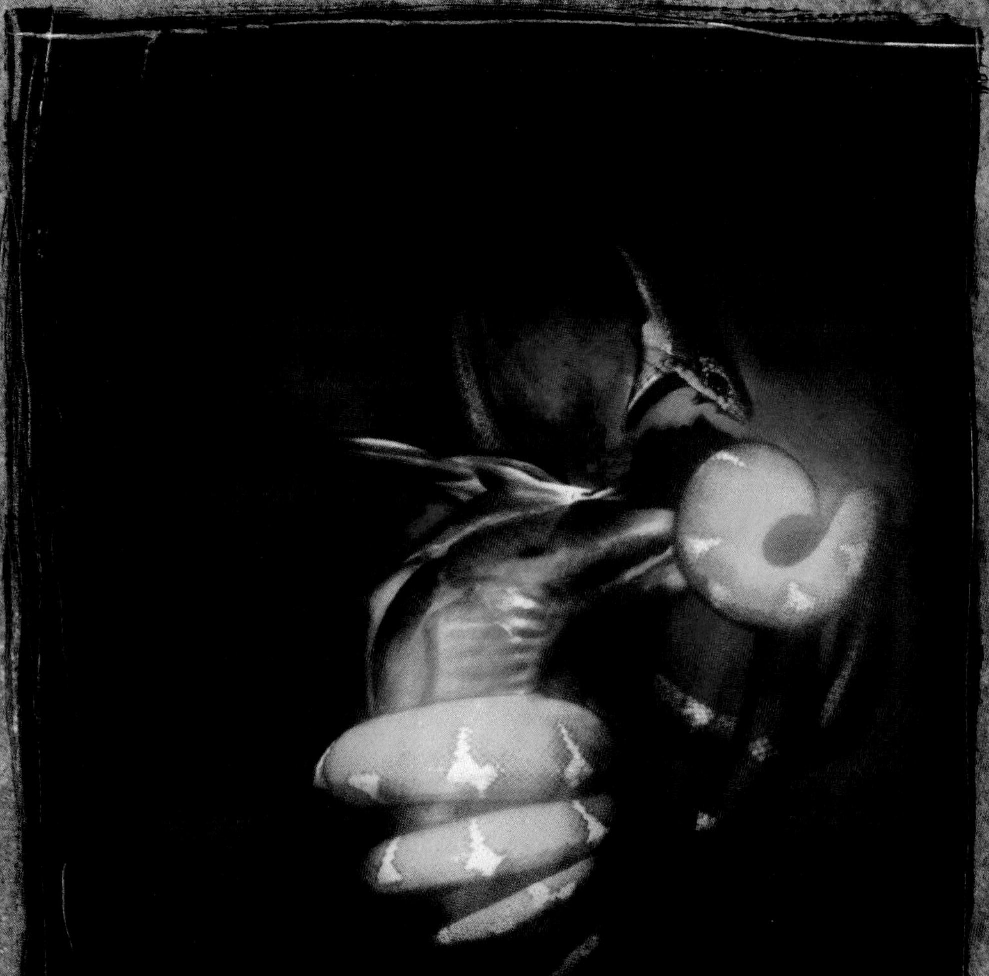

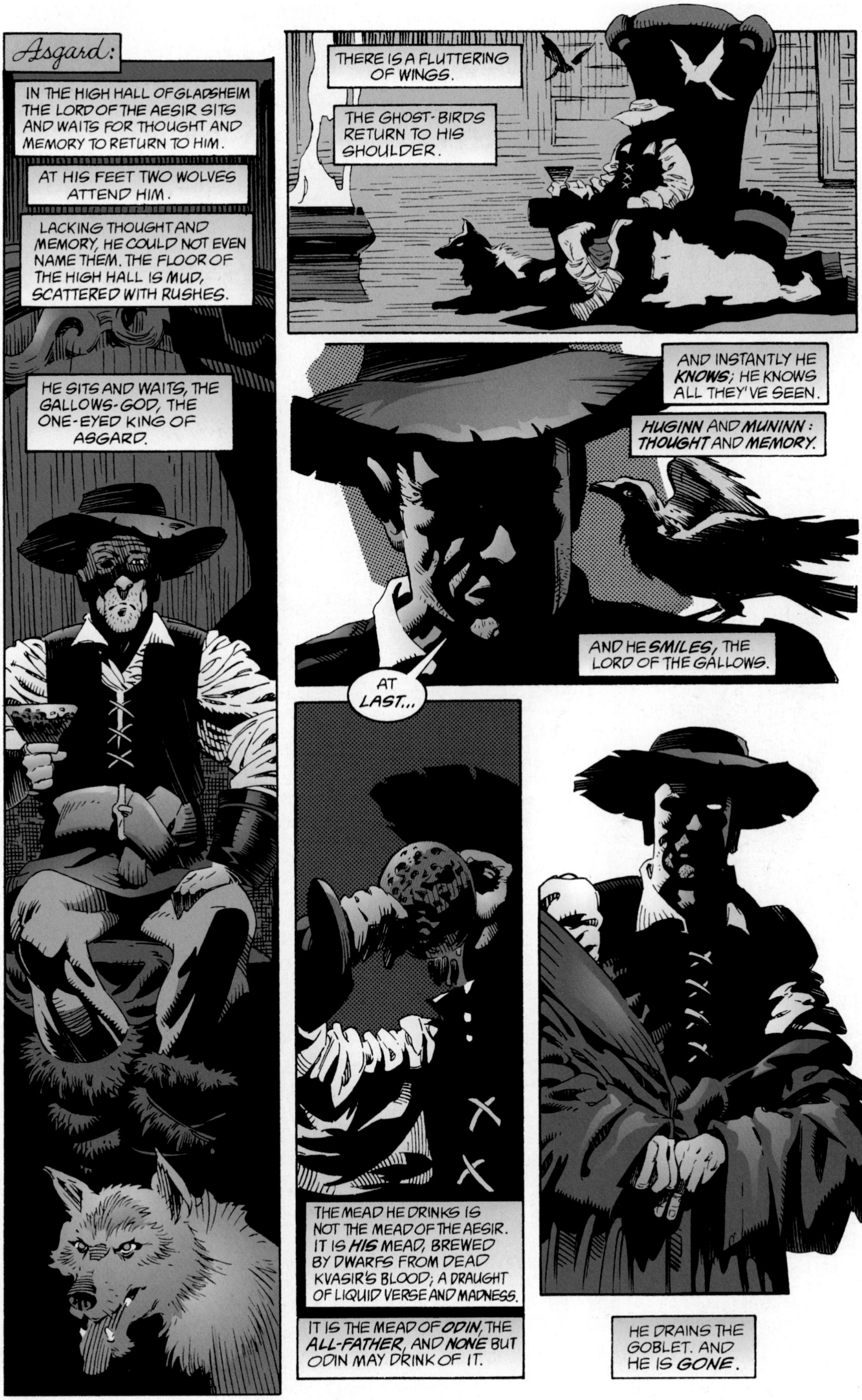
Asgard:
IN THE HIGH HALL OF GLADSHEIM THE LORD OF THE AESIR SITS AND WAITS FOR THOUGHT AND MEMORY TO RETURN TO HIM.
AT HIS FEET TWO WOLVES ATTEND HIM.
LACKING THOUGHT AND MEMORY, HE COULD NOT EVEN NAME THEM. THE FLOOR OF THE HIGH HALL IS MUD, SCATTERED WITH RUSHES.
HE SITS AND WAITS, THE GALLOWS-GOD, THE ONE-EYED KING OF ASGARD.
THERE IS A FLUTTERING OF WINGS.
THE GHOST-BIRDS RETURN TO HIS SHOULDER.
AND INSTANTLY HE KNOWS; HE KNOWS ALL THEY'VE SEEN.
HUGINN AND MUNINN: THOUGHT AND MEMORY.
AND HE SMILES, THE LORD OF THE GALLOWS.
AT LAST...
THE MEAD HE DRINKS IS NOT THE MEAD OF THE AESIR. IT IS HIS MEAD, BREWED BY DWARFS FROM DEAD KVASIR'S BLOOD; A DRAUGHT OF LIQUID VERSE AND MADNESS.
IT IS THE MEAD OF ODIN, THE ALL-FATHER, AND NONE BUT ODIN MAY DRINK OF IT.
HE DRAINS THE GOBLET. AND HE IS GONE.

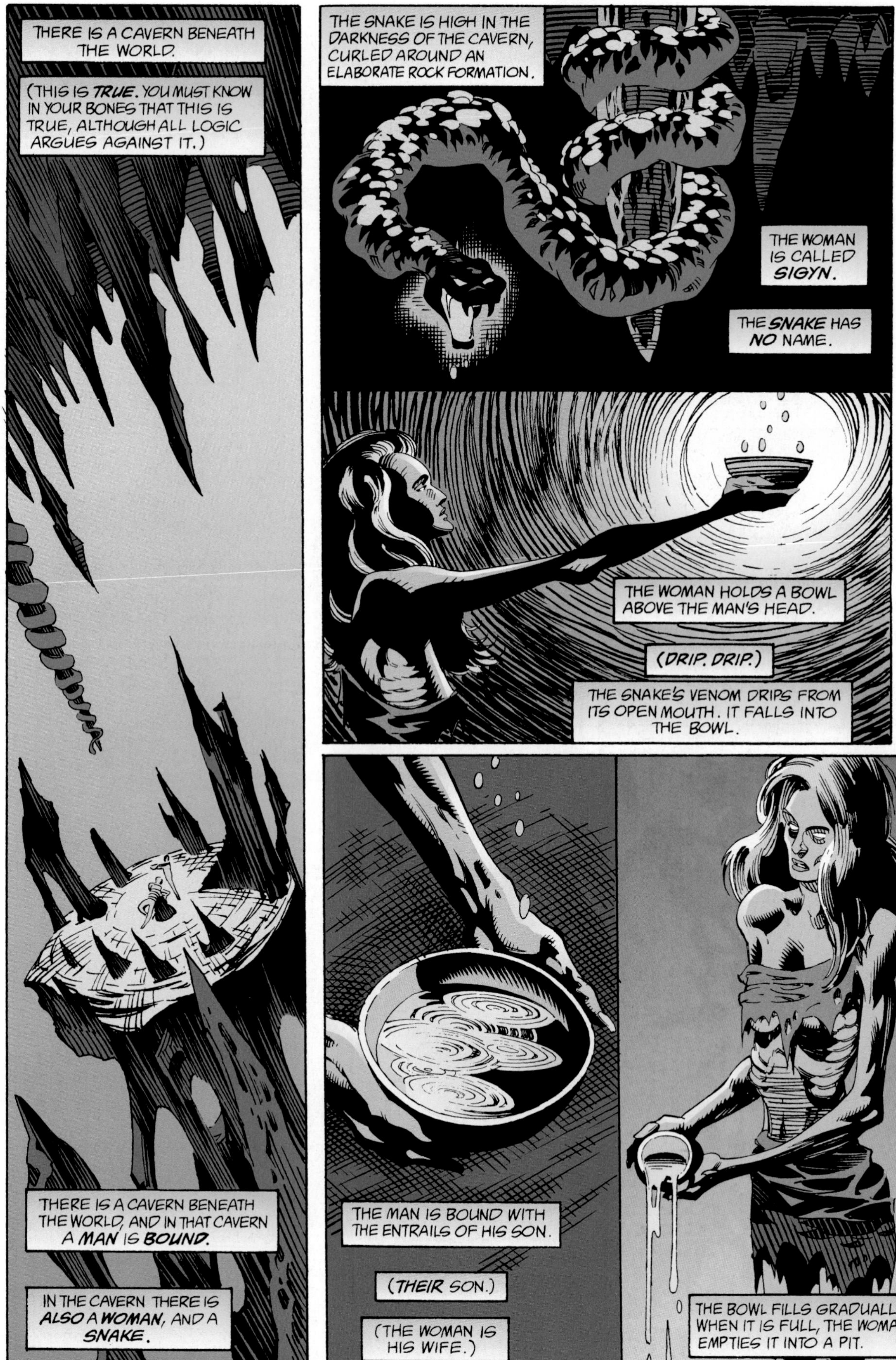
THERE IS A CAVERN BENEATH THE WORLD.
(THIS IS TRUE. YOU MUST KNOW IN YOUR BONES THAT THIS IS TRUE, ALTHOUGH ALL LOGIC ARGUES AGAINST IT.)
THERE IS A CAVERN BENEATH THE WORLD, AND IN THAT CAVERN A MAN IS BOUND.
IN THE CAVERN THERE IS ALSO A WOMAN, AND A SNAKE.
THE SNAKE IS HIGH IN THE DARKNESS OF THE CAVERN, CURLED AROUND AN ELABORATE ROCK FORMATION.
THE WOMAN IS CALLED SIGYN.
THE SNAKE HAS NO NAME.
THE WOMAN HOLDS A BOWL ABOVE THE MAN'S HEAD.
(DRIP. DRIP.)
THE SNAKE'S VENOM DRIPS FROM ITS OPEN MOUTH. IT FALLS INTO THE BOWL.
THE MAN IS BOUND WITH THE ENTRAILS OF HIS SON.
(THEIR SON.)
(THE WOMAN IS HIS WIFE.)
THE BOWL FILLS GRADUALLY WHEN IT IS FULL, THE WOMAN EMPTIES IT INTO A PIT.

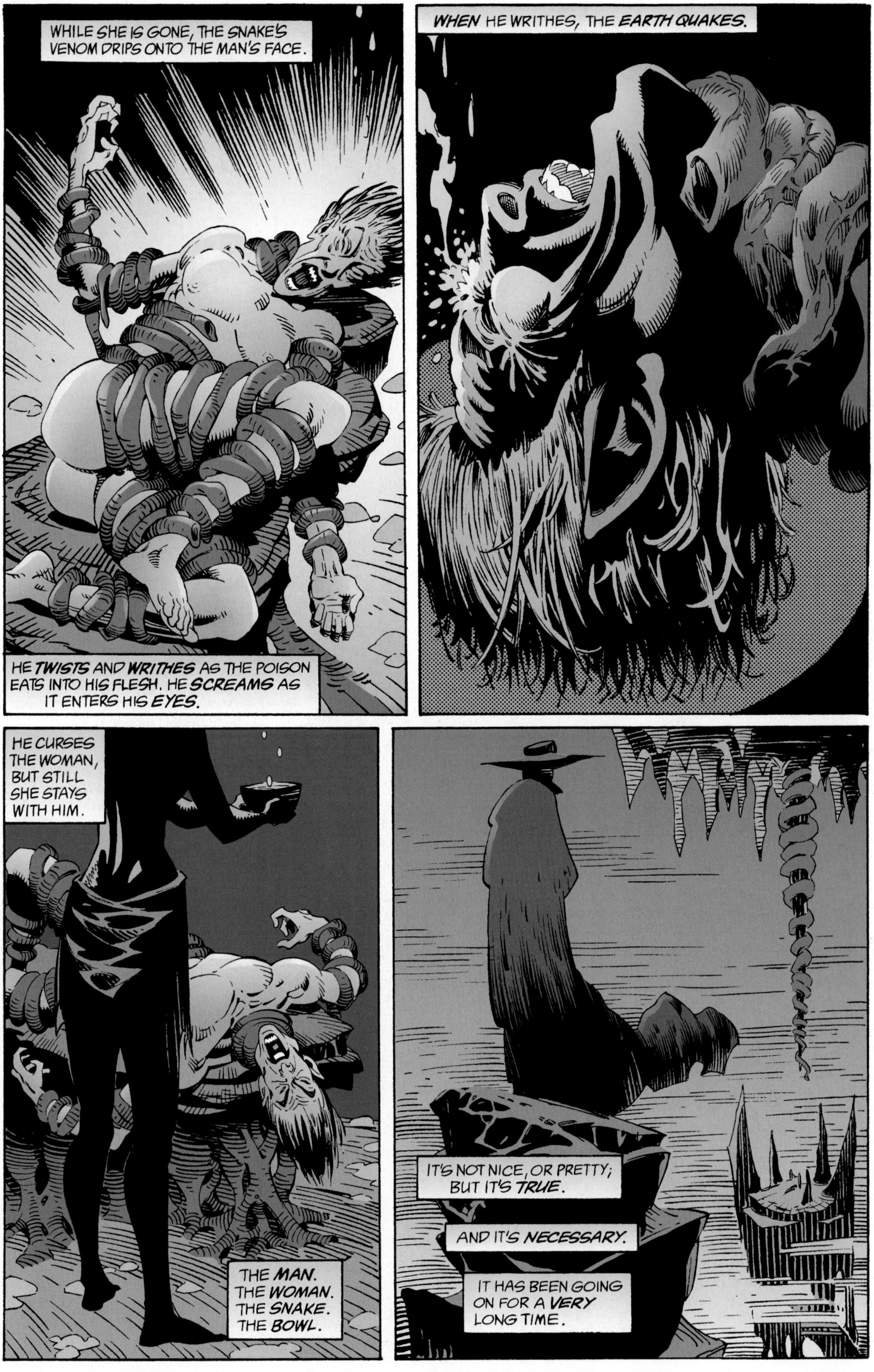
WHILE SHE IS GONE, THE SNAKE'S VENOM DRIPS ONTO THE MAN'S FACE.
HE TWISTS AND WRITHES AS THE POISON EATS INTO HIS FLESH. HE SCREAMS AS IT ENTERS HIS EYES.
WHEN HE WRITHES, THE EARTH QUAKES.
HE CURSES THE WOMAN, BUT STILL SHE STAYS WITH HIM.
THE MAN. THE WOMAN. THE SNAKE. THE BOWL.
IT'S NOT NICE, OR PRETTY; BUT IT'S TRUE.
AND IT'S NECESSARY.
IT HAS BEEN GOING ON FOR A VERY LONG TIME.

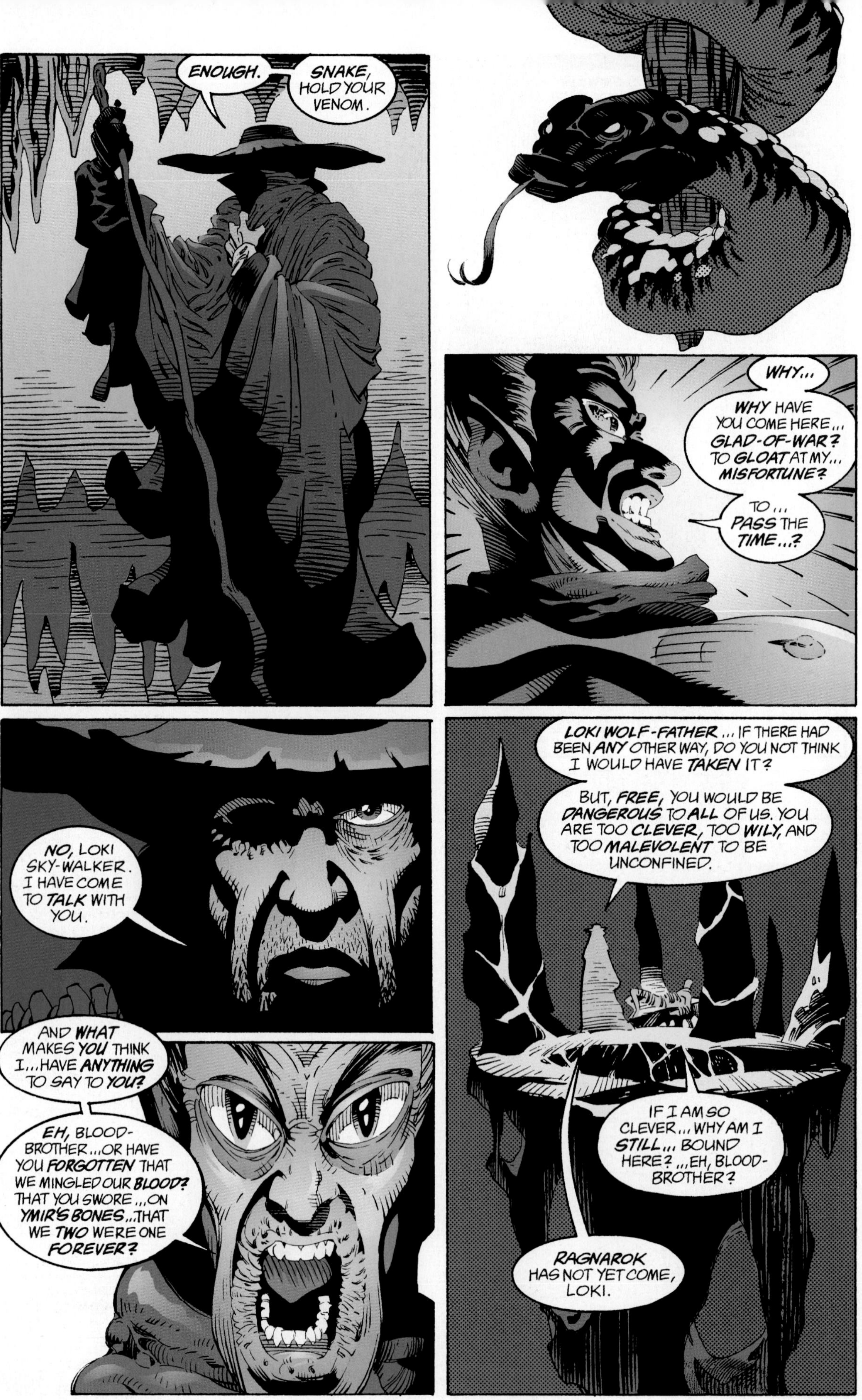
ENOUGH.
SNAKE, HOLD YOUR VENOM.
WHY...
WHY HAVE YOU COME HERE... GLAD-OF-WAR? TO GLOAT AT MY... MISFORTUNE?
TO... PASS THE TIME...?
NO, LOKI SKY-WALKER. I HAVE COME TO TALK WITH YOU.
AND WHAT MAKES YOU THINK I...HAVE ANYTHING TO SAY TO YOU?
EH, BLOOD-BROTHER...OR HAVE YOU FORGOTTEN THAT WE MINGLED OUR BLOOD? THAT YOU SWORE...ON YMIR'S BONES...THAT WE TWO WERE ONE FOREVER?
LOKI WOLF-FATHER... IF THERE HAD BEEN ANY OTHER WAY, DO YOU NOT THINK I WOULD HAVE TAKEN IT?
BUT, FREE, YOU WOULD BE DANGEROUS TO ALL OF US. YOU ARE TOO CLEVER, TOO WILY, AND TOO MALEVOLENT TO BE UNCONFINED.
IF I AM SO CLEVER... WHY AM I STILL... BOUND HERE? ...EH, BLOOD-BROTHER?
RAGNAROK HAS NOT YET COME, LOKI.

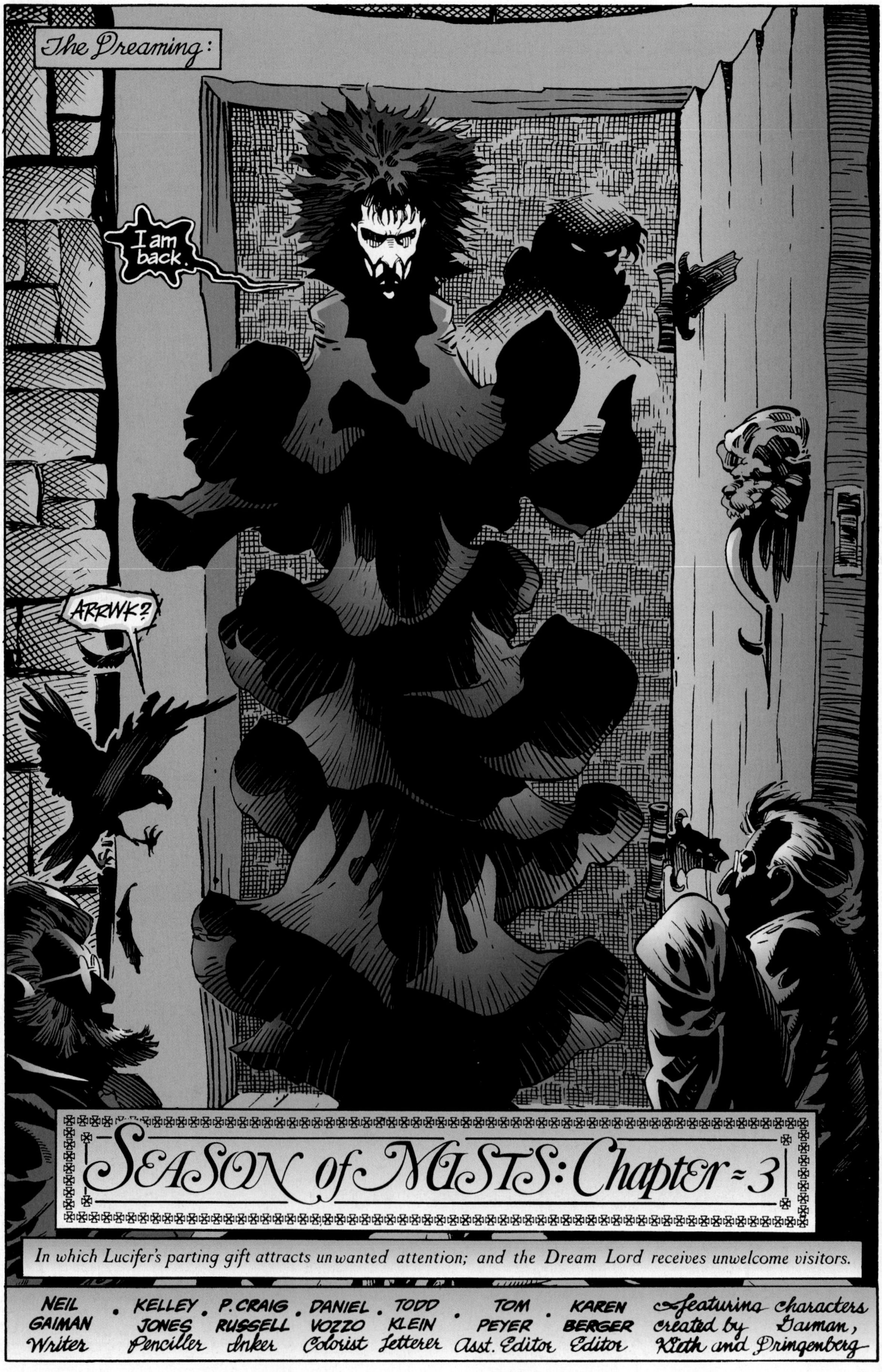

The Dreaming:
I am back.
ARRWK?
SEASON of MISTS: Chapter 3
In which Lucifer's parting gift attracts unwanted attention; and the Dream Lord receives unwelcome visitors.
NEIL GAIMAN Writer
KELLEY JONES Penciller
P. CRAIG RUSSELL Inker
DANIEL VOZZO Colorist
TODD KLEIN Letterer
TOM PEYER Asst. Editor
KAREN BERGER Editor
featuring characters created by Gaiman, Kieth and Dringenberg

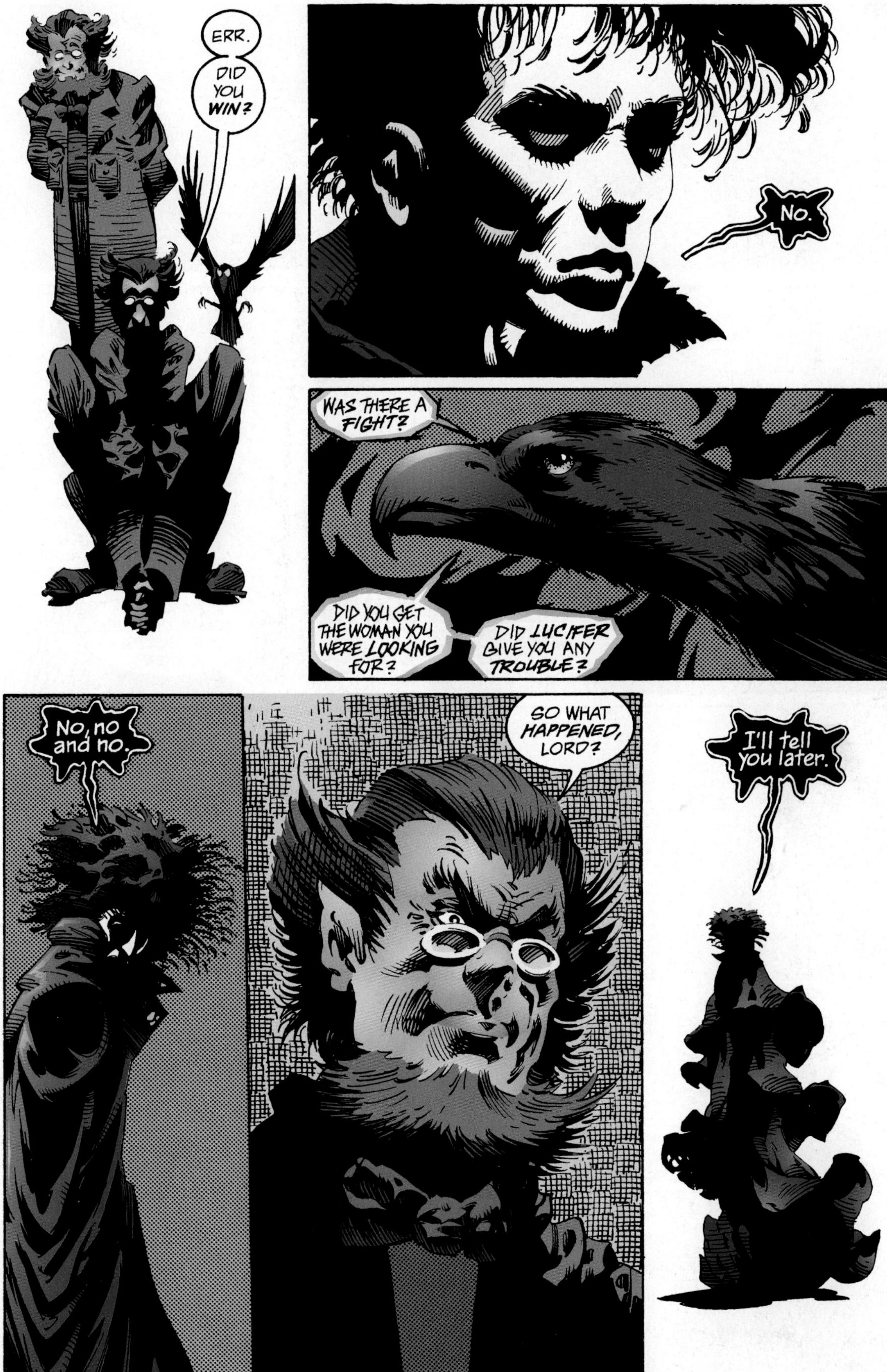
ERR.
DID YOU WIN?
NO.
WAS THERE A FIGHT?
DID YOU GET THE WOMAN YOU WERE LOOKING FOR?
DID LUCIFER GIVE YOU ANY TROUBLE?
No, no and no.
SO WHAT HAPPENED, LORD?
I'll tell you later.

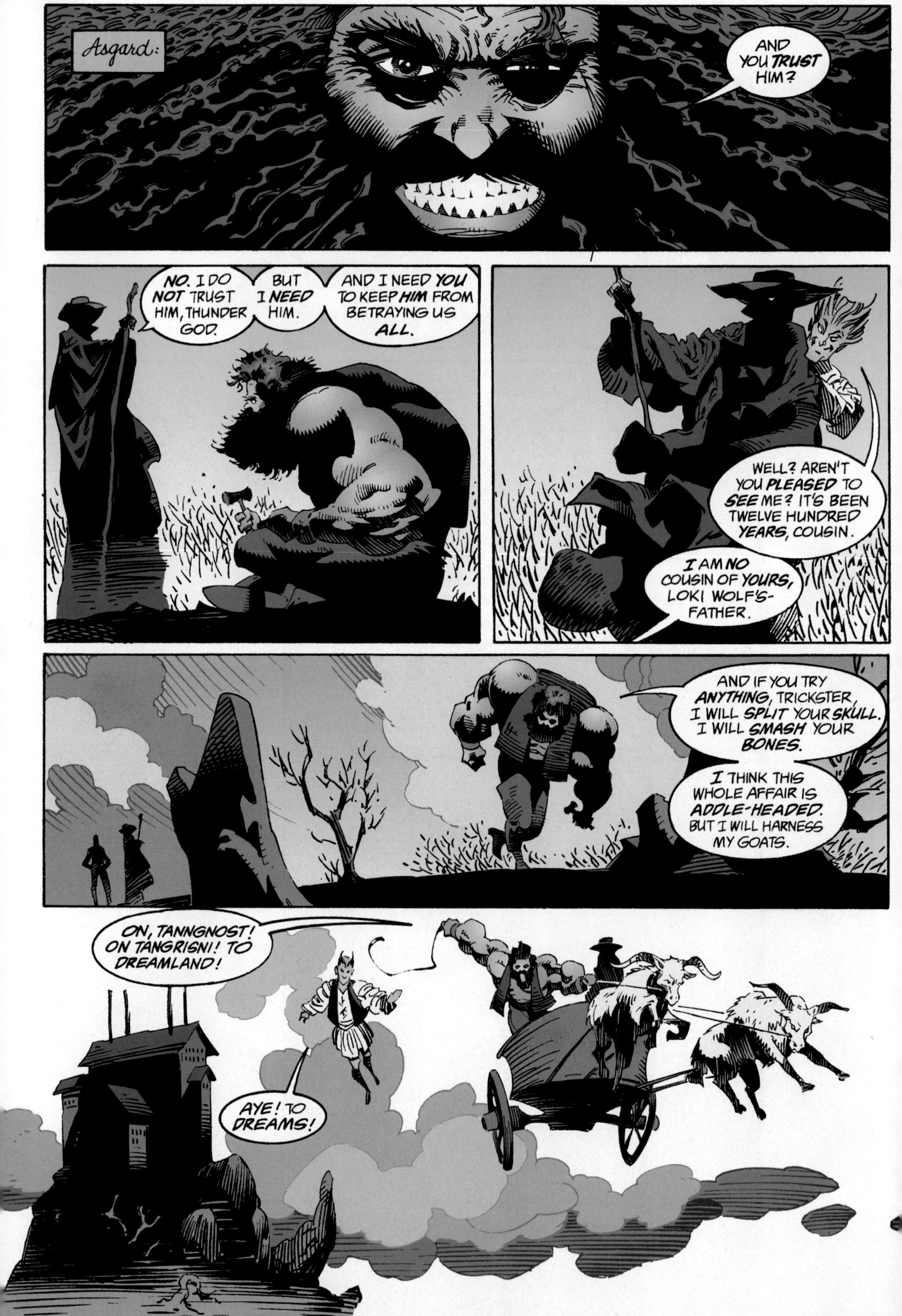
Asgard:
AND YOU TRUST HIM?
NO. I DO NOT TRUST HIM, THUNDER GOD.
BUT I NEED HIM.
AND I NEED YOU TO KEEP HIM FROM BETRAYING US ALL.
WELL? AREN'T YOU PLEASED TO SEE ME? IT'S BEEN TWELVE HUNDRED YEARS, COUSIN.
I AM NO COUSIN OF YOURS, LOKI WOLF'S-FATHER.
AND IF YOU TRY ANYTHING, TRICKSTER, I WILL SPLIT YOUR SKULL. I WILL SMASH YOUR BONES.
I THINK THIS WHOLE AFFAIR IS ADDLE-HEADED. BUT I WILL HARNESS MY GOATS.
ON, TANNGNOST! ON TANGRISNI! TO DREAMLAND!
AYE! TO DREAMS!

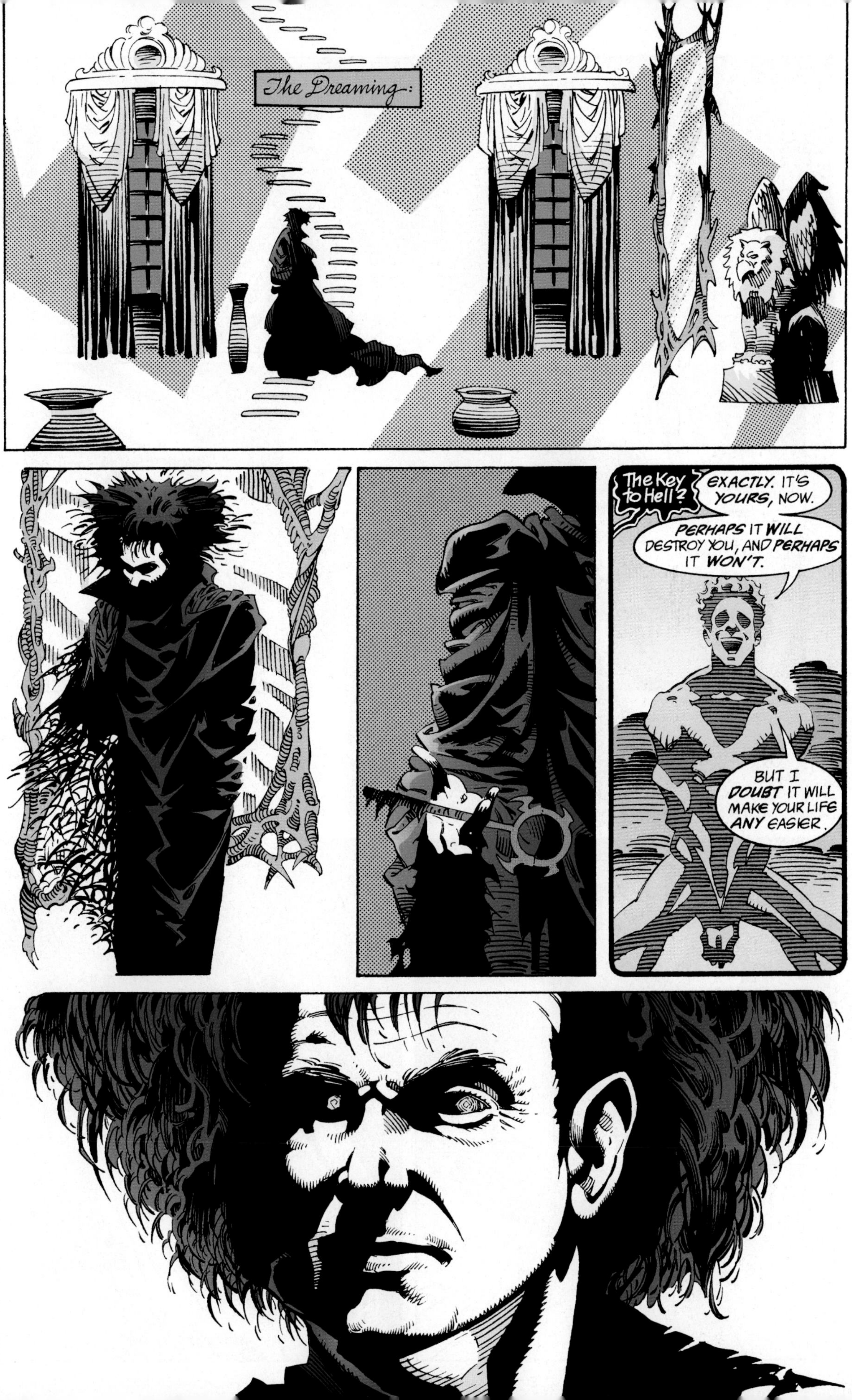
The Dreaming:
The Key to Hell?
EXACTLY. IT'S YOURS, NOW.
PERHAPS IT WILL DESTROY YOU, AND PERHAPS IT WON'T.
BUT I DOUBT IT WILL MAKE YOUR LIFE ANY EASIER.

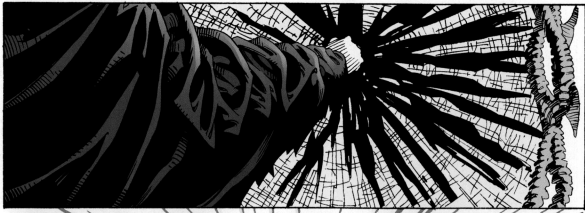

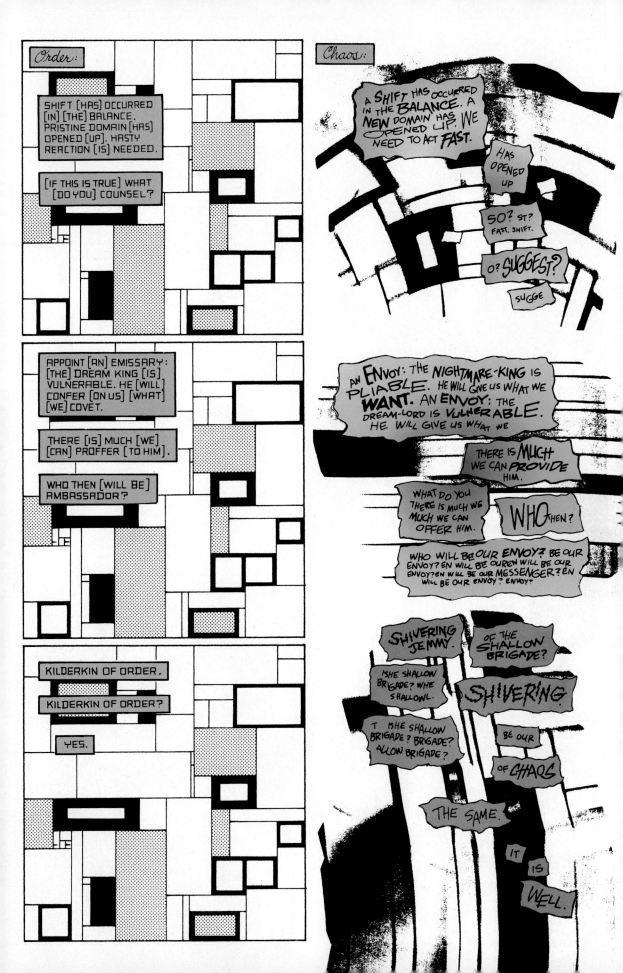

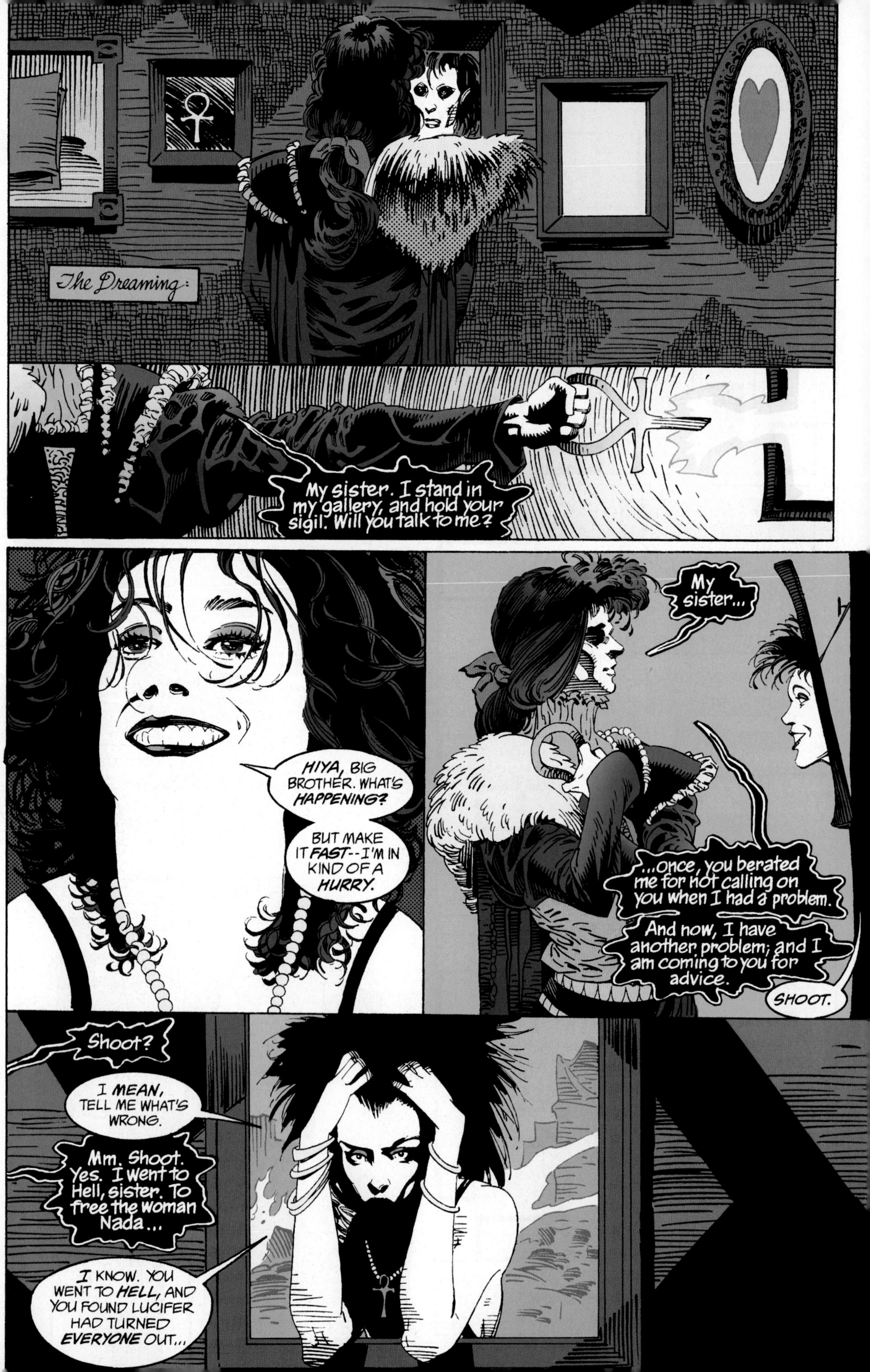

The Dreaming:
My sister. I stand in my gallery, and hold your sigil. Will you talk to me?
HIYA, BIG BROTHER. WHAT'S HAPPENING?
BUT MAKE IT FAST--I'M IN KIND OF A HURRY.
My sister...
...once, you berated me for not calling on you when I had a problem.
And now, I have another problem; and I am coming to you for advice.
SHOOT.
Shoot?
I MEAN, TELL ME WHAT'S WRONG.
Mm. Shoot. Yes. I went to Hell, sister. To free the woman Nada...
I KNOW. YOU WENT TO HELL, AND YOU FOUND LUCIFER HAD TURNED EVERYONE OUT...

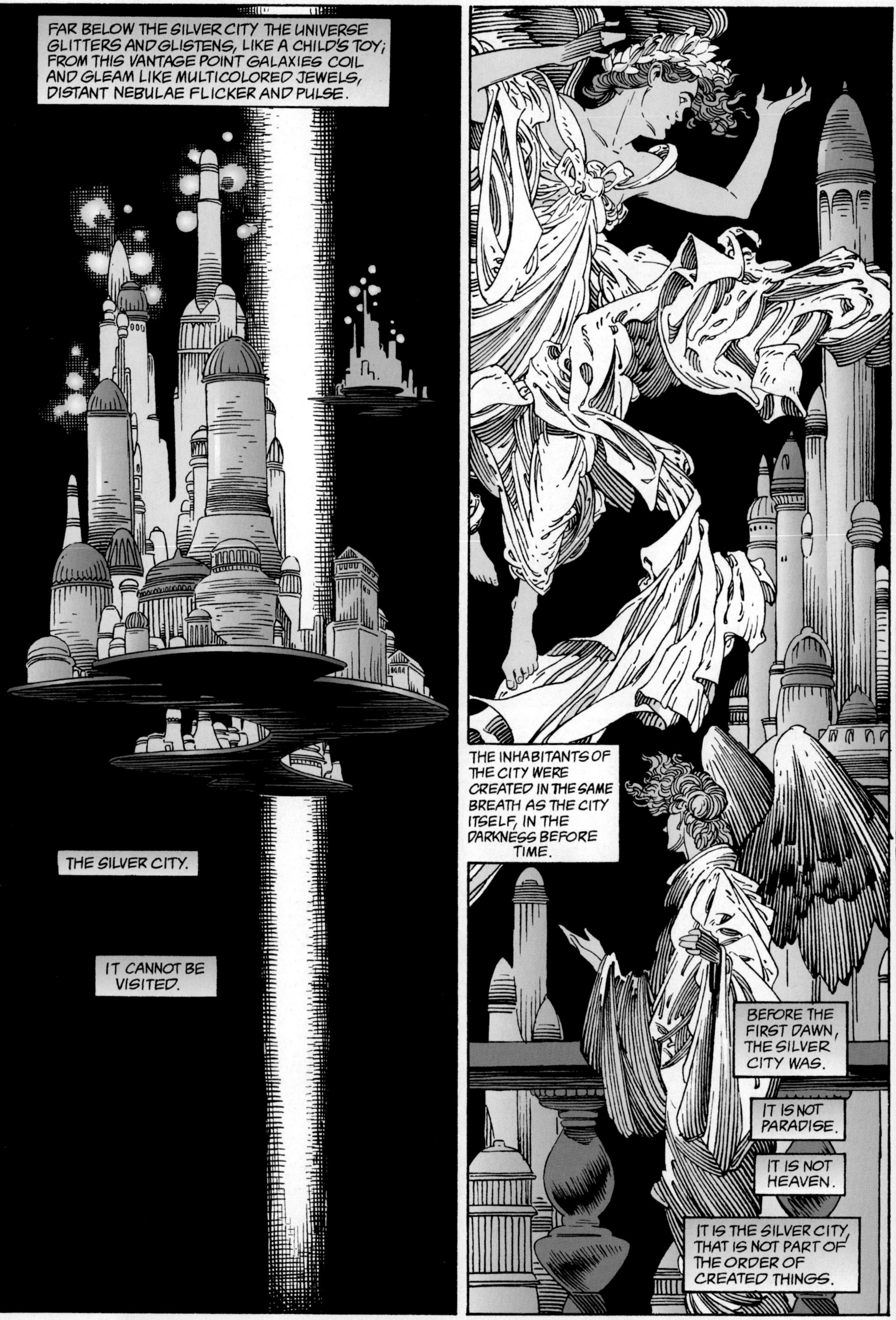
FAR BELOW THE SILVER CITY THE UNIVERSE GLITTERS AND GLISTENS, LIKE A CHILD'S TOY; FROM THIS VANTAGE POINT GALAXIES COIL AND GLEAM LIKE MULTICOLORED JEWELS, DISTANT NEBULAE FLICKER AND PULSE.
THE SILVER CITY.
IT CANNOT BE VISITED.
THE INHABITANTS OF THE CITY WERE CREATED IN THE SAME BREATH AS THE CITY ITSELF, IN THE DARKNESS BEFORE TIME.
BEFORE THE FIRST DAWN, THE SILVER CITY WAS.
IT IS NOT PARADISE.
IT IS NOT HEAVEN.
IT IS THE SILVER CITY, THAT IS NOT PART OF THE ORDER OF CREATED THINGS.

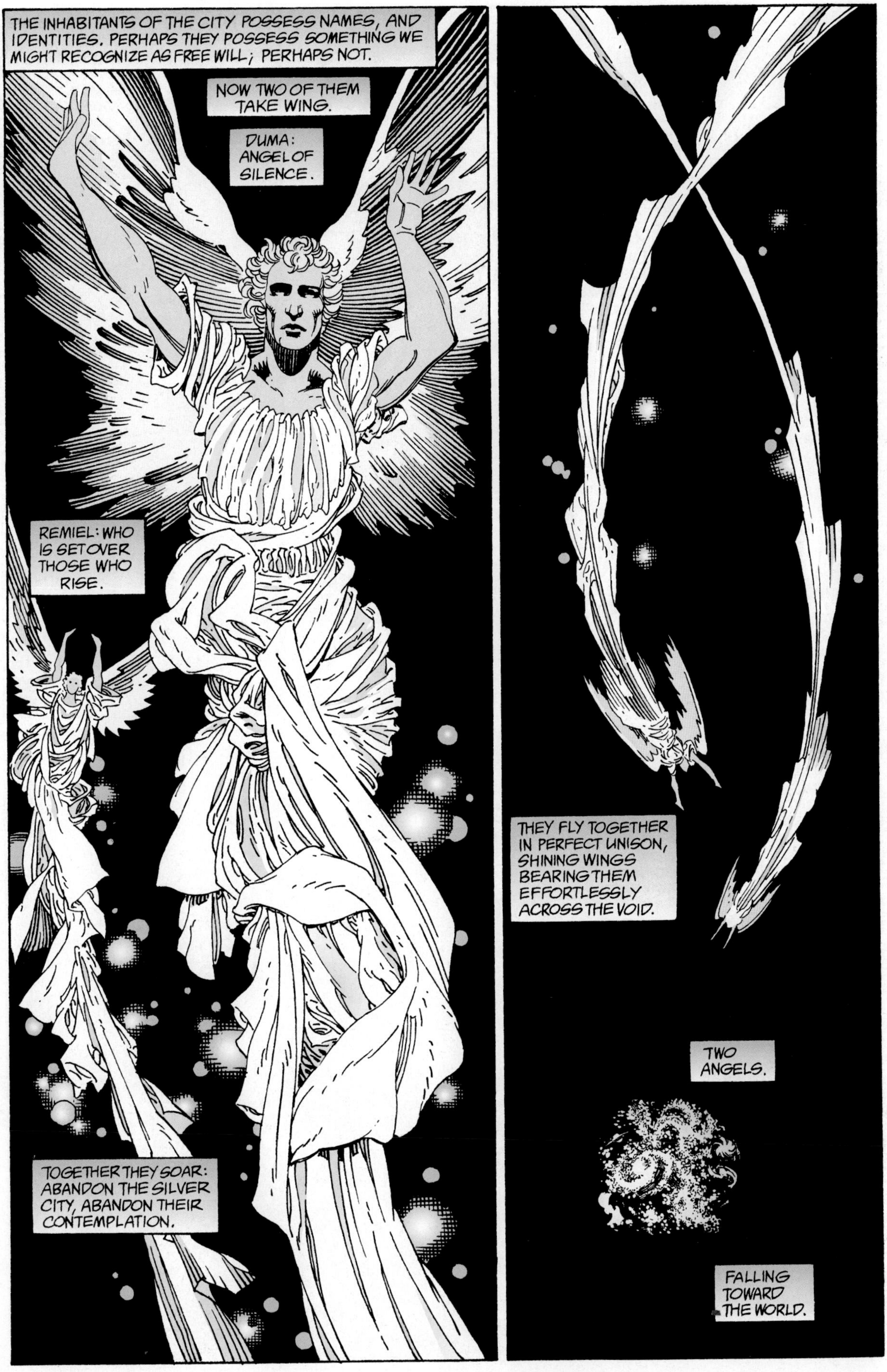
THE INHABITANTS OF THE CITY POSSESS NAMES, AND IDENTITIES. PERHAPS THEY POSSESS SOMETHING WE MIGHT RECOGNIZE AS FREE WILL; PERHAPS NOT.
NOW TWO OF THEM TAKE WING.
DUMA: ANGEL OF SILENCE.
REMIEL: WHO IS SET OVER THOSE WHO RISE.
TOGETHER THEY SOAR: ABANDON THE SILVER CITY, ABANDON THEIR CONTEMPLATION.
THEY FLY TOGETHER IN PERFECT UNISON, SHINING WINGS BEARING THEM EFFORTLESSLY ACROSS THE VOID.
TWO ANGELS.
FALLING TOWARD THE WORLD.

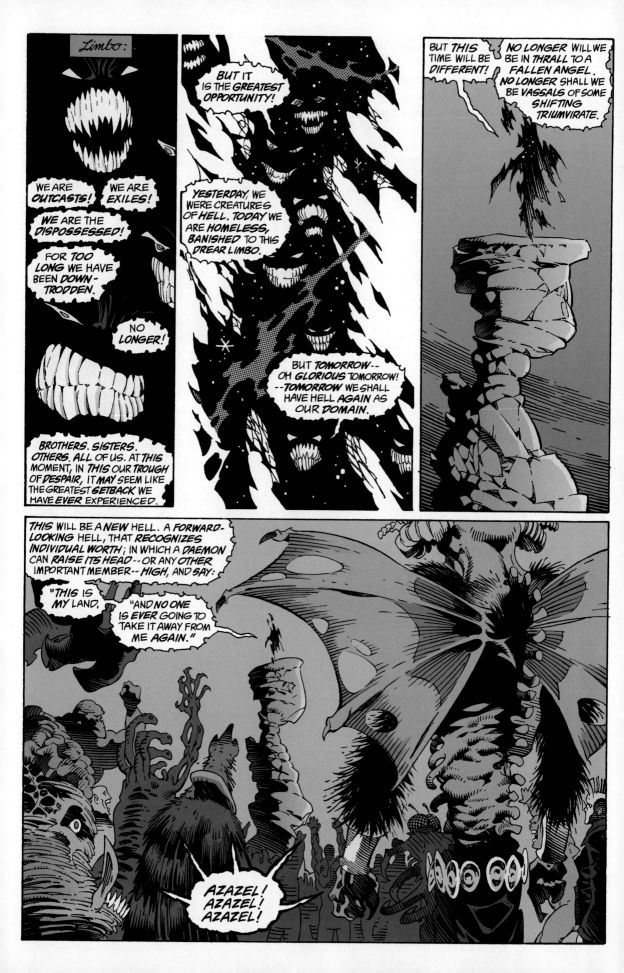

Limbo:

WE ARE OUTCASTS! WE ARE EXILES!

WE ARE THE DISPOSSESSED!

FOR TOO LONG WE HAVE BEEN DOWN-TRODDEN.

NO LONGER!

BROTHERS. SISTERS. OTHERS. ALL OF US. AT THIS MOMENT, IN THIS OUR TROUGH OF DESPAIR, IT MAY SEEM LIKE THE GREATEST SETBACK WE HAVE EVER EXPERIENCED.

BUT IT IS THE GREATEST OPPORTUNITY!

YESTERDAY, WE WERE CREATURES OF HELL. TODAY WE ARE HOMELESS, BANISHED TO THIS DREAR LIMBO.

BUT TOMORROW-- OH GLORIOUS TOMORROW! --TOMORROW WE SHALL HAVE HELL AGAIN AS OUR DOMAIN.

BUT THIS TIME WILL BE DIFFERENT!

NO LONGER WILL WE BE IN THRALL TO A FALLEN ANGEL. NO LONGER SHALL WE BE VASSALS OF SOME SHIFTING TRIUMVIRATE.

THIS WILL BE A NEW HELL. A FORWARD-LOOKING HELL, THAT RECOGNIZES INDIVIDUAL WORTH; IN WHICH A DAEMON CAN RAISE ITS HEAD--OR ANY OTHER IMPORTANT MEMBER--HIGH, AND SAY:

"THIS IS MY LAND.

"AND NO ONE IS EVER GOING TO TAKE IT AWAY FROM ME AGAIN."

AZAZEL! AZAZEL! AZAZEL!

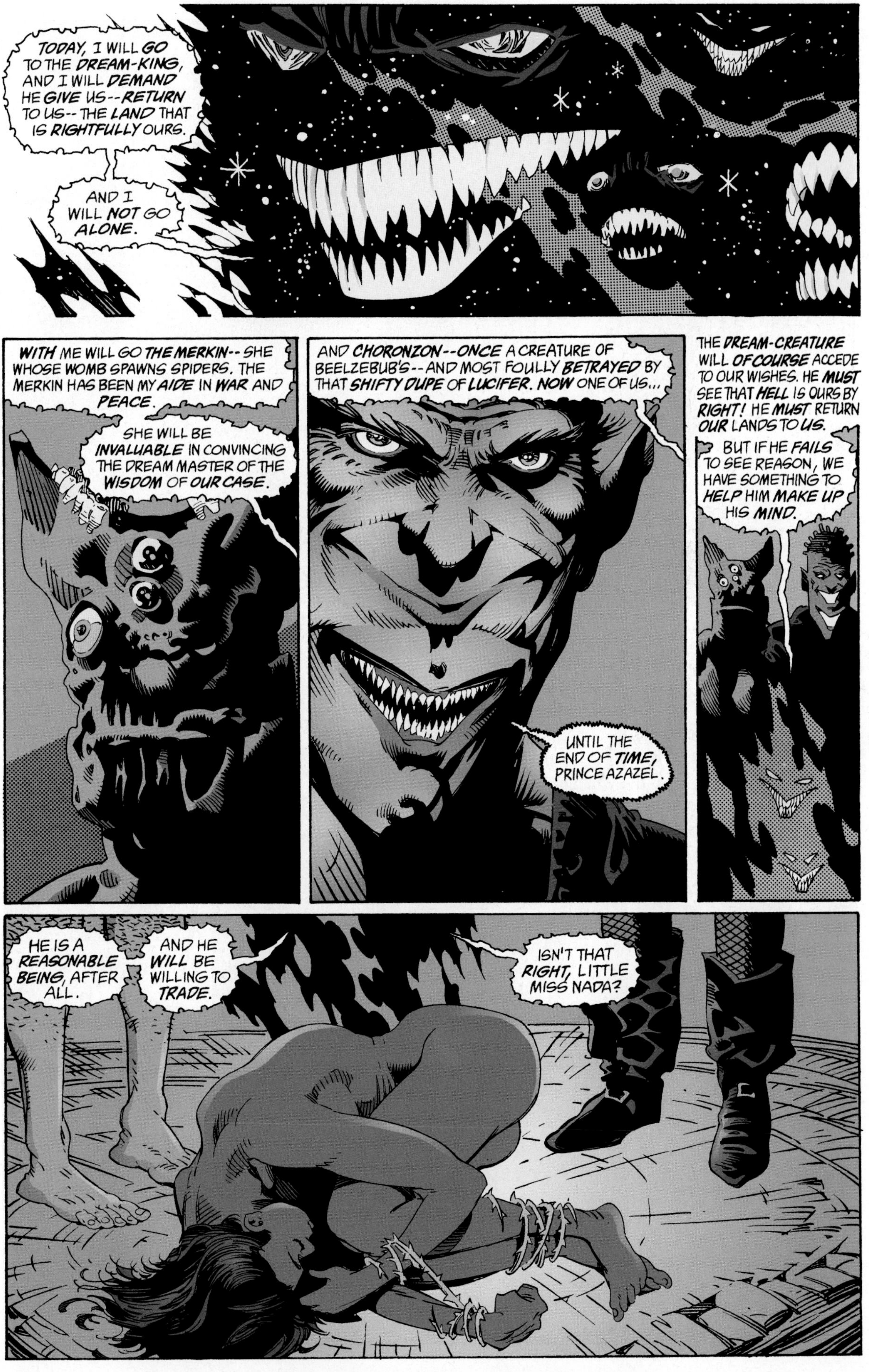
TODAY, I WILL GO TO THE DREAM-KING, AND I WILL DEMAND HE GIVE US--RETURN TO US--THE LAND THAT IS RIGHTFULLY OURS.
AND I WILL NOT GO ALONE.
WITH ME WILL GO THE MERKIN--SHE WHOSE WOMB SPAWNS SPIDERS. THE MERKIN HAS BEEN MY AIDE IN WAR AND PEACE.
SHE WILL BE INVALUABLE IN CONVINCING THE DREAM MASTER OF THE WISDOM OF OUR CASE.
AND CHORONZON--ONCE A CREATURE OF BEELZEBUB'S--AND MOST FOULLY BETRAYED BY THAT SHIFTY DUPE OF LUCIFER. NOW ONE OF US...
UNTIL THE END OF TIME, PRINCE AZAZEL.
THE DREAM-CREATURE WILL OF COURSE ACCEDE TO OUR WISHES. HE MUST SEE THAT HELL IS OURS BY RIGHT! HE MUST RETURN OUR LANDS TO US.
BUT IF HE FAILS TO SEE REASON, WE HAVE SOMETHING TO HELP HIM MAKE UP HIS MIND.
HE IS A REASONABLE BEING, AFTER ALL.
AND HE WILL BE WILLING TO TRADE.
ISN'T THAT RIGHT, LITTLE MISS NADA?

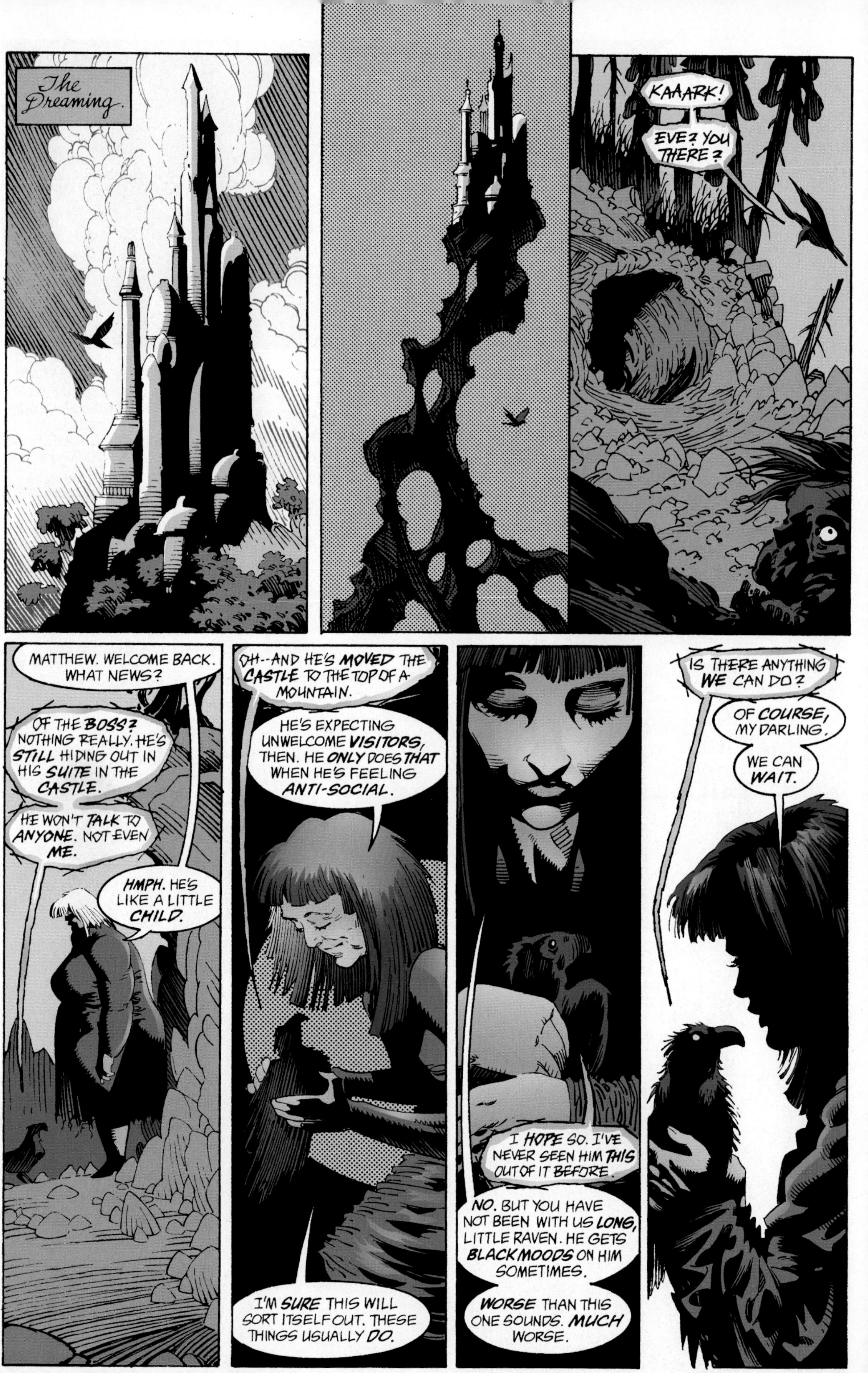
The Dreaming.
KAAARK!
EVE? YOU THERE?
MATTHEW. WELCOME BACK. WHAT NEWS?
OF THE BOSS? NOTHING REALLY. HE'S STILL HIDING OUT IN HIS SUITE IN THE CASTLE.
HE WON'T TALK TO ANYONE. NOT EVEN ME.
HMPH. HE'S LIKE A LITTLE CHILD.
OH--AND HE'S MOVED THE CASTLE TO THE TOP OF A MOUNTAIN.
HE'S EXPECTING UNWELCOME VISITORS, THEN. HE ONLY DOES THAT WHEN HE'S FEELING ANTI-SOCIAL.
I'M SURE THIS WILL SORT ITSELF OUT. THESE THINGS USUALLY DO.
I HOPE SO. I'VE NEVER SEEN HIM THIS OUT OF IT BEFORE.
NO. BUT YOU HAVE NOT BEEN WITH US LONG, LITTLE RAVEN. HE GETS BLACK MOODS ON HIM SOMETIMES.
WORSE THAN THIS ONE SOUNDS. MUCH WORSE.
IS THERE ANYTHING WE CAN DO?
OF COURSE, MY DARLING.
WE CAN WAIT.

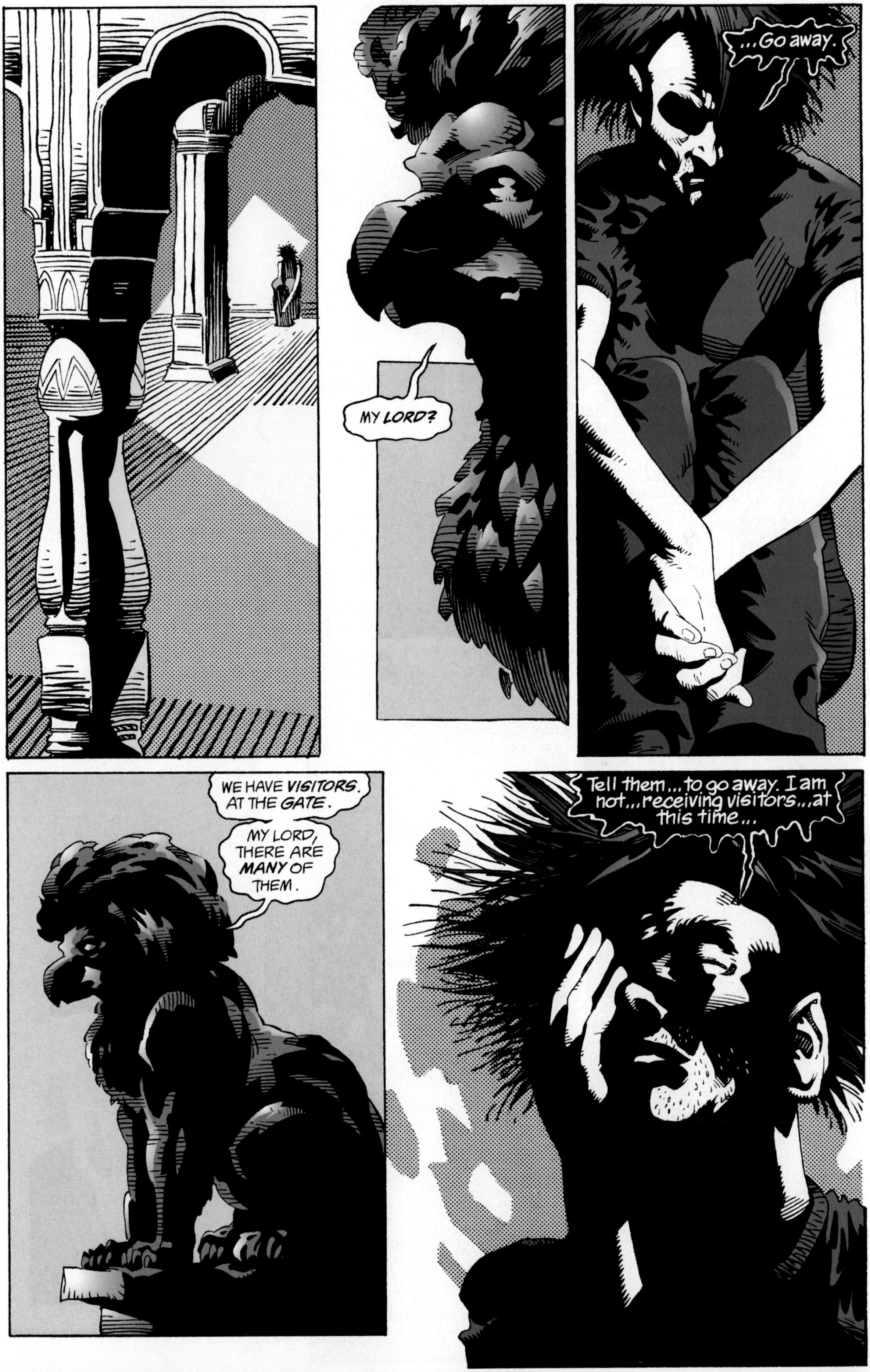
MY LORD?
...Go away.
WE HAVE VISITORS. AT THE GATE.
MY LORD, THERE ARE MANY OF THEM.
Tell them...to go away. I am not...receiving visitors...at this time...

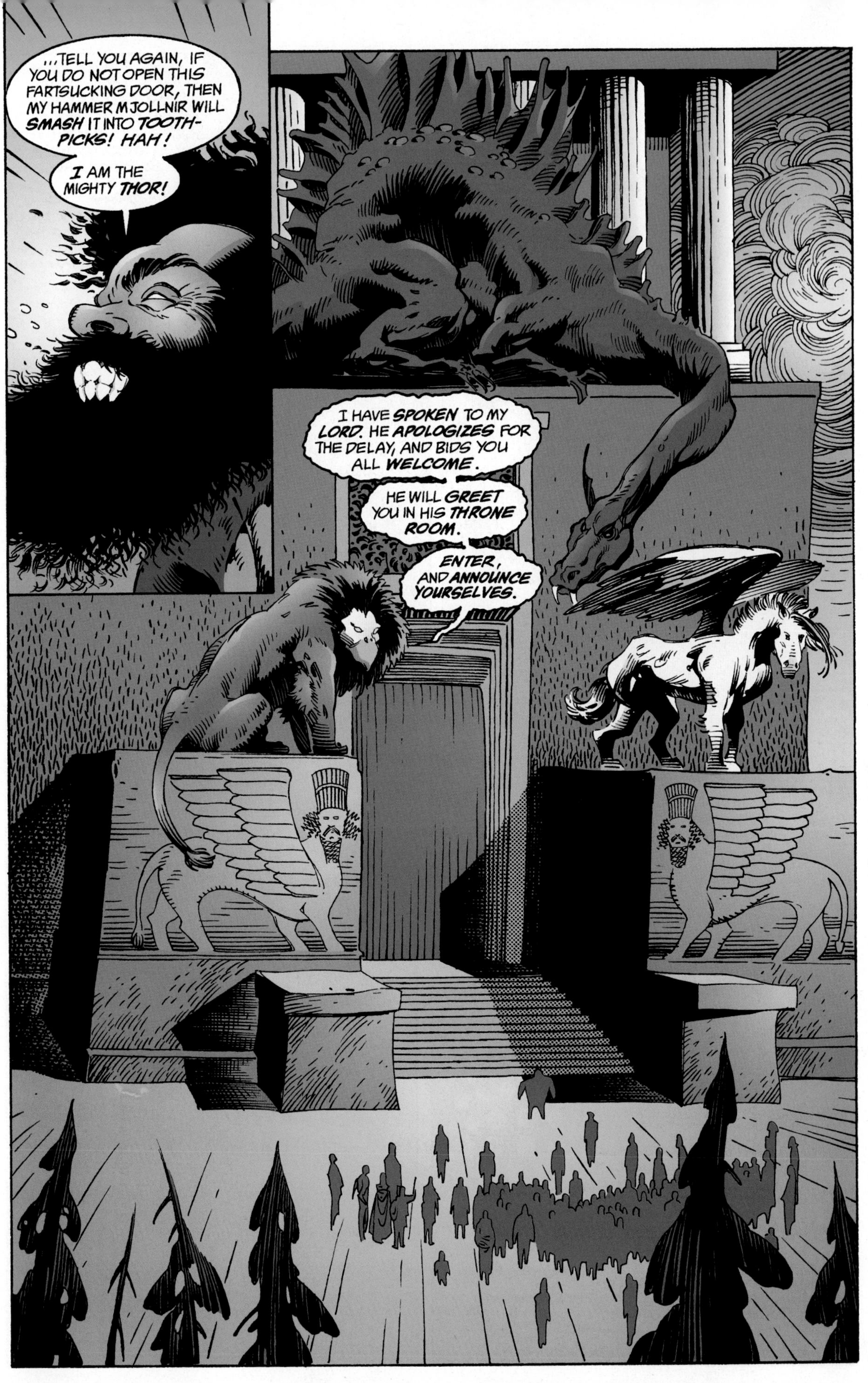
...TELL YOU AGAIN, IF YOU DO NOT OPEN THIS FARTSUCKING DOOR, THEN MY HAMMER MJOLLNIR WILL SMASH IT INTO TOOTH-PICKS! HAH!
I AM THE MIGHTY THOR!
I HAVE SPOKEN TO MY LORD. HE APOLOGIZES FOR THE DELAY, AND BIDS YOU ALL WELCOME.
HE WILL GREET YOU IN HIS THRONE ROOM.
ENTER, AND ANNOUNCE YOURSELVES.

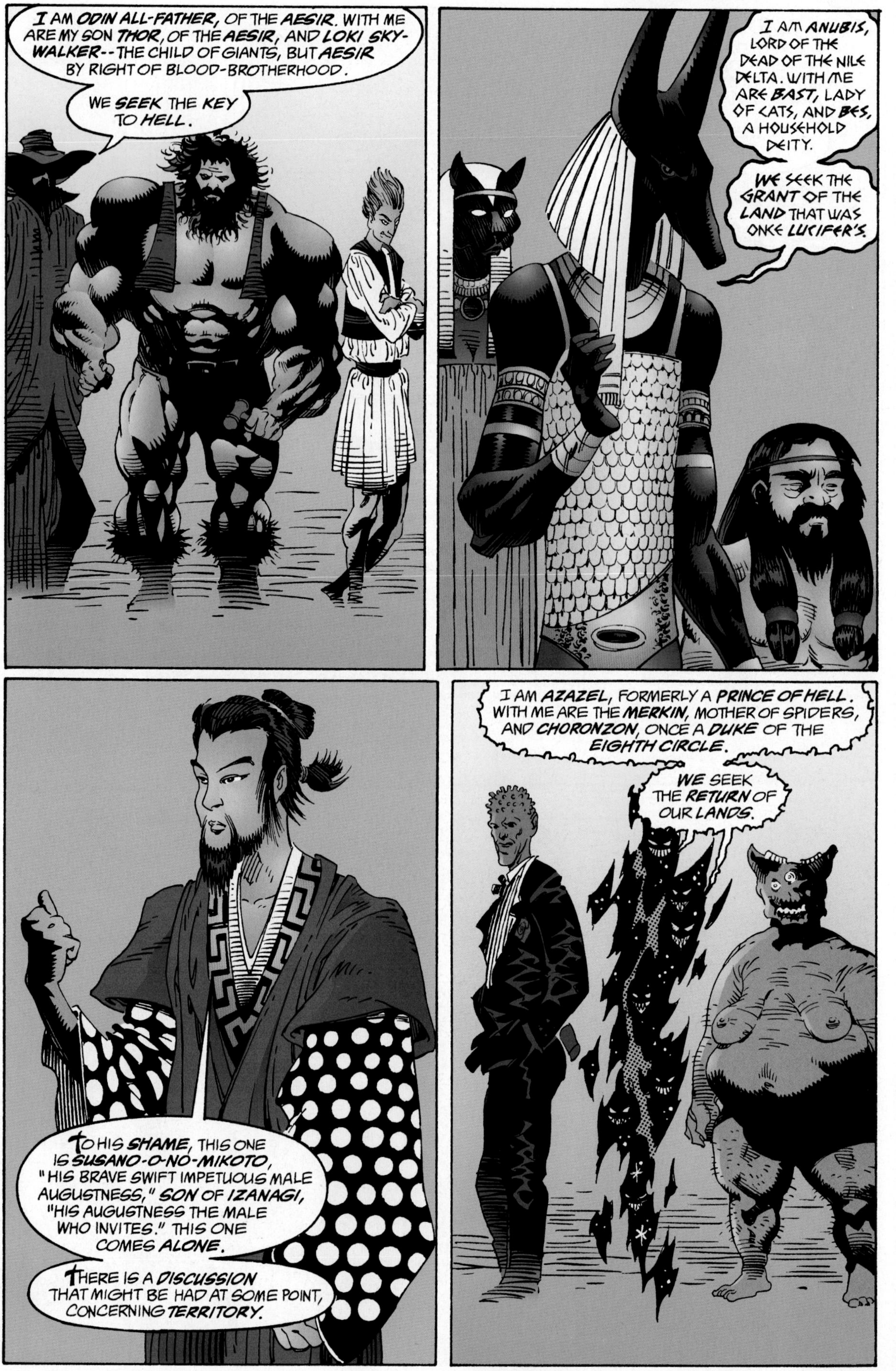
I AM ODIN ALL-FATHER, OF THE AESIR. WITH ME ARE MY SON THOR, OF THE AESIR, AND LOKI SKY-WALKER--THE CHILD OF GIANTS, BUT AESIR BY RIGHT OF BLOOD-BROTHERHOOD.
WE SEEK THE KEY TO HELL.
I AM ANUBIS, LORD OF THE DEAD OF THE NILE DELTA. WITH ME ARE BAST, LADY OF CATS, AND BES, A HOUSEHOLD DEITY.
WE SEEK THE GRANT OF THE LAND THAT WAS ONCE LUCIFER'S.
TO HIS SHAME, THIS ONE IS SUSANO-O-NO-MIKOTO, "HIS BRAVE SWIFT IMPETUOUS MALE AUGUSTNESS," SON OF IZANAGI, "HIS AUGUSTNESS THE MALE WHO INVITES." THIS ONE COMES ALONE.
THERE IS A DISCUSSION THAT MIGHT BE HAD AT SOME POINT, CONCERNING TERRITORY.
I AM AZAZEL, FORMERLY A PRINCE OF HELL. WITH ME ARE THE MERKIN, MOTHER OF SPIDERS, AND CHORONZON, ONCE A DUKE OF THE EIGHTH CIRCLE.
WE SEEK THE RETURN OF OUR LANDS.

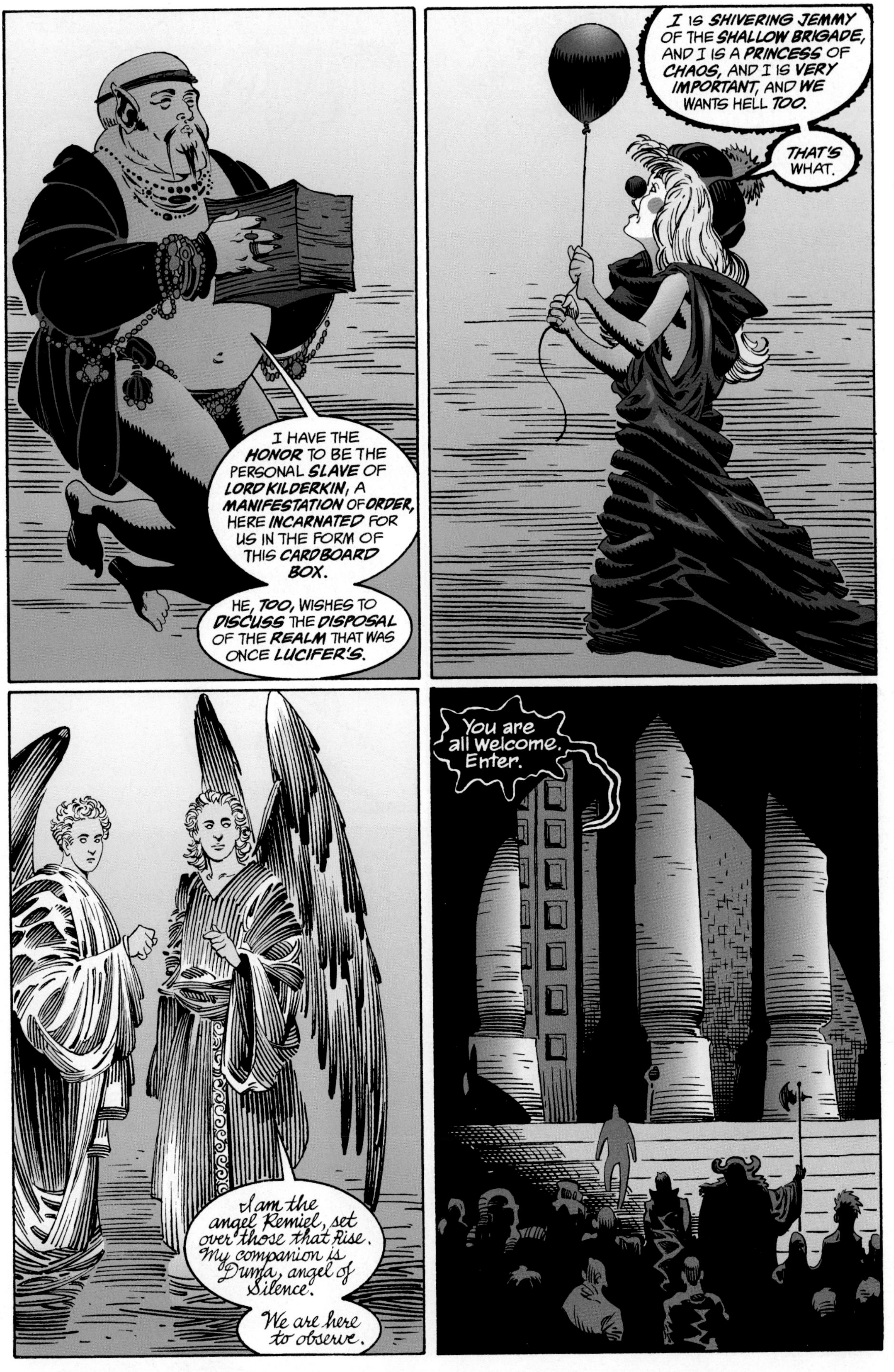
I HAVE THE HONOR TO BE THE PERSONAL SLAVE OF LORD KILDERKIN, A MANIFESTATION OF ORDER, HERE INCARNATED FOR US IN THE FORM OF THIS CARDBOARD BOX.
HE, TOO, WISHES TO DISCUSS THE DISPOSAL OF THE REALM THAT WAS ONCE LUCIFER'S.
I IS SHIVERING JEMMY OF THE SHALLOW BRIGADE, AND I IS A PRINCESS OF CHAOS, AND I IS VERY IMPORTANT, AND WE WANTS HELL TOO.
THAT'S WHAT.
I am the angel Remiel, set over those that Rise. My companion is Duma, angel of Silence.
We are here to observe.
You are all welcome. Enter.

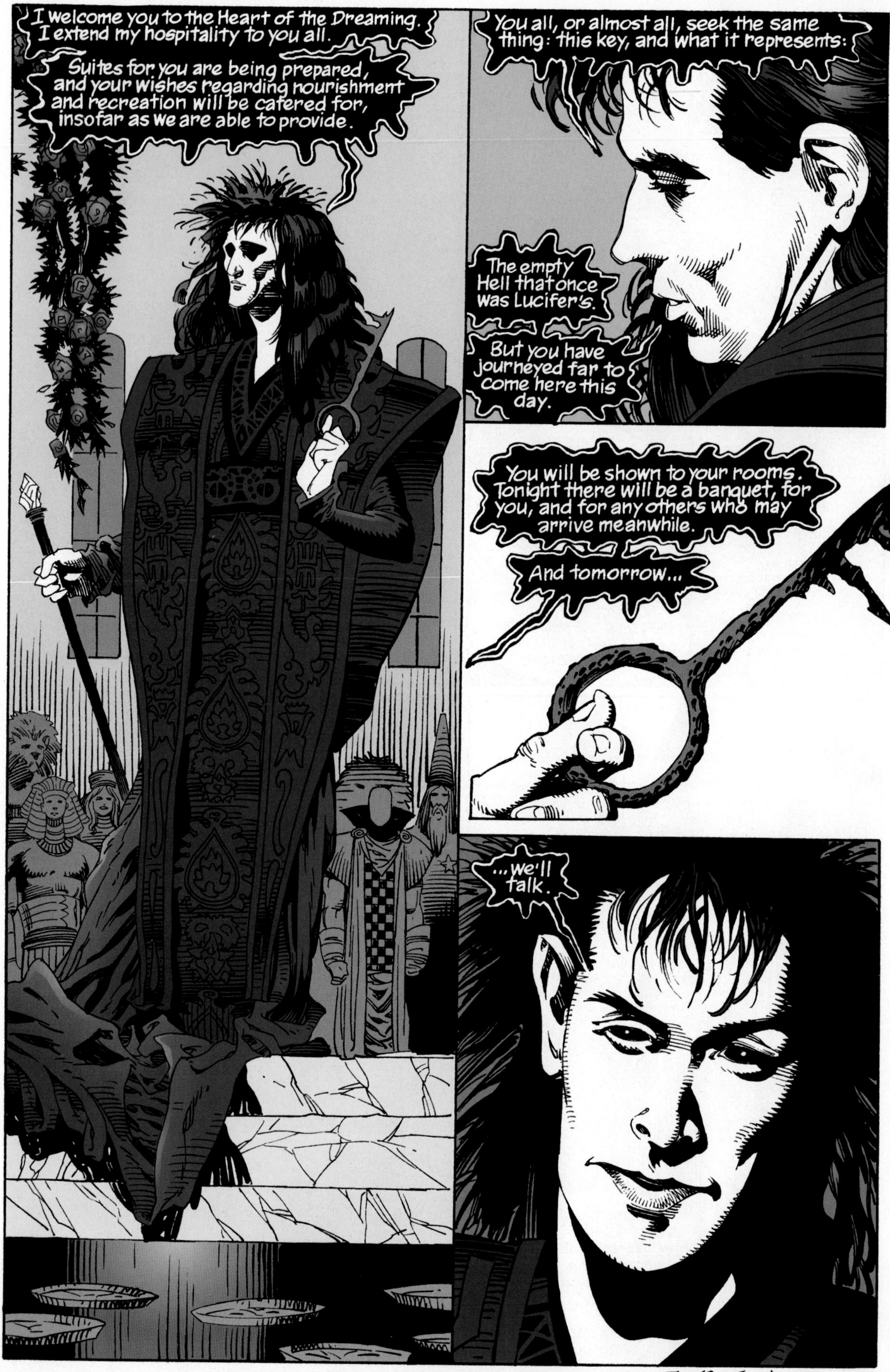
I welcome you to the Heart of the Dreaming. I extend my hospitality to you all.
Suites for you are being prepared, and your wishes regarding nourishment and recreation will be catered for, insofar as we are able to provide.
You all, or almost all, seek the same thing: this key, and what it represents:
The empty Hell that once was Lucifer's.
But you have journeyed far to come here this day.
You will be shown to your rooms. Tonight there will be a banquet, for you, and for any others who may arrive meanwhile.
And tomorrow...
...we'll talk.

To Be Continued

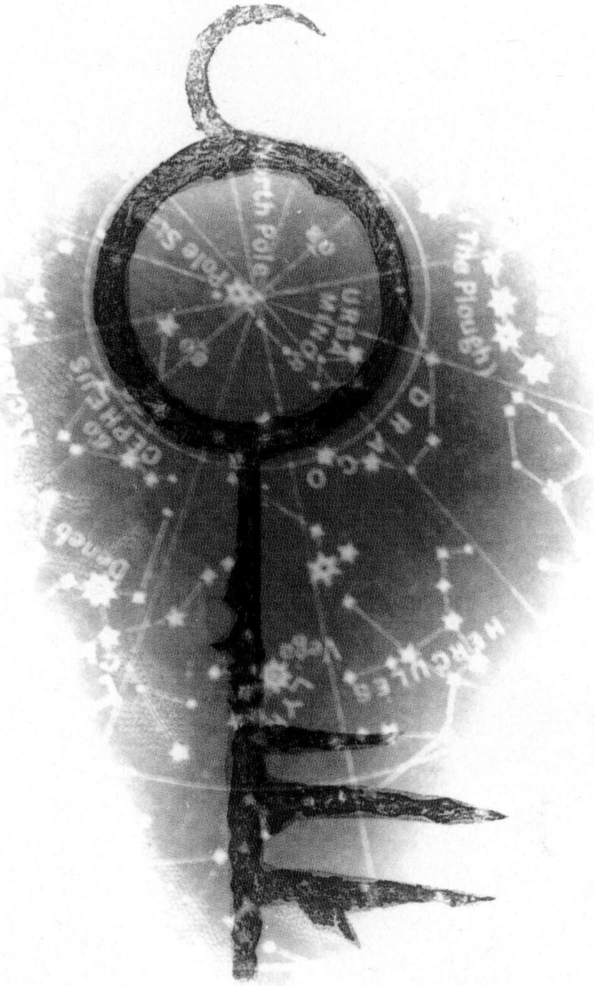
(The Plough)
URSA MINOR
DRACO
CEPHEUS
Deneb
Vega
HERCULES

N WHICH THE DEAD RETURN;
AND CHARLES ROWLAND
CONCLUDES HIS EDUCATION.

EPISODE 4

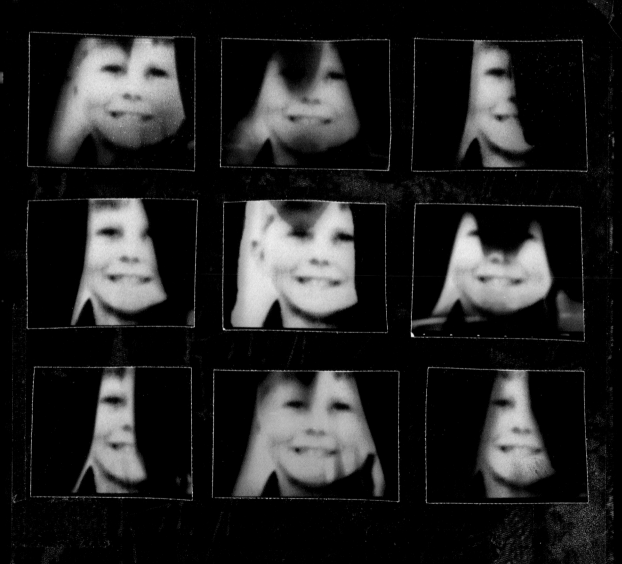

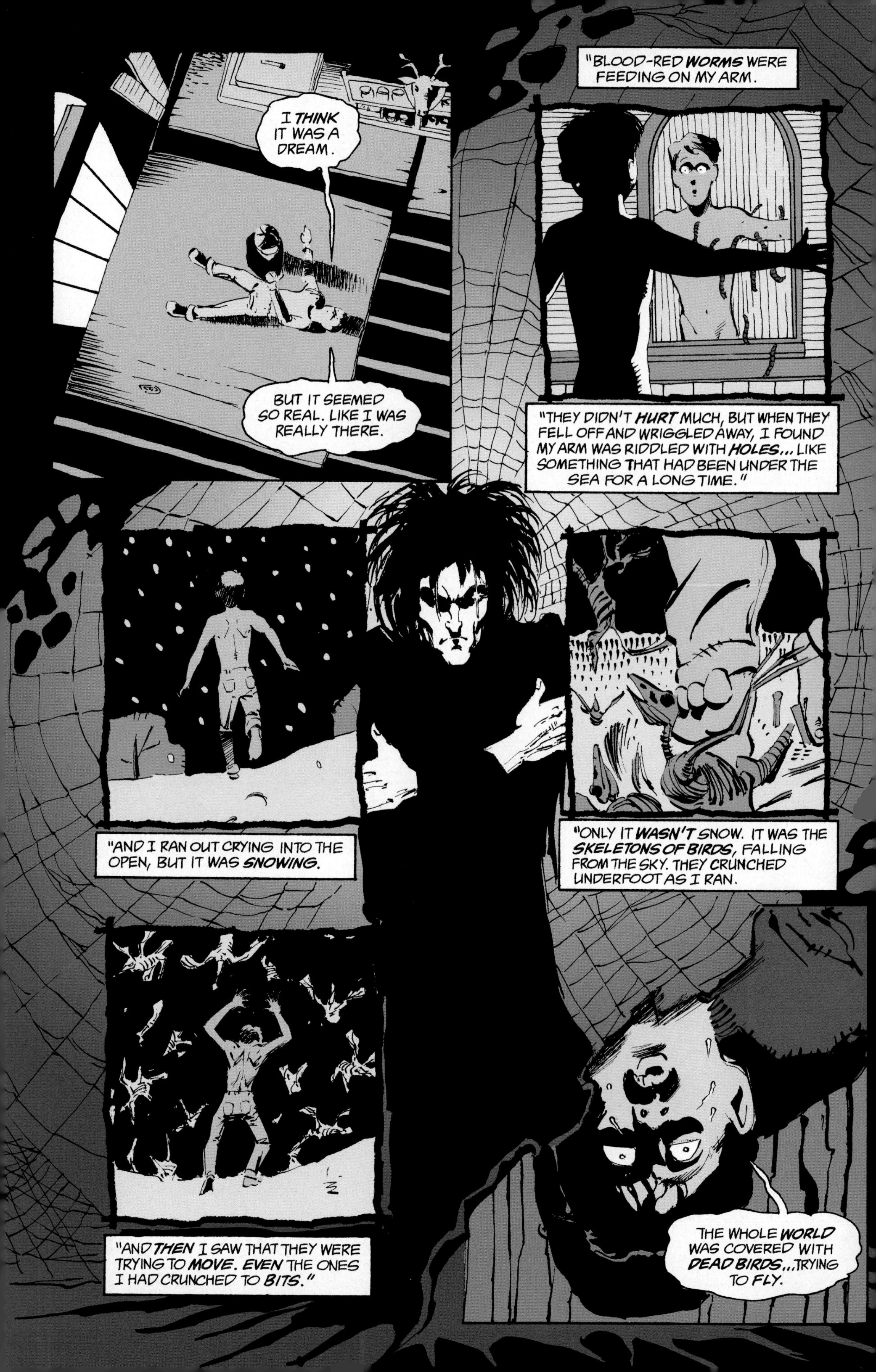
I THINK IT WAS A DREAM.
BUT IT SEEMED SO REAL. LIKE I WAS REALLY THERE.
"BLOOD-RED WORMS WERE FEEDING ON MY ARM.
"THEY DIDN'T HURT MUCH, BUT WHEN THEY FELL OFF AND WRIGGLED AWAY, I FOUND MY ARM WAS RIDDLED WITH HOLES... LIKE SOMETHING THAT HAD BEEN UNDER THE SEA FOR A LONG TIME."
"AND I RAN OUT CRYING INTO THE OPEN, BUT IT WAS SNOWING.
"ONLY IT WASN'T SNOW. IT WAS THE SKELETONS OF BIRDS, FALLING FROM THE SKY. THEY CRUNCHED UNDERFOOT AS I RAN.
"AND THEN I SAW THAT THEY WERE TRYING TO MOVE. EVEN THE ONES I HAD CRUNCHED TO BITS."
THE WHOLE WORLD WAS COVERED WITH DEAD BIRDS...TRYING TO FLY.

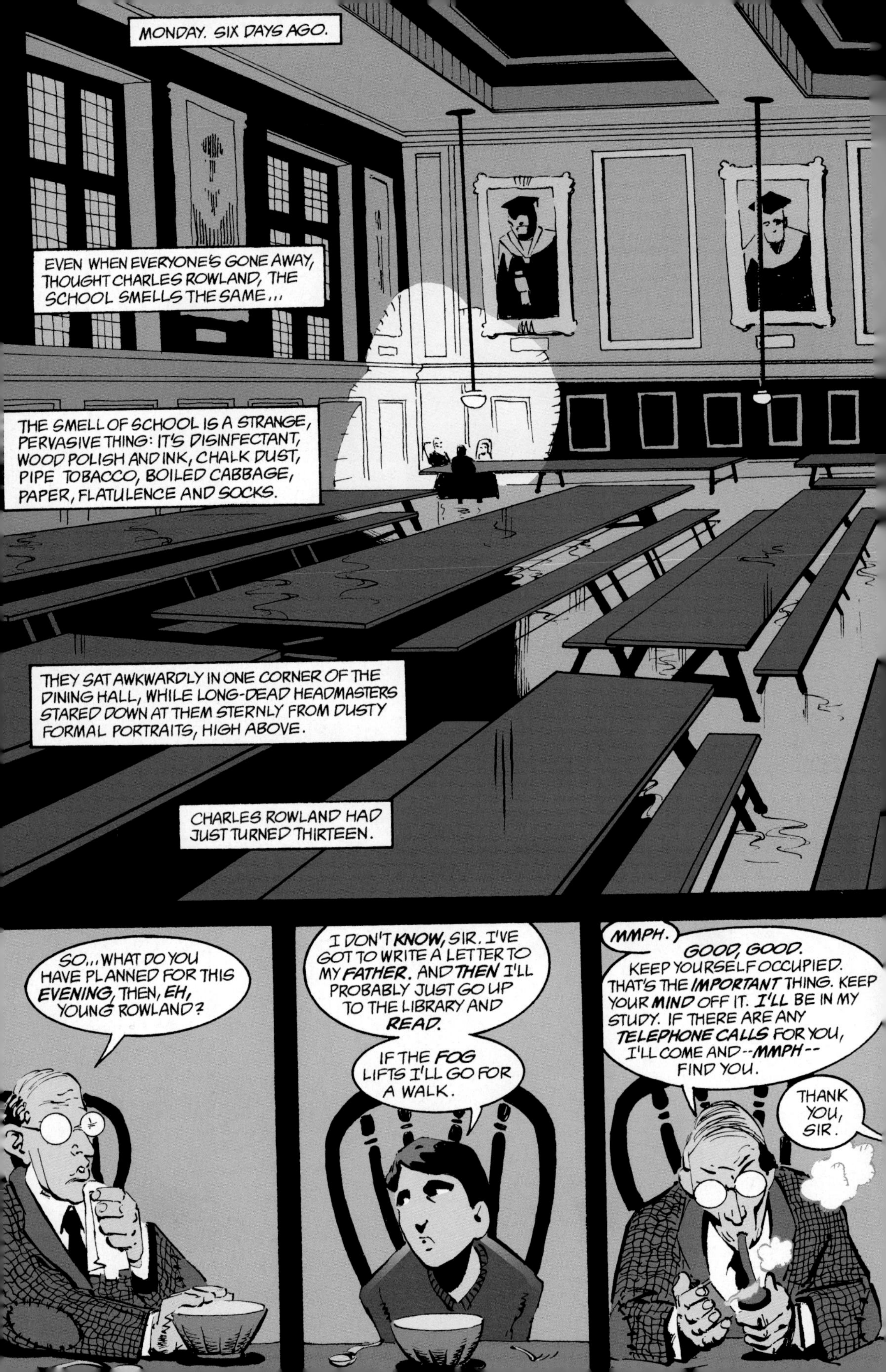
MONDAY. SIX DAYS AGO.
EVEN WHEN EVERYONE'S GONE AWAY, THOUGHT CHARLES ROWLAND, THE SCHOOL SMELLS THE SAME...
THE SMELL OF SCHOOL IS A STRANGE, PERVASIVE THING: IT'S DISINFECTANT, WOOD POLISH AND INK, CHALK DUST, PIPE TOBACCO, BOILED CABBAGE, PAPER, FLATULENCE AND SOCKS.
THEY SAT AWKWARDLY IN ONE CORNER OF THE DINING HALL, WHILE LONG-DEAD HEADMASTERS STARED DOWN AT THEM STERNLY FROM DUSTY FORMAL PORTRAITS, HIGH ABOVE.
CHARLES ROWLAND HAD JUST TURNED THIRTEEN.
SO... WHAT DO YOU HAVE PLANNED FOR THIS EVENING, THEN, EH, YOUNG ROWLAND?
I DON'T KNOW, SIR. I'VE GOT TO WRITE A LETTER TO MY FATHER. AND THEN I'LL PROBABLY JUST GO UP TO THE LIBRARY AND READ.
IF THE FOG LIFTS I'LL GO FOR A WALK.
MMPH.
GOOD, GOOD. KEEP YOURSELF OCCUPIED. THAT'S THE IMPORTANT THING. KEEP YOUR MIND OFF IT. I'LL BE IN MY STUDY. IF THERE ARE ANY TELEPHONE CALLS FOR YOU, I'LL COME AND --MMPH-- FIND YOU.
THANK YOU, SIR.

ROWLAND'S FATHER WAS IN KUWAIT.

EVEN SO, I *MUST* SAY, THIS IS *MOST* AWKWARD. ARE YOU *QUITE* SURE YOU HAVE NO RELATIVES TO WHOM YOU COULD BE SENT, FOR THE REST OF --MMMPH-- SCHOOL HOLIDAYS?

THERE'S NO ONE THAT I *KNOW* OF, SIR.

FATHER WAS GOING TO FLY ME OUT TO KUWAIT, IN THE HOLS. I'VE *ALWAYS* SPENT THE HOLIDAYS WITH HIM. UNTIL *NOW*.

MMPH.

DON'T BE *HARD* ON THE BOY, HEADMASTER. WHAT *I* SAY IS, IT'S *ALL* THAT SADDAM HUSSEIN'S FAULT. POOR MISTER ROWLAND DIDN'T *ASK* TO BE A HOSTAGE, *DID* HE?

IT'S A GOOD THING THAT *WE'RE* BOTH STAYING ON AT SCHOOL OVER THE HOLIDAYS, OTHERWISE I DON'T KNOW *WHERE* THE LAD COULD GO.

YOU'RE *RIGHT*, OF COURSE, MISS GRIBBLE.

OF *COURSE* I AM. AND *ROWLAND* CAN KEEP HIMSELF *OCCUPIED*, CAN'T YOU, DEAR?

YES, MATRON.

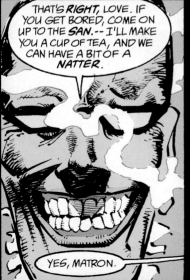

THAT'S *RIGHT*, LOVE. IF YOU GET BORED, COME ON UP TO THE *SAN*.-- I'LL MAKE YOU A CUP OF TEA, AND WE CAN HAVE A BIT OF A *NATTER*.

YES, MATRON.

RIGHT. NOW, YOU RUN ALONG. DON'T WORRY ABOUT THE PLATES. ALFRED WILL CLEAN UP LATER.

ALL RIGHT. THANK YOU, MATRON. THANK YOU, SIR.

REV. A.N. PARKINSON, M.A. (OXON) HEADMASTER 1901-1916

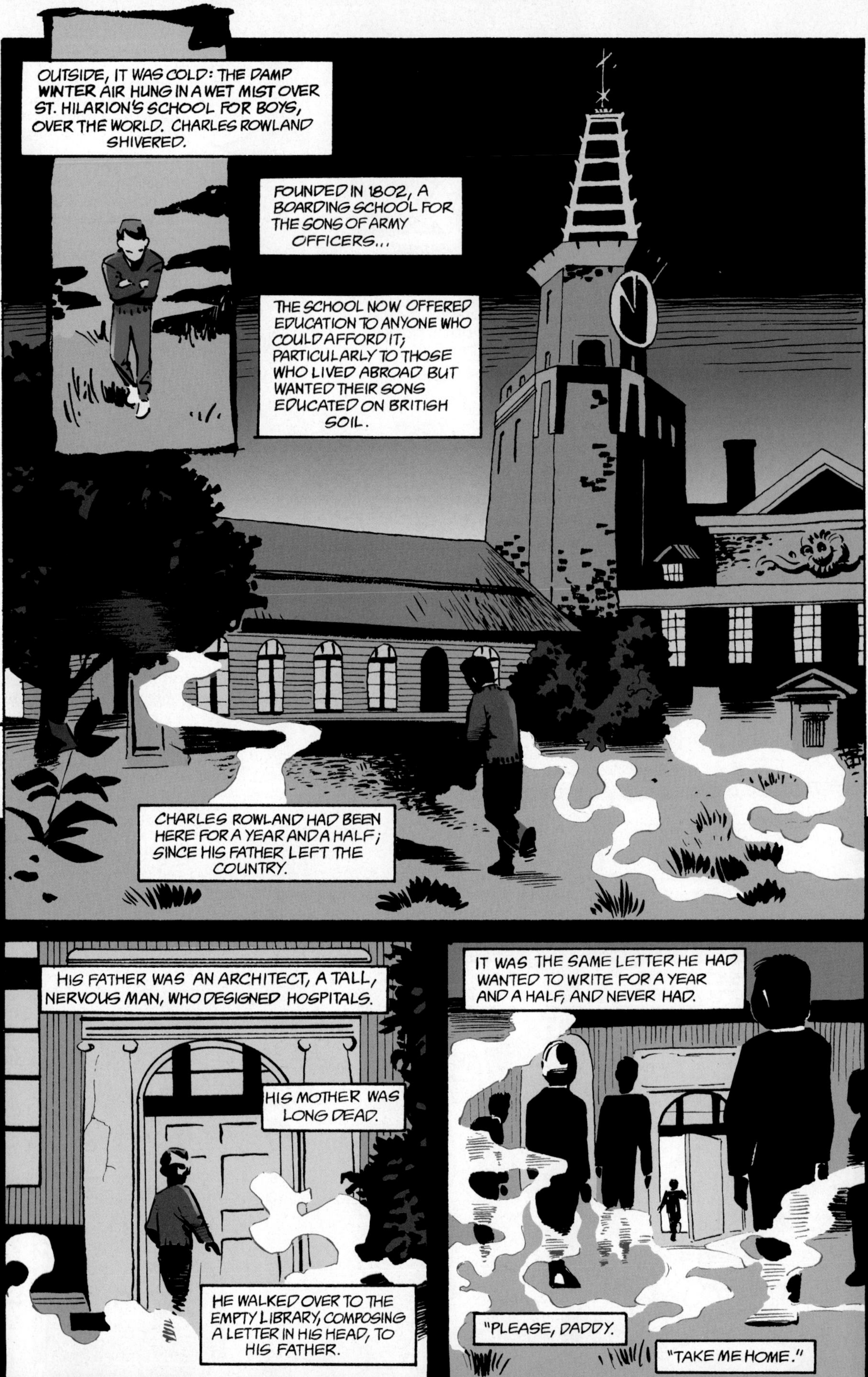
OUTSIDE, IT WAS COLD: THE DAMP WINTER AIR HUNG IN A WET MIST OVER ST. HILARION'S SCHOOL FOR BOYS, OVER THE WORLD. CHARLES ROWLAND SHIVERED.
FOUNDED IN 1802, A BOARDING SCHOOL FOR THE SONS OF ARMY OFFICERS...
THE SCHOOL NOW OFFERED EDUCATION TO ANYONE WHO COULD AFFORD IT; PARTICULARLY TO THOSE WHO LIVED ABROAD BUT WANTED THEIR SONS EDUCATED ON BRITISH SOIL.
CHARLES ROWLAND HAD BEEN HERE FOR A YEAR AND A HALF; SINCE HIS FATHER LEFT THE COUNTRY.
HIS FATHER WAS AN ARCHITECT, A TALL, NERVOUS MAN, WHO DESIGNED HOSPITALS.
HIS MOTHER WAS LONG DEAD.
HE WALKED OVER TO THE EMPTY LIBRARY, COMPOSING A LETTER IN HIS HEAD, TO HIS FATHER.
IT WAS THE SAME LETTER HE HAD WANTED TO WRITE FOR A YEAR AND A HALF, AND NEVER HAD.
"PLEASE, DADDY.
"TAKE ME HOME."

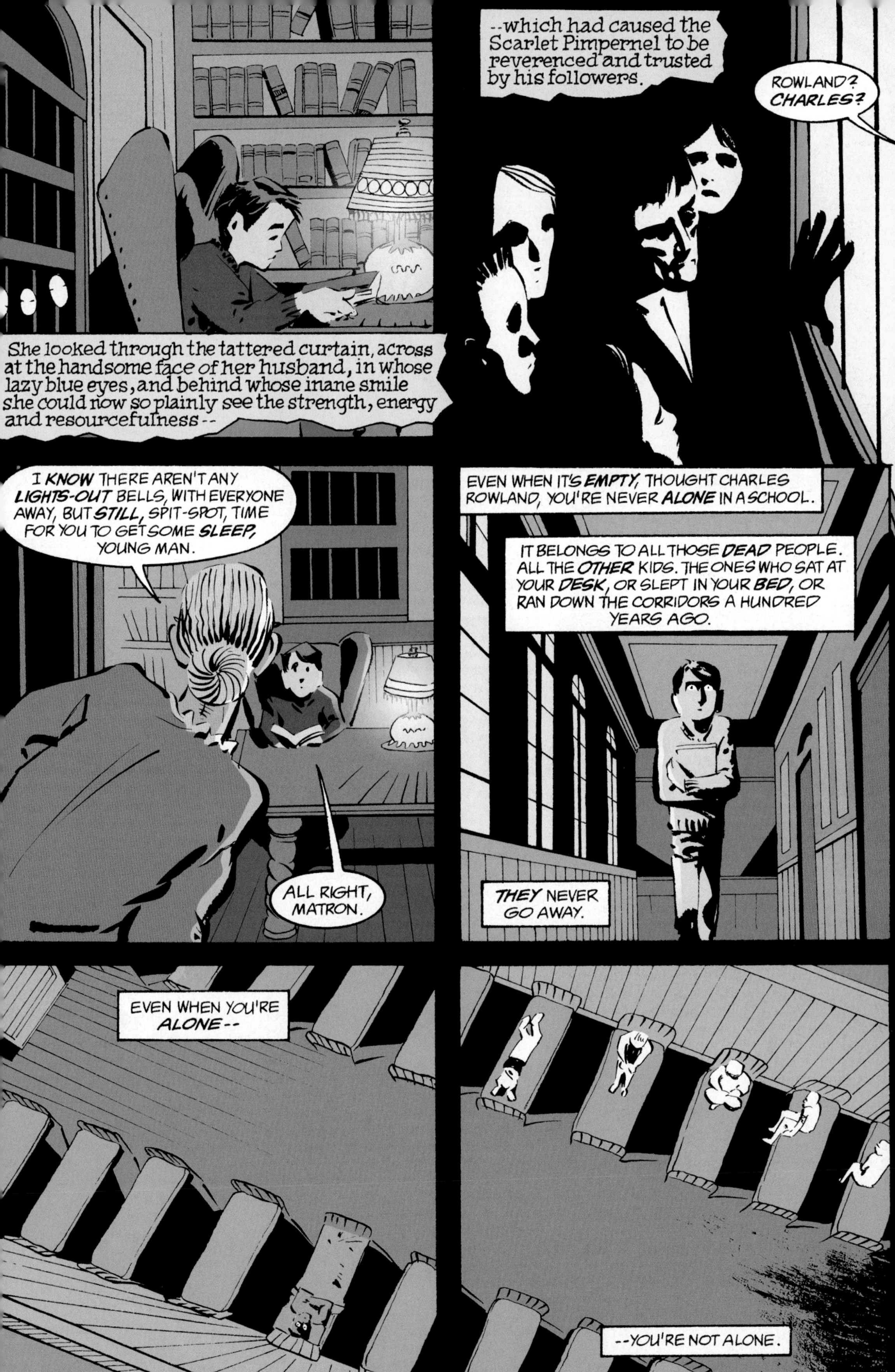
She looked through the tattered curtain, across at the handsome face of her husband, in whose lazy blue eyes, and behind whose inane smile she could now so plainly see the strength, energy and resourcefulness --
--which had caused the Scarlet Pimpernel to be reverenced and trusted by his followers.
ROWLAND? CHARLES?
I KNOW THERE AREN'T ANY LIGHTS-OUT BELLS, WITH EVERYONE AWAY, BUT STILL, SPIT-SPOT, TIME FOR YOU TO GET SOME SLEEP, YOUNG MAN.
ALL RIGHT, MATRON.
EVEN WHEN IT'S EMPTY, THOUGHT CHARLES ROWLAND, YOU'RE NEVER ALONE IN A SCHOOL.
IT BELONGS TO ALL THOSE DEAD PEOPLE. ALL THE OTHER KIDS. THE ONES WHO SAT AT YOUR DESK, OR SLEPT IN YOUR BED, OR RAN DOWN THE CORRIDORS A HUNDRED YEARS AGO.
THEY NEVER GO AWAY.
EVEN WHEN YOU'RE ALONE--
--YOU'RE NOT ALONE.

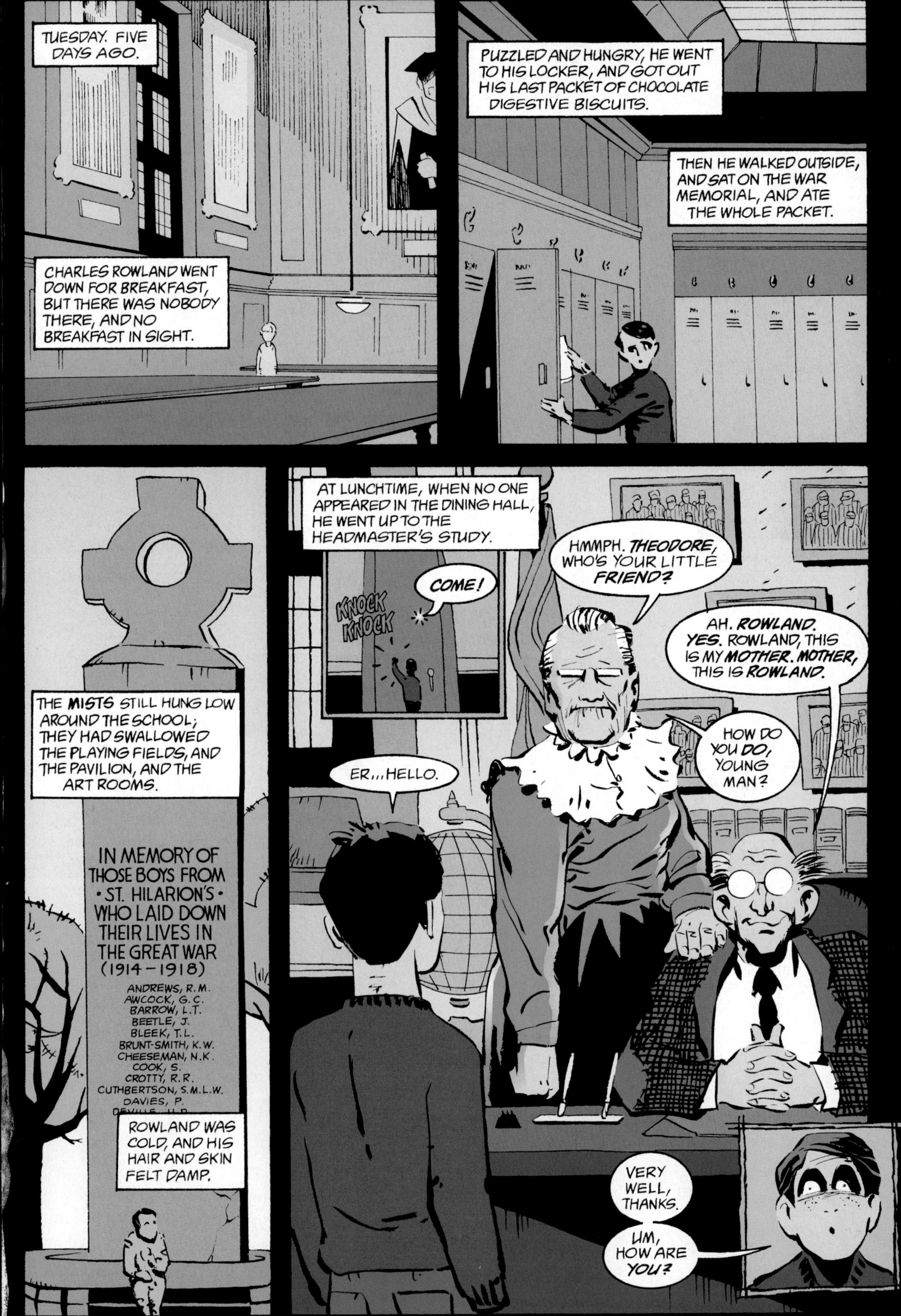
TUESDAY. FIVE DAYS AGO.
CHARLES ROWLAND WENT DOWN FOR BREAKFAST, BUT THERE WAS NOBODY THERE, AND NO BREAKFAST IN SIGHT.
PUZZLED AND HUNGRY, HE WENT TO HIS LOCKER, AND GOT OUT HIS LAST PACKET OF CHOCOLATE DIGESTIVE BISCUITS.
THEN HE WALKED OUTSIDE, AND SAT ON THE WAR MEMORIAL, AND ATE THE WHOLE PACKET.
THE MISTS STILL HUNG LOW AROUND THE SCHOOL; THEY HAD SWALLOWED THE PLAYING FIELDS, AND THE PAVILION, AND THE ART ROOMS.
IN MEMORY OF THOSE BOYS FROM • ST. HILARION'S • WHO LAID DOWN THEIR LIVES IN THE GREAT WAR (1914–1918)
ANDREWS, R.M.
AWCOCK, G.C.
BARROW, L.T.
BEETLE, J.
BLEEK, T.L.
BRUNT-SMITH, K.W.
CHEESEMAN, N.K.
COOK, S.
CROTTY, R.R.
CUTHBERTSON, S.M.L.W.
DAVIES, P.
ROWLAND WAS COLD, AND HIS HAIR AND SKIN FELT DAMP.
AT LUNCHTIME, WHEN NO ONE APPEARED IN THE DINING HALL, HE WENT UP TO THE HEADMASTER'S STUDY.
KNOCK KNOCK
COME!
HMMPH. THEODORE, WHO'S YOUR LITTLE FRIEND?
AH. ROWLAND. YES. ROWLAND, THIS IS MY MOTHER. MOTHER, THIS IS ROWLAND.
HOW DO YOU DO, YOUNG MAN?
ER... HELLO.
VERY WELL, THANKS.
UM, HOW ARE YOU?

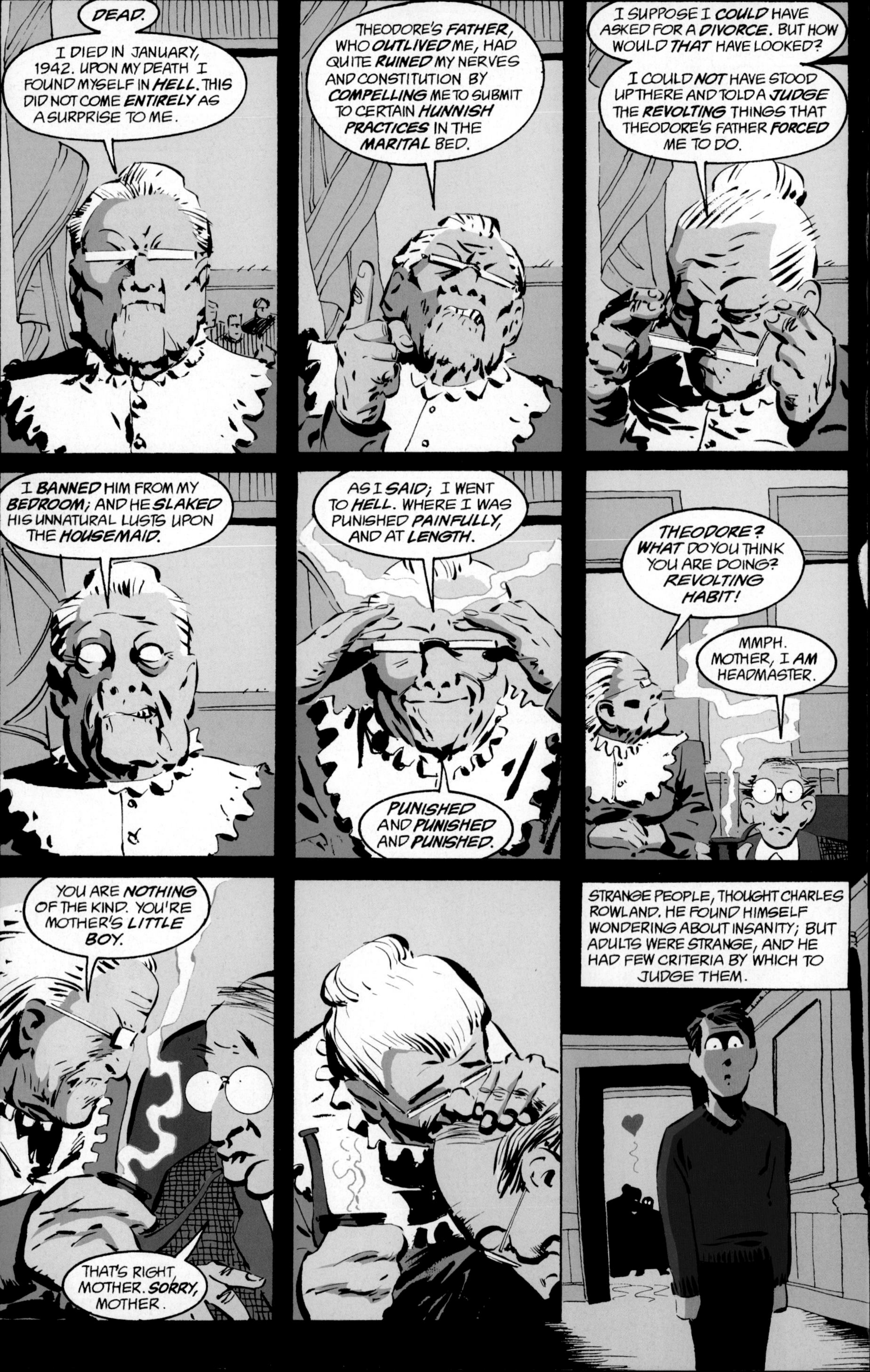
DEAD.
I DIED IN JANUARY, 1942. UPON MY DEATH I FOUND MYSELF IN HELL. THIS DID NOT COME ENTIRELY AS A SURPRISE TO ME.
THEODORE'S FATHER, WHO OUTLIVED ME, HAD QUITE RUINED MY NERVES AND CONSTITUTION BY COMPELLING ME TO SUBMIT TO CERTAIN HUNNISH PRACTICES IN THE MARITAL BED.
I SUPPOSE I COULD HAVE ASKED FOR A DIVORCE. BUT HOW WOULD THAT HAVE LOOKED?
I COULD NOT HAVE STOOD UP THERE AND TOLD A JUDGE THE REVOLTING THINGS THAT THEODORE'S FATHER FORCED ME TO DO.
I BANNED HIM FROM MY BEDROOM; AND HE SLAKED HIS UNNATURAL LUSTS UPON THE HOUSEMAID.
AS I SAID; I WENT TO HELL. WHERE I WAS PUNISHED PAINFULLY, AND AT LENGTH.
PUNISHED AND PUNISHED AND PUNISHED.
THEODORE? WHAT DO YOU THINK YOU ARE DOING? REVOLTING HABIT!
MMPH. MOTHER, I AM HEADMASTER.
YOU ARE NOTHING OF THE KIND. YOU'RE MOTHER'S LITTLE BOY.
THAT'S RIGHT, MOTHER. SORRY, MOTHER.
STRANGE PEOPLE, THOUGHT CHARLES ROWLAND. HE FOUND HIMSELF WONDERING ABOUT INSANITY; BUT ADULTS WERE STRANGE, AND HE HAD FEW CRITERIA BY WHICH TO JUDGE THEM.

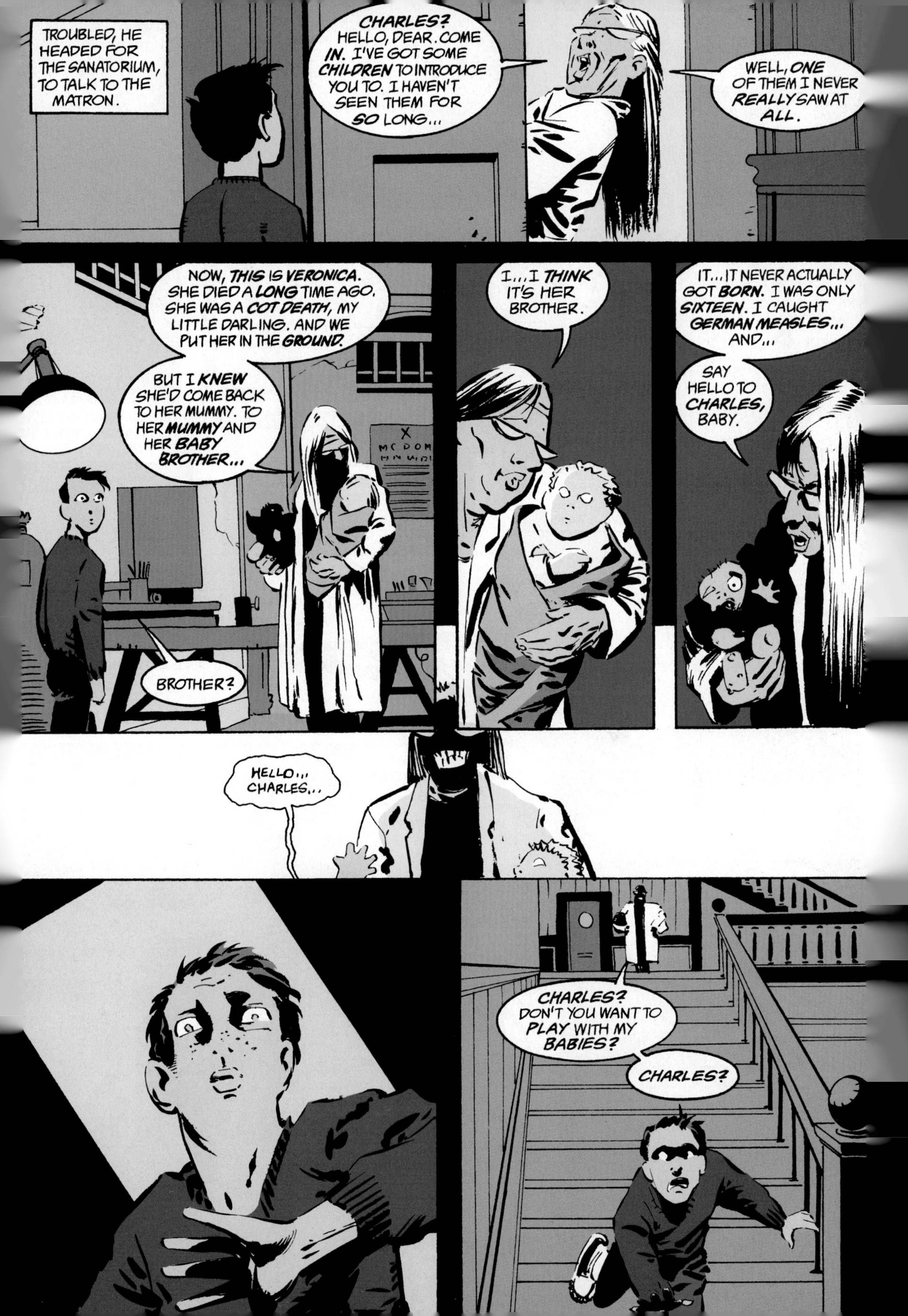
TROUBLED, HE HEADED FOR THE SANATORIUM, TO TALK TO THE MATRON.
CHARLES? HELLO, DEAR. COME IN. I'VE GOT SOME CHILDREN TO INTRODUCE YOU TO. I HAVEN'T SEEN THEM FOR SO LONG...
WELL, ONE OF THEM I NEVER REALLY SAW AT ALL.
NOW, THIS IS VERONICA. SHE DIED A LONG TIME AGO. SHE WAS A COT DEATH, MY LITTLE DARLING. AND WE PUT HER IN THE GROUND.
BUT I KNEW SHE'D COME BACK TO HER MUMMY. TO HER MUMMY AND HER BABY BROTHER...
BROTHER?
I...I THINK IT'S HER BROTHER.
IT...IT NEVER ACTUALLY GOT BORN. I WAS ONLY SIXTEEN. I CAUGHT GERMAN MEASLES... AND...
SAY HELLO TO CHARLES, BABY.
HELLO... CHARLES...
CHARLES? DON'T YOU WANT TO PLAY WITH MY BABIES?
CHARLES?

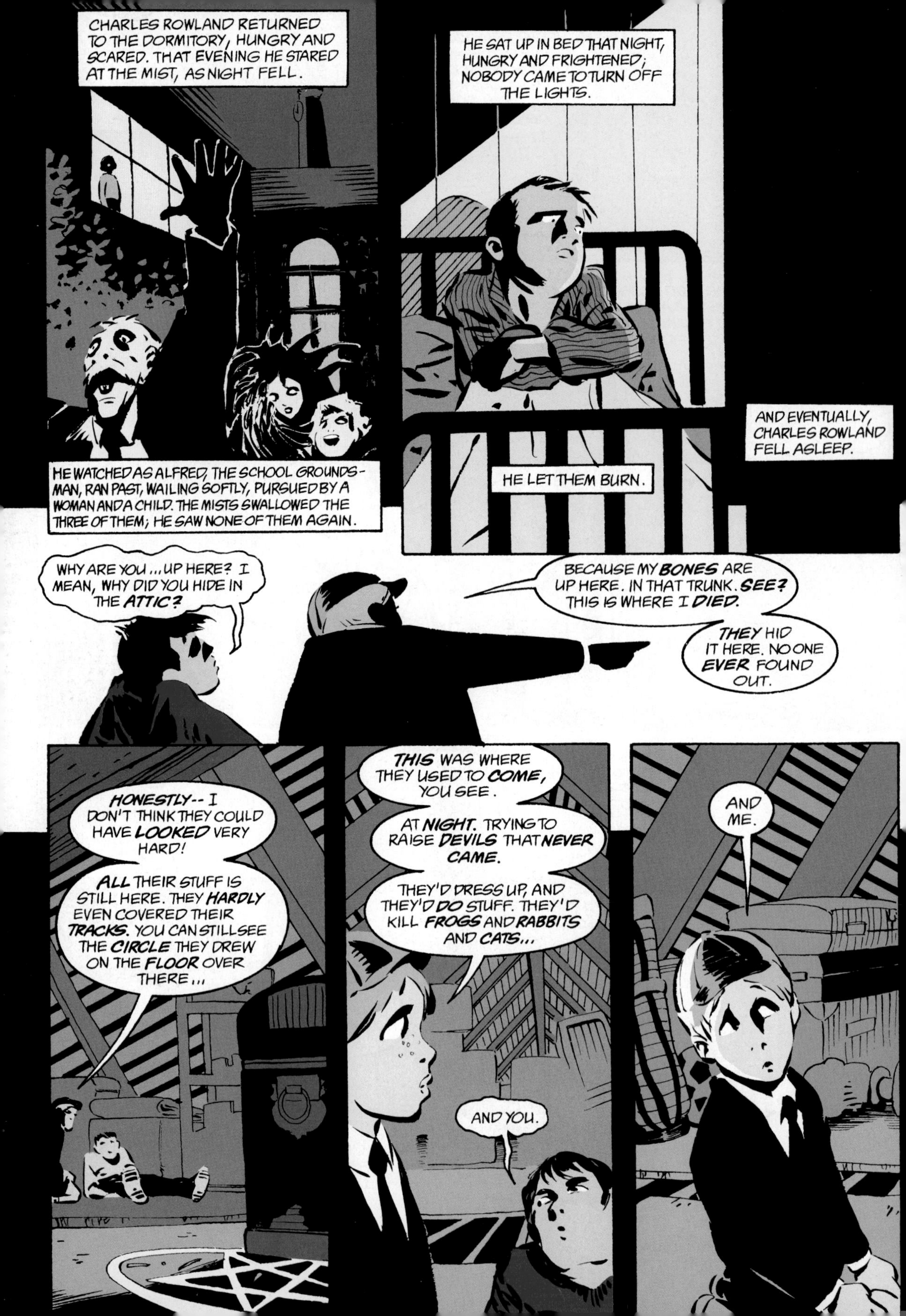

CHARLES ROWLAND RETURNED TO THE DORMITORY, HUNGRY AND SCARED. THAT EVENING HE STARED AT THE MIST, AS NIGHT FELL.
HE WATCHED AS ALFRED, THE SCHOOL GROUNDS-MAN, RAN PAST, WAILING SOFTLY, PURSUED BY A WOMAN AND A CHILD. THE MISTS SWALLOWED THE THREE OF THEM; HE SAW NONE OF THEM AGAIN.
HE SAT UP IN BED THAT NIGHT, HUNGRY AND FRIGHTENED; NOBODY CAME TO TURN OFF THE LIGHTS.
HE LET THEM BURN.
AND EVENTUALLY, CHARLES ROWLAND FELL ASLEEP.
WHY ARE YOU ...UP HERE? I MEAN, WHY DID YOU HIDE IN THE ATTIC?
BECAUSE MY BONES ARE UP HERE. IN THAT TRUNK. SEE? THIS IS WHERE I DIED.
THEY HID IT HERE. NO ONE EVER FOUND OUT.
HONESTLY-- I DON'T THINK THEY COULD HAVE LOOKED VERY HARD!
ALL THEIR STUFF IS STILL HERE. THEY HARDLY EVEN COVERED THEIR TRACKS. YOU CAN STILL SEE THE CIRCLE THEY DREW ON THE FLOOR OVER THERE...
THIS WAS WHERE THEY USED TO COME, YOU SEE.
AT NIGHT. TRYING TO RAISE DEVILS THAT NEVER CAME.
THEY'D DRESS UP, AND THEY'D DO STUFF. THEY'D KILL FROGS AND RABBITS AND CATS...
AND YOU.
AND ME.

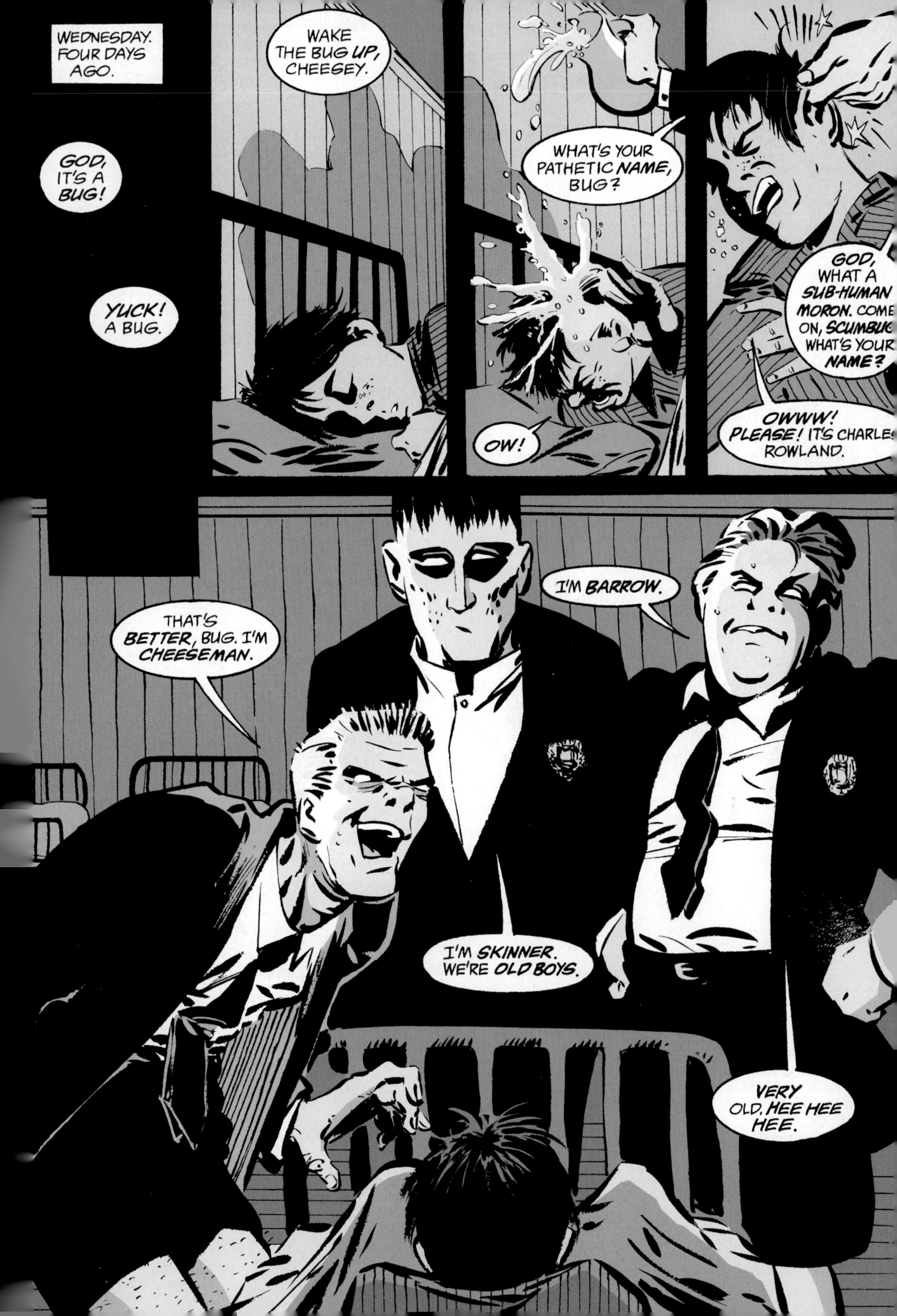
WEDNESDAY. FOUR DAYS AGO.
GOD, IT'S A BUG!
YUCK! A BUG.
WAKE THE BUG UP, CHEESEY.
WHAT'S YOUR PATHETIC NAME, BUG?
OW!
GOD, WHAT A SUB-HUMAN MORON. COME ON, SCUMBUG WHAT'S YOUR NAME?
OWWW! PLEASE! IT'S CHARLES ROWLAND.
THAT'S BETTER, BUG. I'M CHEESEMAN.
I'M BARROW.
I'M SKINNER. WE'RE OLD BOYS.
VERY OLD, HEE HEE HEE.

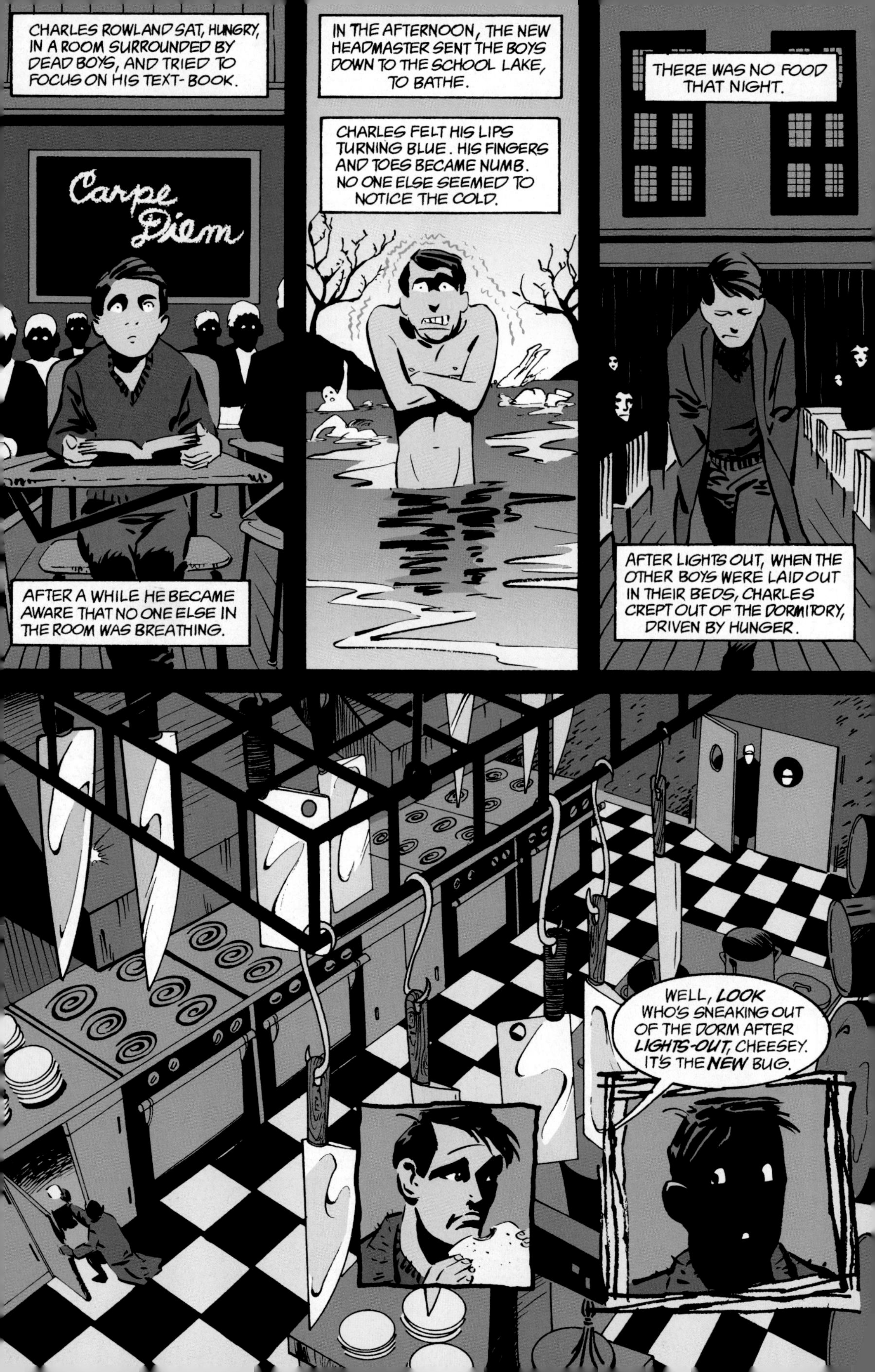
CHARLES ROWLAND SAT, HUNGRY, IN A ROOM SURROUNDED BY DEAD BOYS, AND TRIED TO FOCUS ON HIS TEXT-BOOK.
Carpe Diem
AFTER A WHILE HE BECAME AWARE THAT NO ONE ELSE IN THE ROOM WAS BREATHING.
IN THE AFTERNOON, THE NEW HEADMASTER SENT THE BOYS DOWN TO THE SCHOOL LAKE, TO BATHE.
CHARLES FELT HIS LIPS TURNING BLUE. HIS FINGERS AND TOES BECAME NUMB. NO ONE ELSE SEEMED TO NOTICE THE COLD.
THERE WAS NO FOOD THAT NIGHT.
AFTER LIGHTS OUT, WHEN THE OTHER BOYS WERE LAID OUT IN THEIR BEDS, CHARLES CREPT OUT OF THE DORMITORY, DRIVEN BY HUNGER.
WELL, LOOK WHO'S SNEAKING OUT OF THE DORM AFTER LIGHTS-OUT, CHEESEY. IT'S THE NEW BUG.

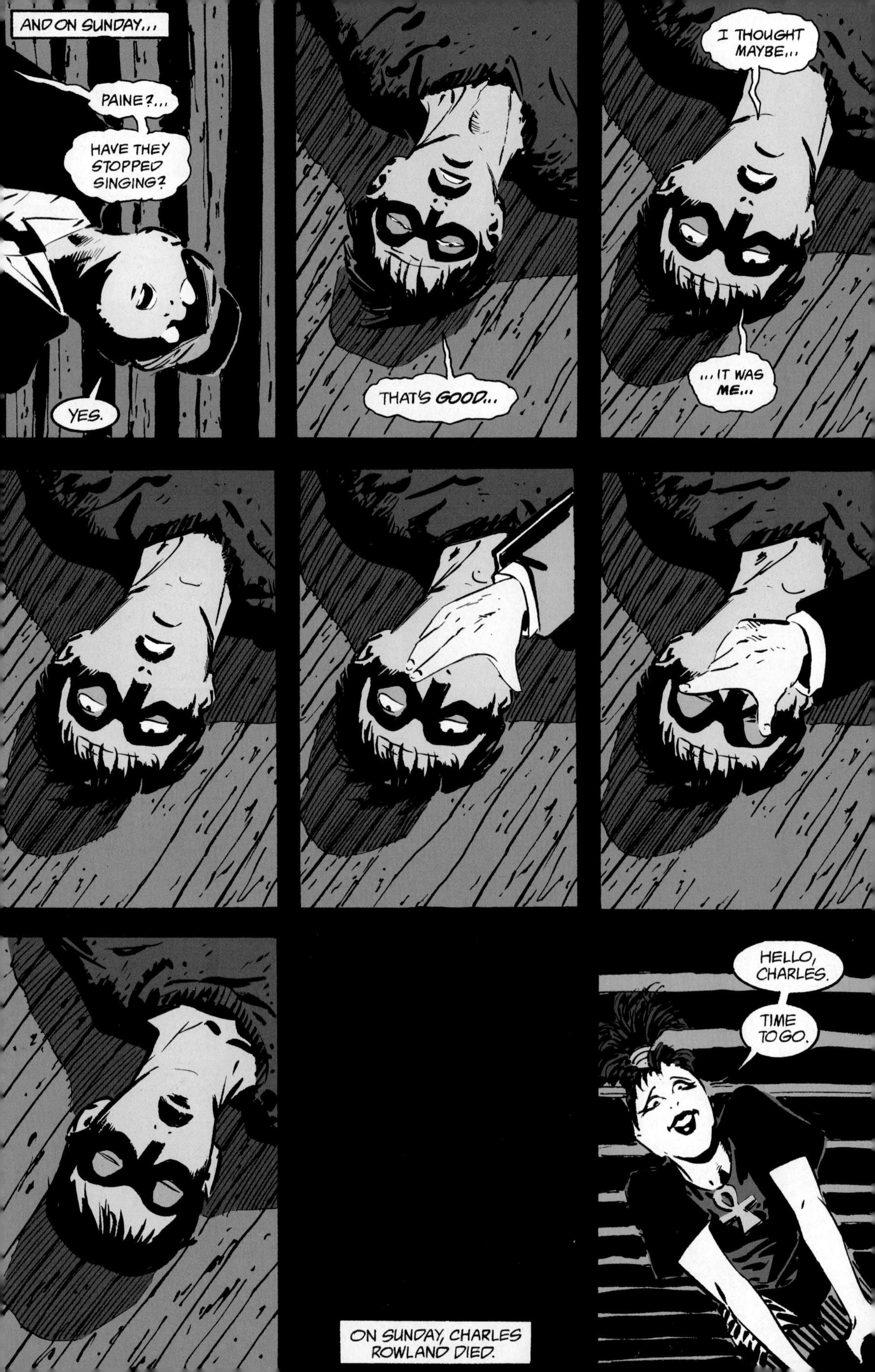

AND ON SUNDAY...
PAINE?...
HAVE THEY STOPPED SINGING?
YES.
THAT'S GOOD...
I THOUGHT MAYBE...
...IT WAS ME...
ON SUNDAY, CHARLES ROWLAND DIED.
HELLO, CHARLES.
TIME TO GO.

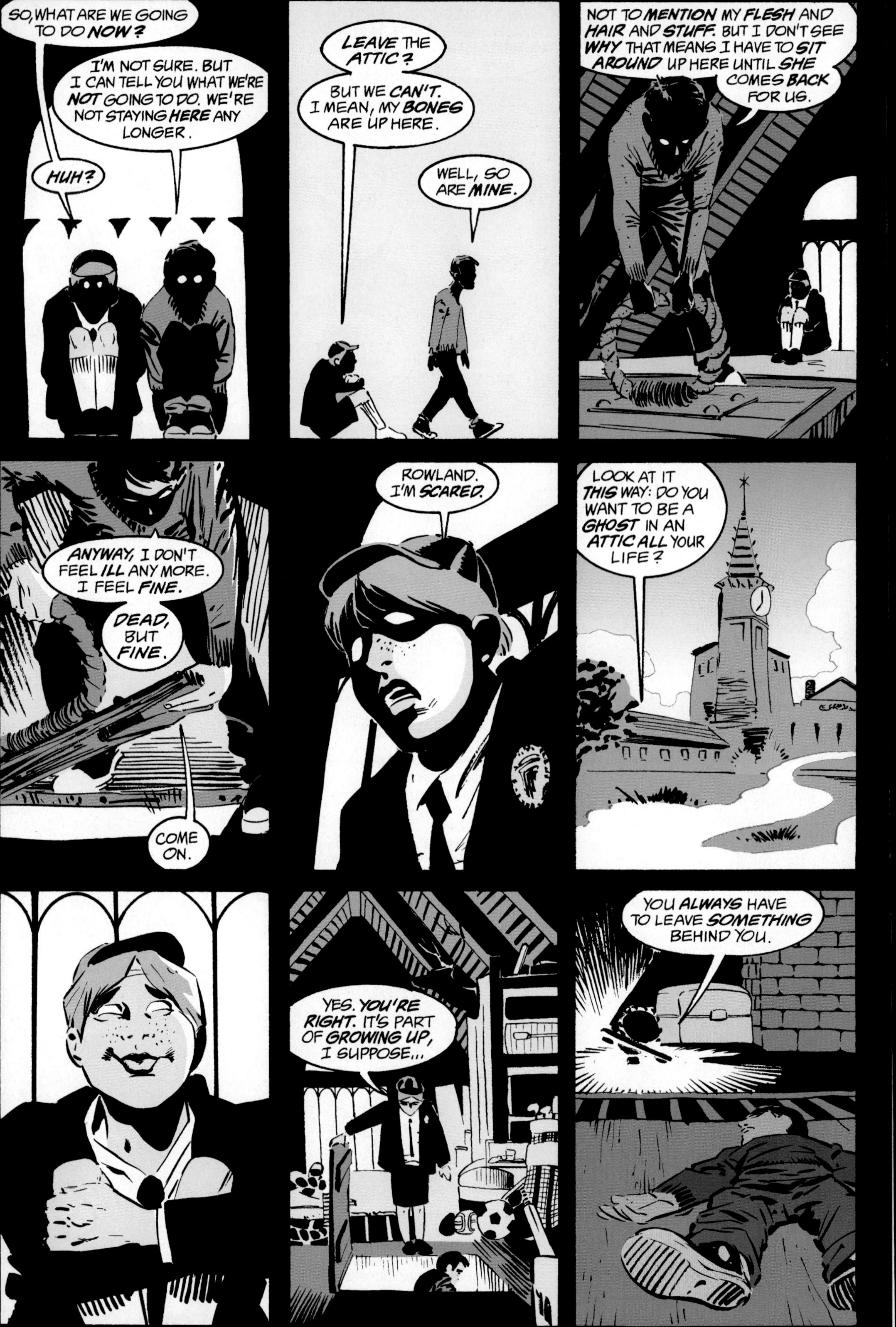
SO, WHAT ARE WE GOING TO DO NOW?
I'M NOT SURE. BUT I CAN TELL YOU WHAT WE'RE NOT GOING TO DO. WE'RE NOT STAYING HERE ANY LONGER.
HUH?
LEAVE THE ATTIC?
BUT WE CAN'T. I MEAN, MY BONES ARE UP HERE.
WELL, SO ARE MINE.
NOT TO MENTION MY FLESH AND HAIR AND STUFF. BUT I DON'T SEE WHY THAT MEANS I HAVE TO SIT AROUND UP HERE UNTIL SHE COMES BACK FOR US.
ANYWAY, I DON'T FEEL ILL ANY MORE. I FEEL FINE.
DEAD, BUT FINE.
COME ON.
ROWLAND. I'M SCARED.
LOOK AT IT THIS WAY: DO YOU WANT TO BE A GHOST IN AN ATTIC ALL YOUR LIFE?
YES. YOU'RE RIGHT. IT'S PART OF GROWING UP, I SUPPOSE...
YOU ALWAYS HAVE TO LEAVE SOMETHING BEHIND YOU.

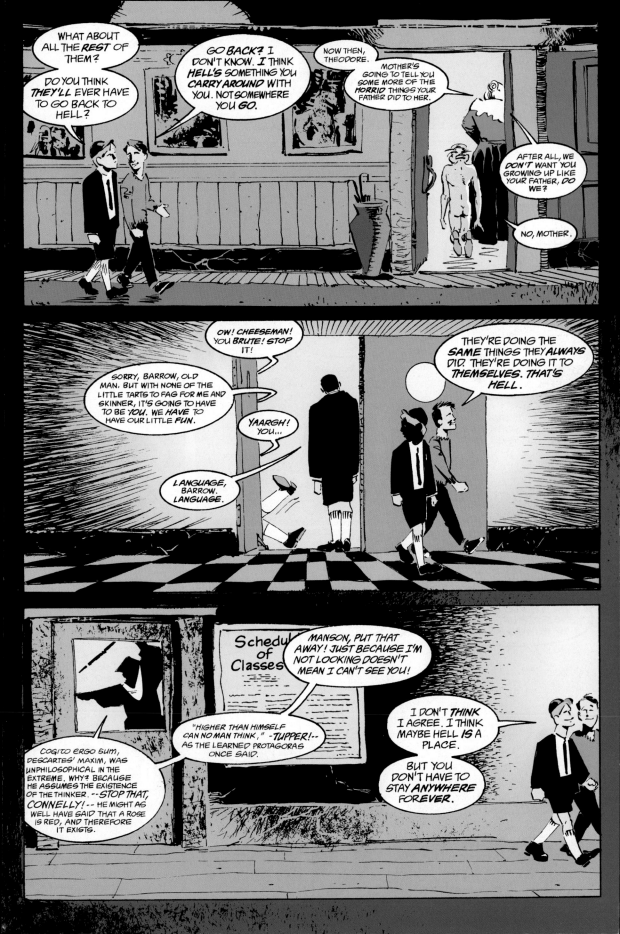

To Be Continued.

In which a banquet is held, and of what comes after; concerning diplomacy and bedrooms, blackmail and threats; and an unusual recipe for sausages.

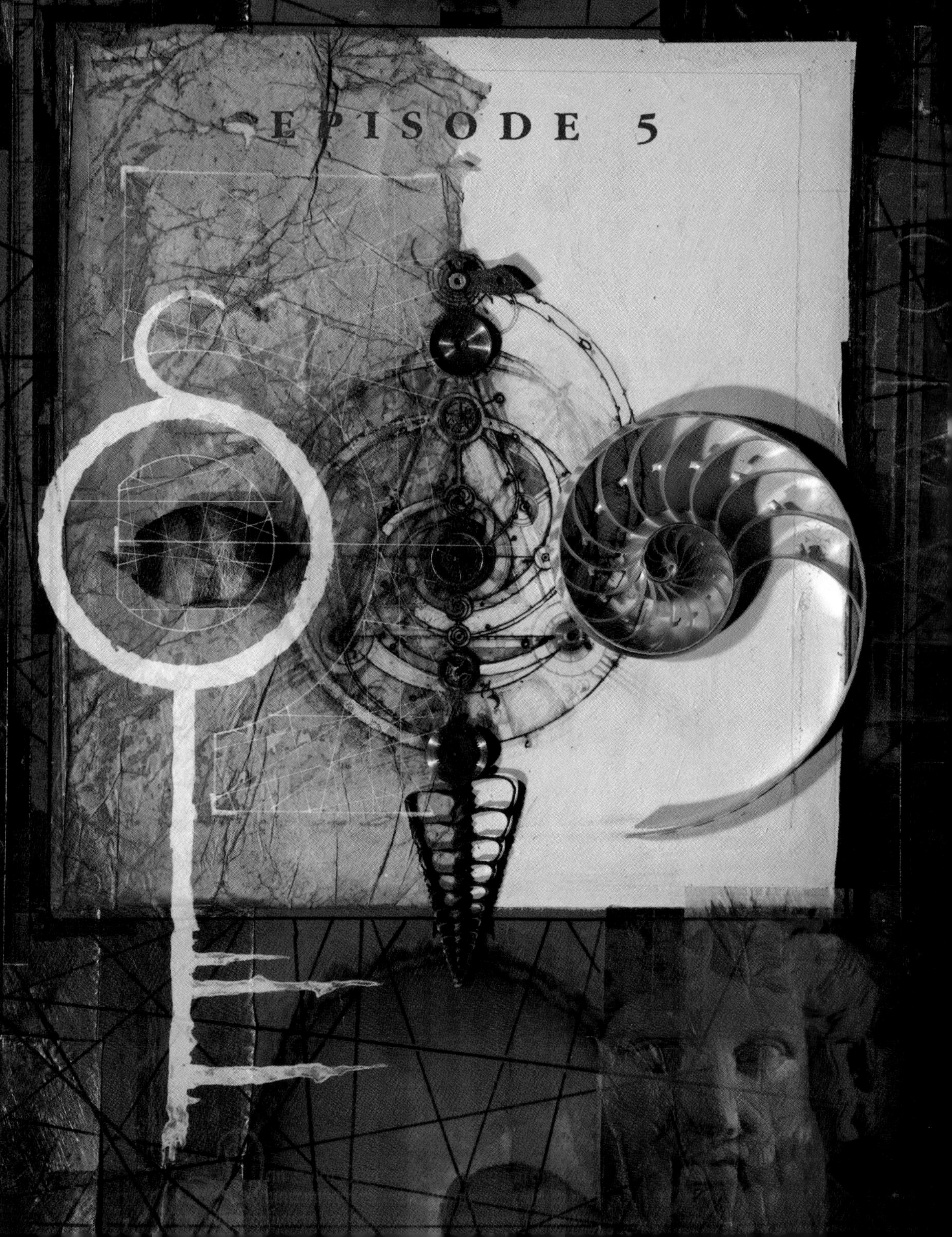
EPISODE 5

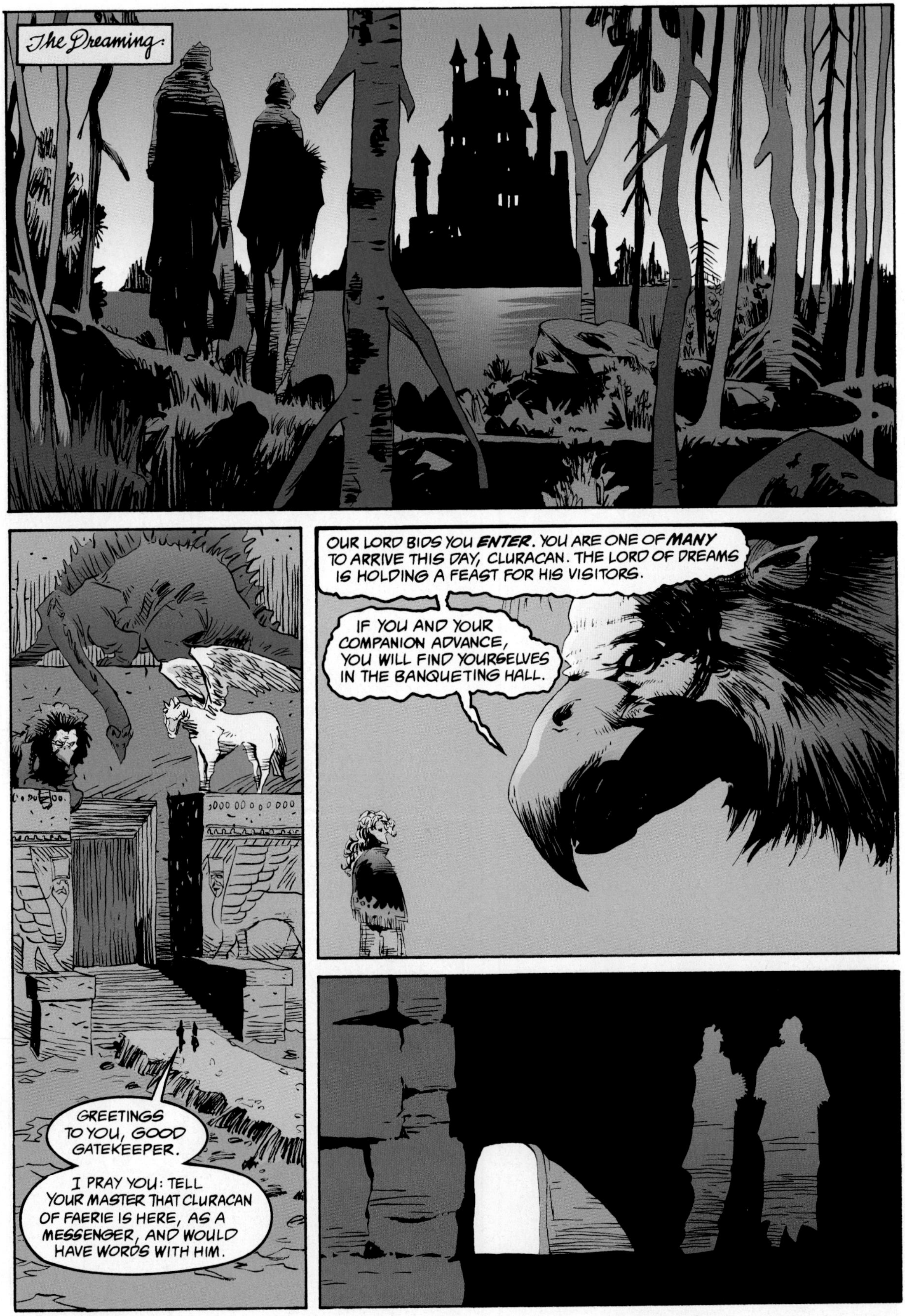
The Dreaming:
GREETINGS TO YOU, GOOD GATEKEEPER.
I PRAY YOU: TELL YOUR MASTER THAT CLURACAN OF FAERIE IS HERE, AS A MESSENGER, AND WOULD HAVE WORDS WITH HIM.
OUR LORD BIDS YOU **ENTER**. YOU ARE ONE OF **MANY** TO ARRIVE THIS DAY, CLURACAN. THE LORD OF DREAMS IS HOLDING A FEAST FOR HIS VISITORS.
IF YOU AND YOUR COMPANION ADVANCE, YOU WILL FIND YOURSELVES IN THE BANQUETING HALL.

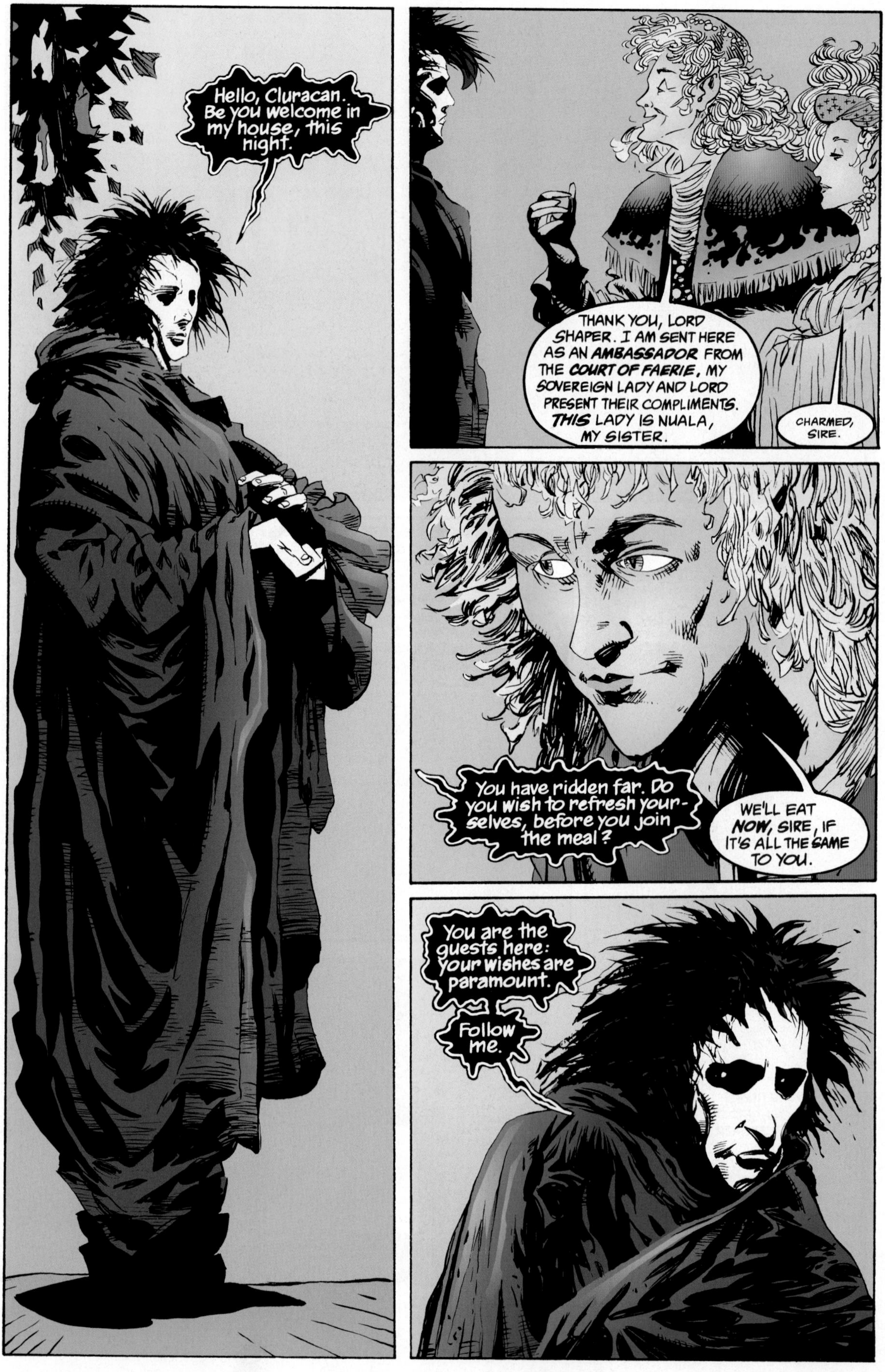
Hello, Cluracan. Be you welcome in my house, this night.
THANK YOU, LORD SHAPER. I AM SENT HERE AS AN **AMBASSADOR** FROM THE **COURT OF FAERIE**, MY SOVEREIGN LADY AND LORD PRESENT THEIR COMPLIMENTS. **THIS** LADY IS NUALA, MY SISTER.
CHARMED, SIRE.
You have ridden far. Do you wish to refresh yourselves, before you join the meal?
WE'LL EAT **NOW**, SIRE, IF IT'S ALL THE SAME TO YOU.
You are the guests here: your wishes are paramount.
Follow me.

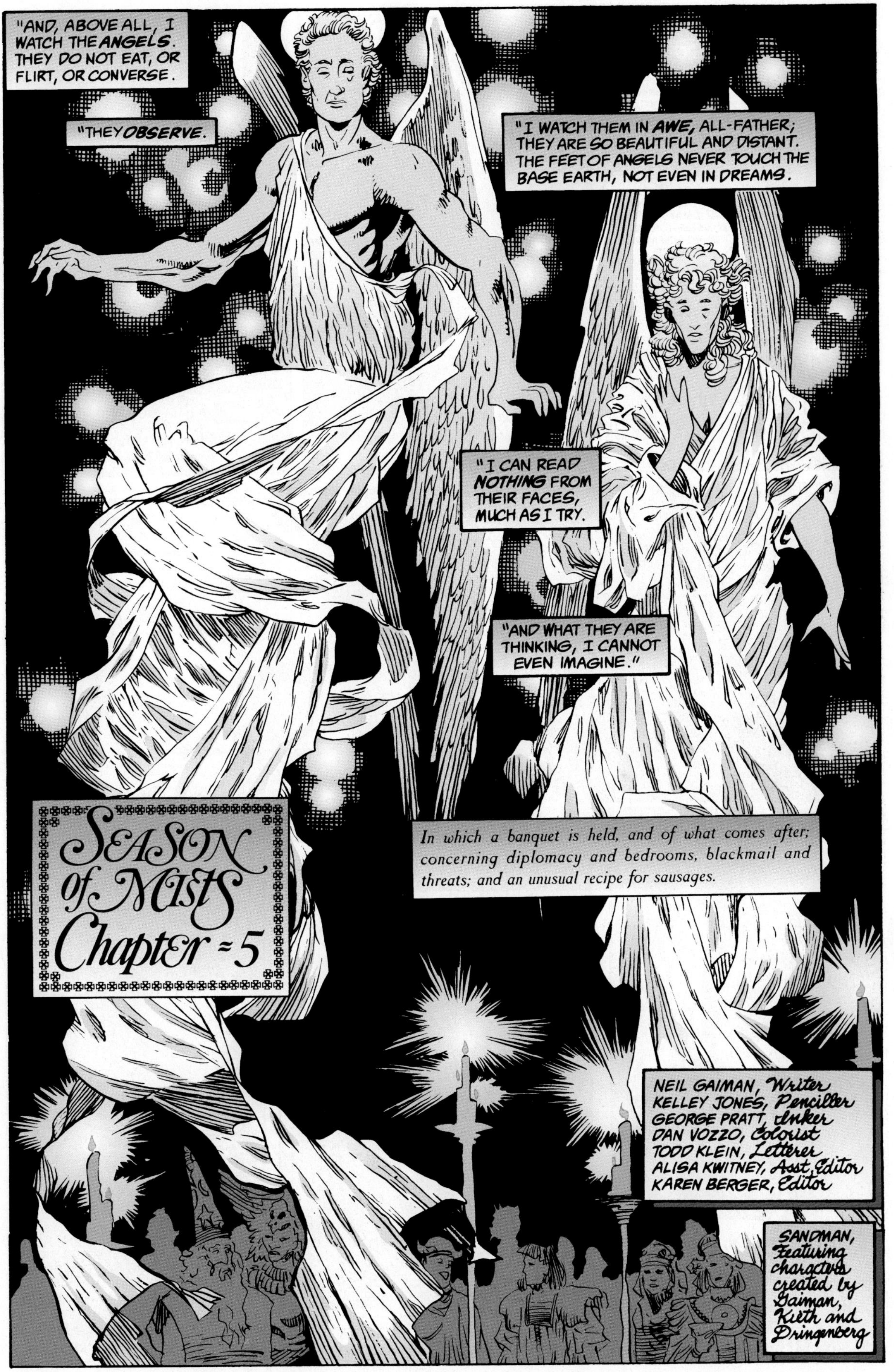

"AND, ABOVE ALL, I WATCH THE ANGELS. THEY DO NOT EAT, OR FLIRT, OR CONVERSE.
"THEY OBSERVE.
"I WATCH THEM IN AWE, ALL-FATHER; THEY ARE SO BEAUTIFUL AND DISTANT. THE FEET OF ANGELS NEVER TOUCH THE BASE EARTH, NOT EVEN IN DREAMS.
"I CAN READ NOTHING FROM THEIR FACES, MUCH AS I TRY.
"AND WHAT THEY ARE THINKING, I CANNOT EVEN IMAGINE."
SEASON of MISTS Chapter 5
In which a banquet is held, and of what comes after; concerning diplomacy and bedrooms, blackmail and threats; and an unusual recipe for sausages.
NEIL GAIMAN, Writer
KELLEY JONES, Penciller
GEORGE PRATT, Inker
DAN VOZZO, Colorist
TODD KLEIN, Letterer
ALISA KWITNEY, Asst. Editor
KAREN BERGER, Editor
SANDMAN, Featuring characters created by Gaiman, Kieth and Dringenberg

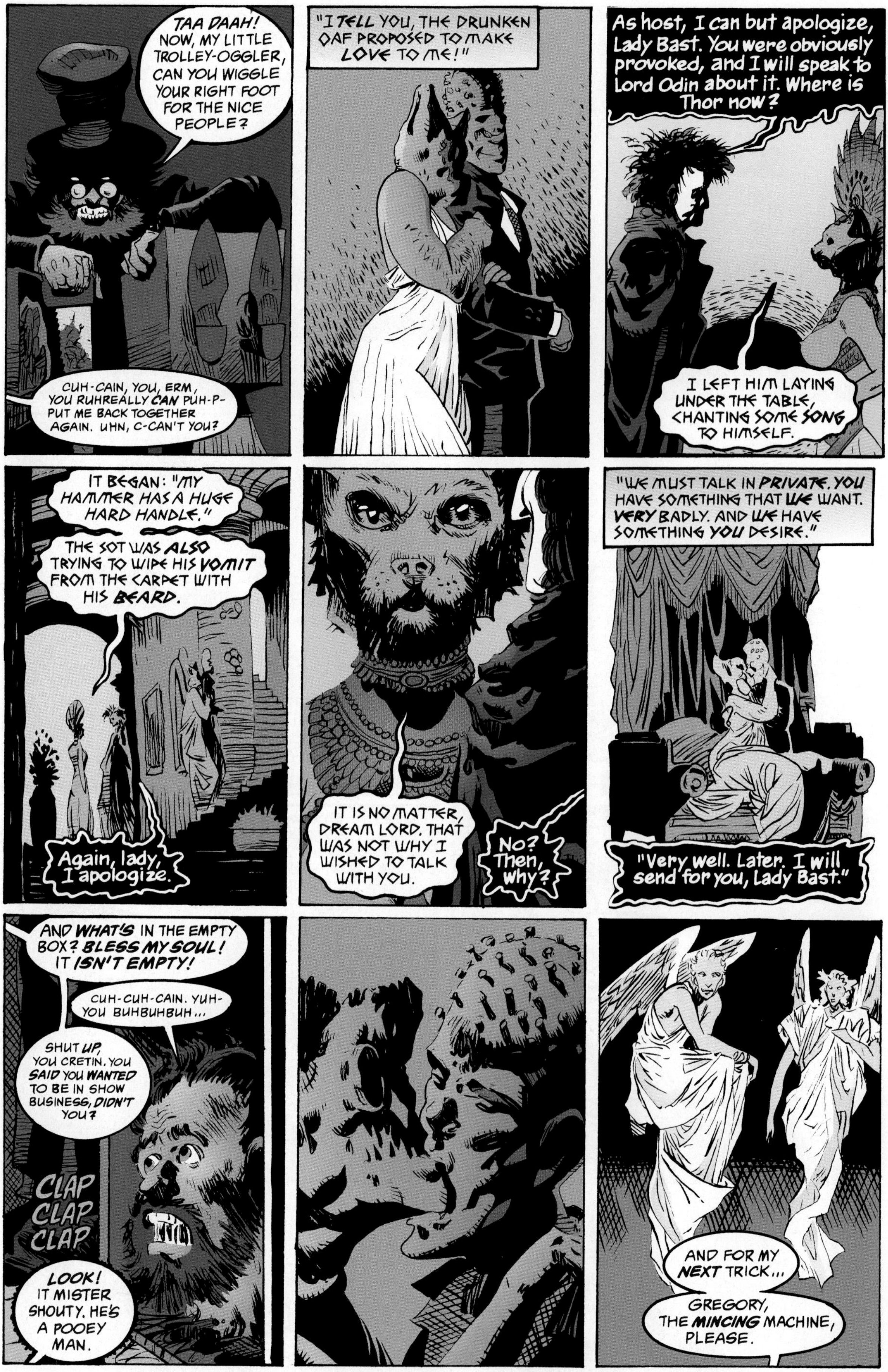
TAA DAAH! NOW, MY LITTLE TROLLEY-OGGLER, CAN YOU WIGGLE YOUR RIGHT FOOT FOR THE NICE PEOPLE?
CUH-CAIN, YOU, ERM, YOU RUHREALLY CAN PUH-P-PUT ME BACK TOGETHER AGAIN. UHN, C-CAN'T YOU?
"I TELL YOU, THE DRUNKEN OAF PROPOSED TO MAKE LOVE TO ME!"
As host, I can but apologize, Lady Bast. You were obviously provoked, and I will speak to Lord Odin about it. Where is Thor now?
I LEFT HIM LAYING UNDER THE TABLE, CHANTING SOME SONG TO HIMSELF.
IT BEGAN: "MY HAMMER HAS A HUGE HARD HANDLE."
THE SOT WAS ALSO TRYING TO WIPE HIS VOMIT FROM THE CARPET WITH HIS BEARD.
Again, lady, I apologize.
IT IS NO MATTER, DREAM LORD. THAT WAS NOT WHY I WISHED TO TALK WITH YOU.
No? Then, why?
"WE MUST TALK IN PRIVATE. YOU HAVE SOMETHING THAT WE WANT. VERY BADLY. AND WE HAVE SOMETHING YOU DESIRE."
"Very well. Later. I will send for you, Lady Bast."
AND WHAT'S IN THE EMPTY BOX? BLESS MY SOUL! IT ISN'T EMPTY!
CUH-CUH-CAIN. YUH-YOU BUHBUHBUH...
SHUT UP, YOU CRETIN. YOU SAID YOU WANTED TO BE IN SHOW BUSINESS, DIDN'T YOU?
CLAP CLAP CLAP
LOOK! IT MISTER SHOUTY. HE'S A POOEY MAN.
AND FOR MY NEXT TRICK...
GREGORY, THE MINCING MACHINE, PLEASE.

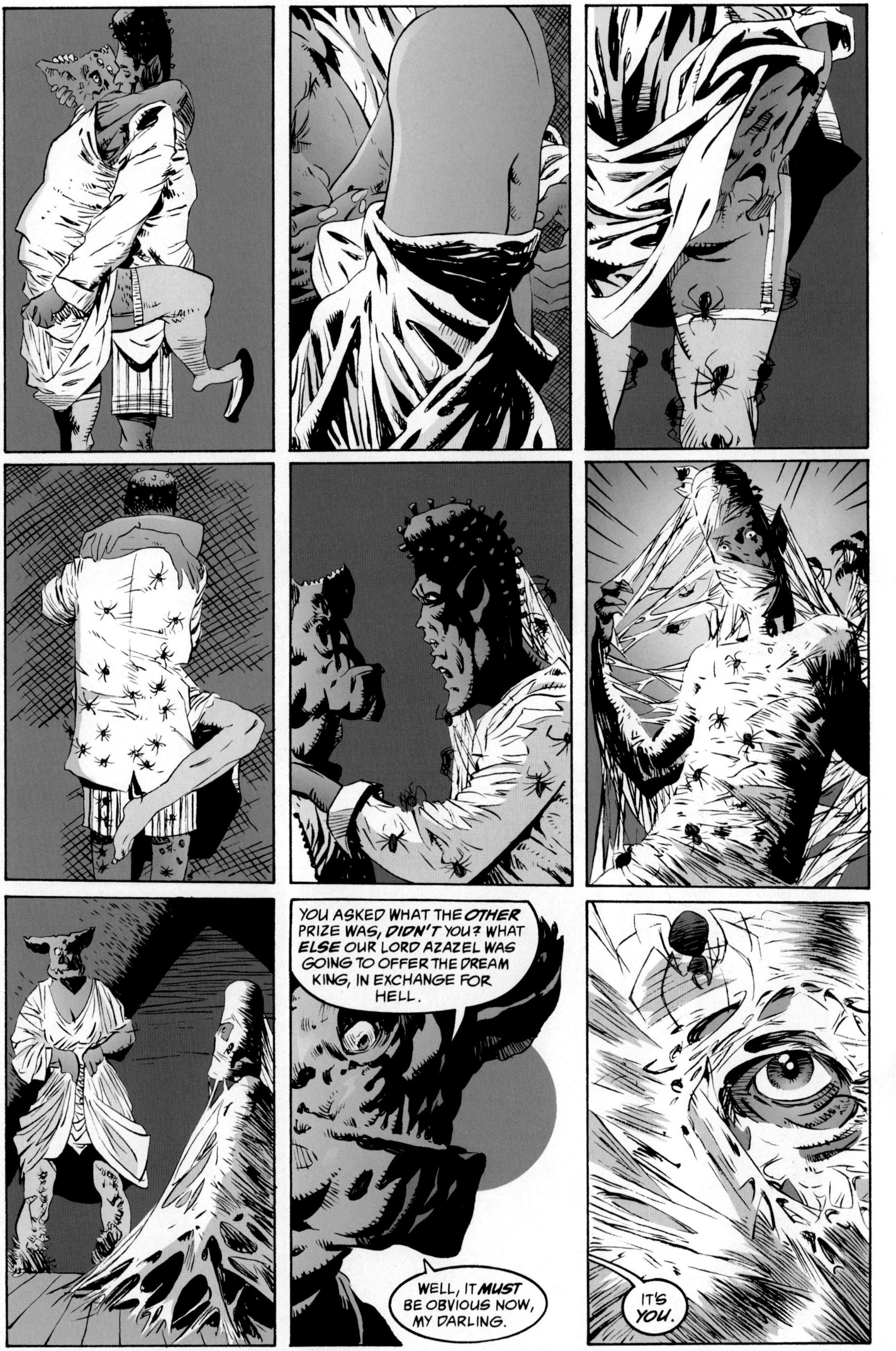
YOU ASKED WHAT THE OTHER PRIZE WAS, DIDN'T YOU? WHAT ELSE OUR LORD AZAZEL WAS GOING TO OFFER THE DREAM KING, IN EXCHANGE FOR HELL.
WELL, IT MUST BE OBVIOUS NOW, MY DARLING.
IT'S YOU.

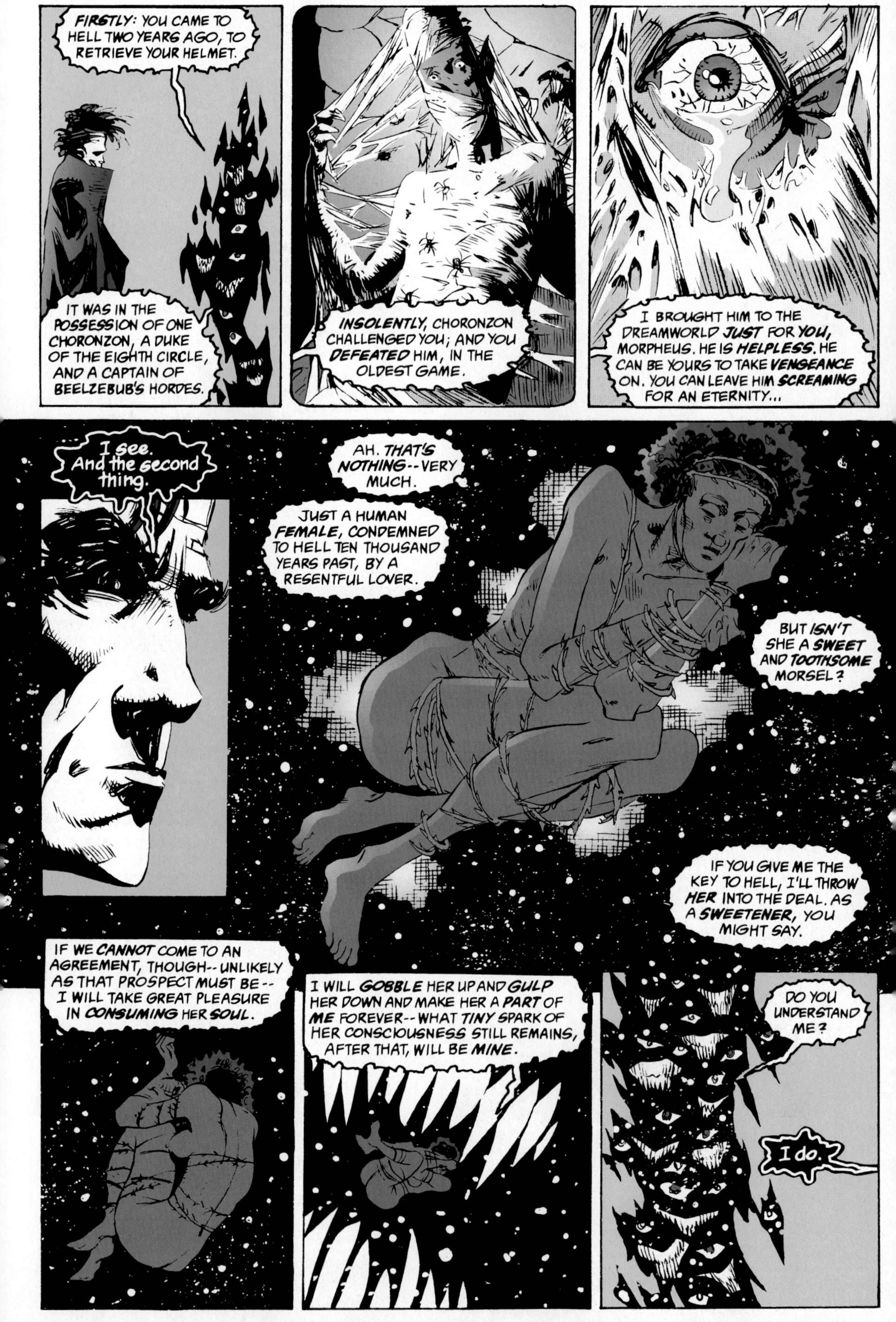
FIRSTLY: YOU CAME TO HELL TWO YEARS AGO, TO RETRIEVE YOUR HELMET.
IT WAS IN THE POSSESSION OF ONE CHORONZON, A DUKE OF THE EIGHTH CIRCLE, AND A CAPTAIN OF BEELZEBUB'S HORDES.
INSOLENTLY, CHORONZON CHALLENGED YOU; AND YOU DEFEATED HIM, IN THE OLDEST GAME.
I BROUGHT HIM TO THE DREAMWORLD JUST FOR YOU, MORPHEUS. HE IS HELPLESS. HE CAN BE YOURS TO TAKE VENGEANCE ON. YOU CAN LEAVE HIM SCREAMING FOR AN ETERNITY...
I see. And the second thing.
AH. THAT'S NOTHING--VERY MUCH.
JUST A HUMAN FEMALE, CONDEMNED TO HELL TEN THOUSAND YEARS PAST, BY A RESENTFUL LOVER.
BUT ISN'T SHE A SWEET AND TOOTHSOME MORSEL?
IF YOU GIVE ME THE KEY TO HELL, I'LL THROW HER INTO THE DEAL. AS A SWEETENER, YOU MIGHT SAY.
IF WE CANNOT COME TO AN AGREEMENT, THOUGH--UNLIKELY AS THAT PROSPECT MUST BE--I WILL TAKE GREAT PLEASURE IN CONSUMING HER SOUL.
I WILL GOBBLE HER UP AND GULP HER DOWN AND MAKE HER A PART OF ME FOREVER--WHAT TINY SPARK OF HER CONSCIOUSNESS STILL REMAINS, AFTER THAT, WILL BE MINE.
DO YOU UNDERSTAND ME?
I do.

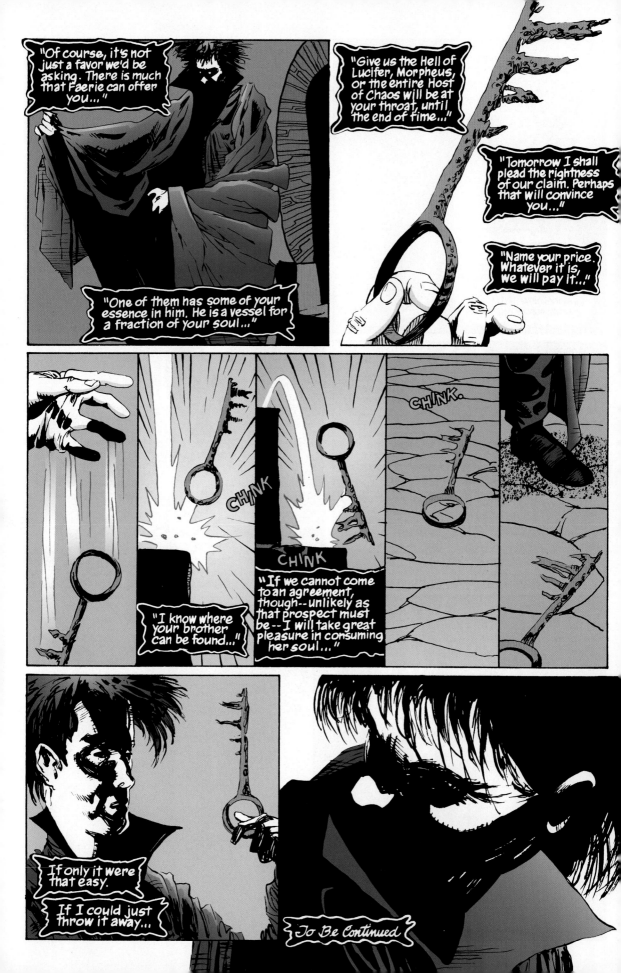

In which the vexing question of the sovereignty of Hell is finally settled, to the satisfaction of some; the finer points of hospitality; and in which it is demonstrated that while some may fall, others are pushed.

EPISODE 6

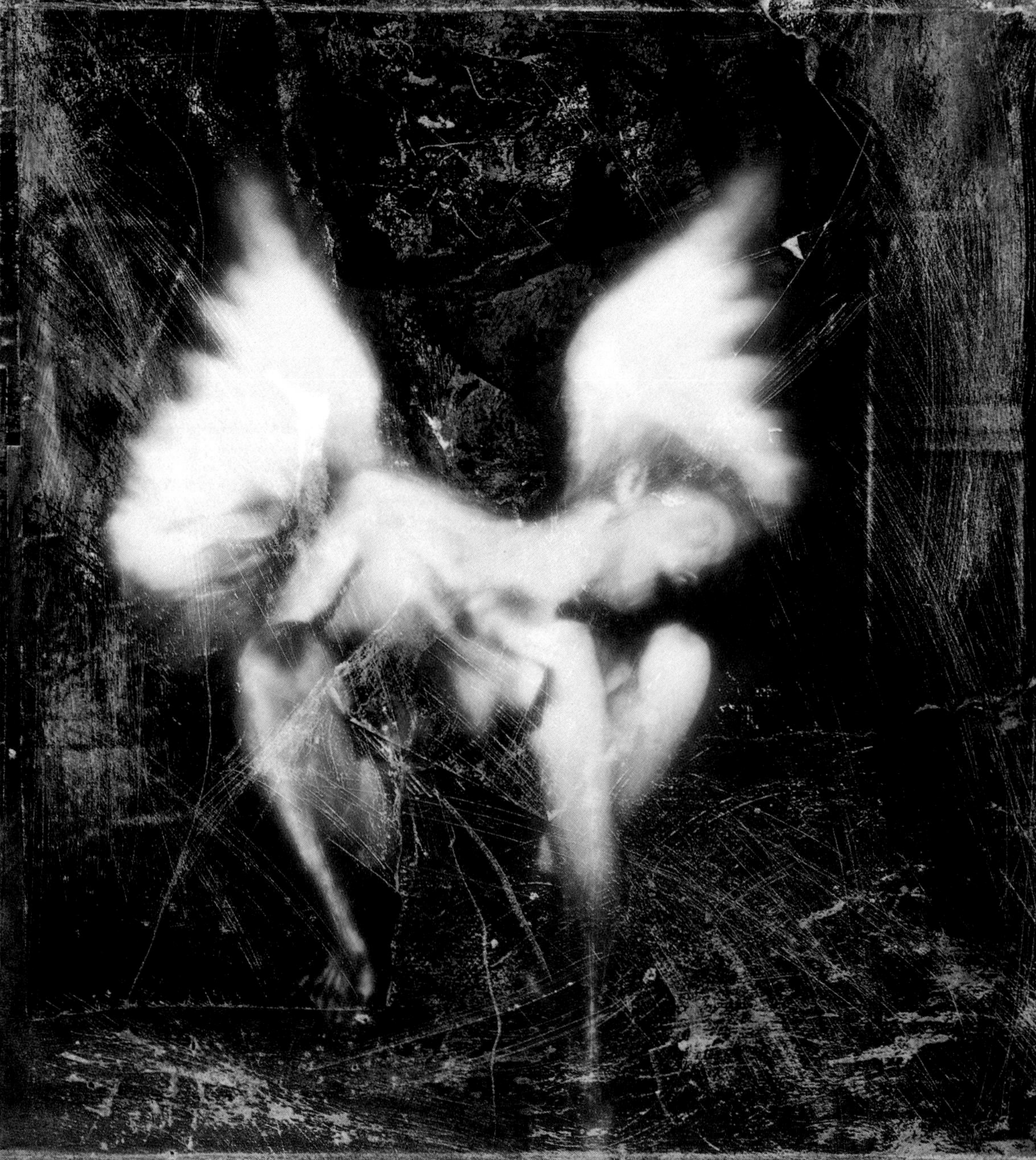

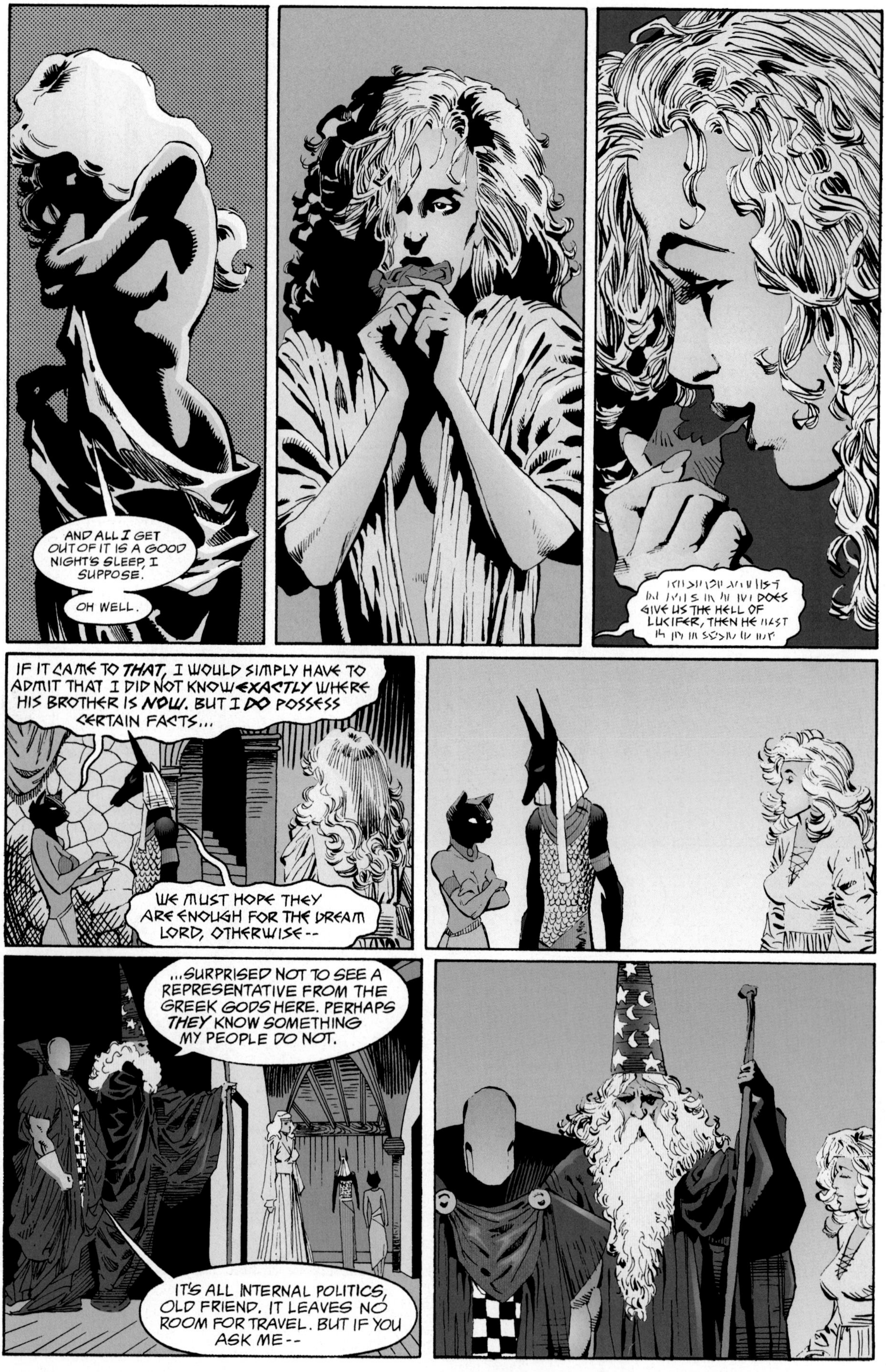
AND ALL I GET OUT OF IT IS A GOOD NIGHT'S SLEEP, I SUPPOSE.
OH WELL.
DOES GIVE US THE HELL OF LUCIFER, THEN HE
IF IT CAME TO THAT, I WOULD SIMPLY HAVE TO ADMIT THAT I DID NOT KNOW EXACTLY WHERE HIS BROTHER IS NOW. BUT I DO POSSESS CERTAIN FACTS...
WE MUST HOPE THEY ARE ENOUGH FOR THE DREAM LORD, OTHERWISE--
...SURPRISED NOT TO SEE A REPRESENTATIVE FROM THE GREEK GODS HERE. PERHAPS THEY KNOW SOMETHING MY PEOPLE DO NOT.
IT'S ALL INTERNAL POLITICS, OLD FRIEND. IT LEAVES NO ROOM FOR TRAVEL. BUT IF YOU ASK ME--

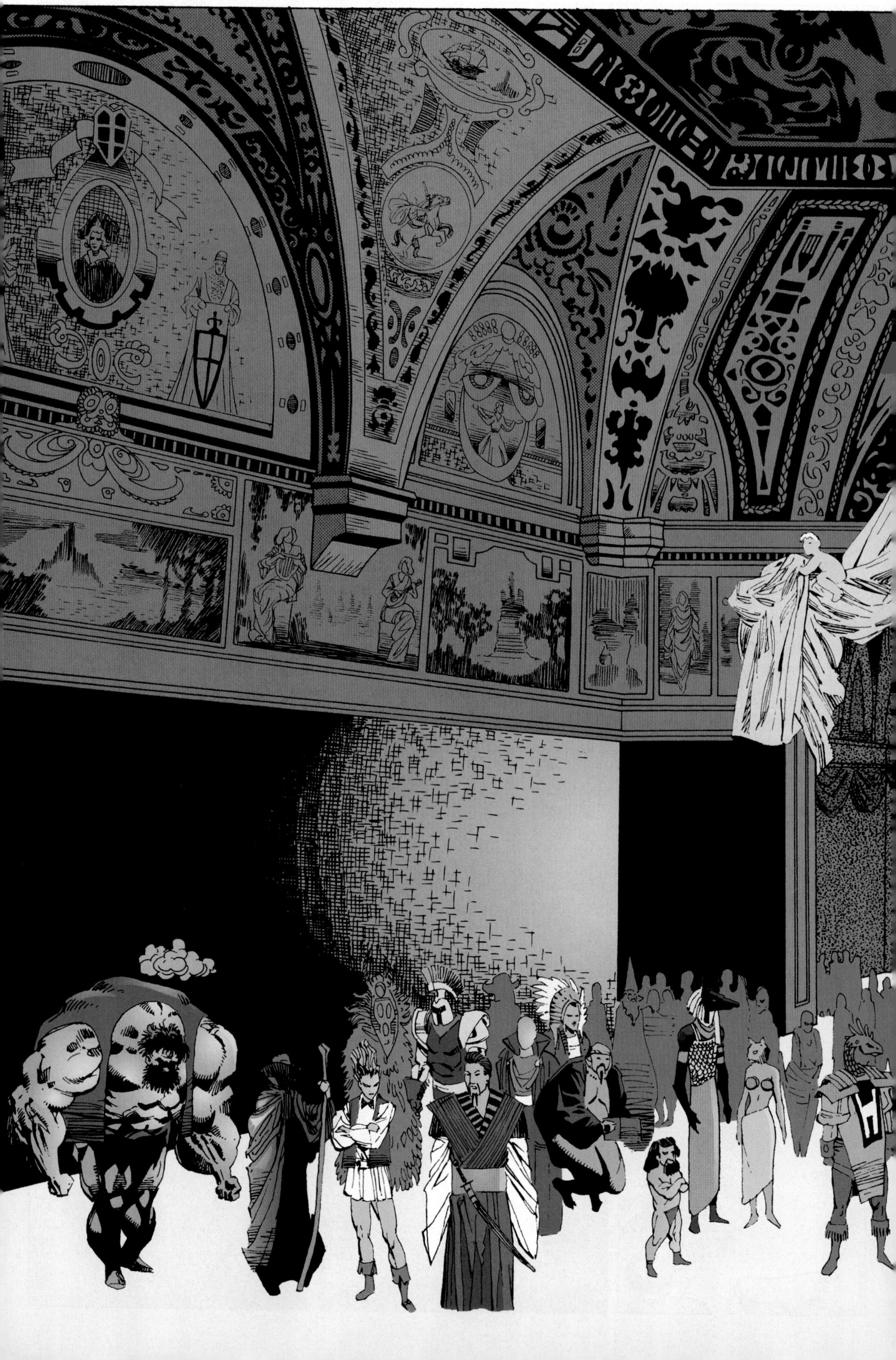

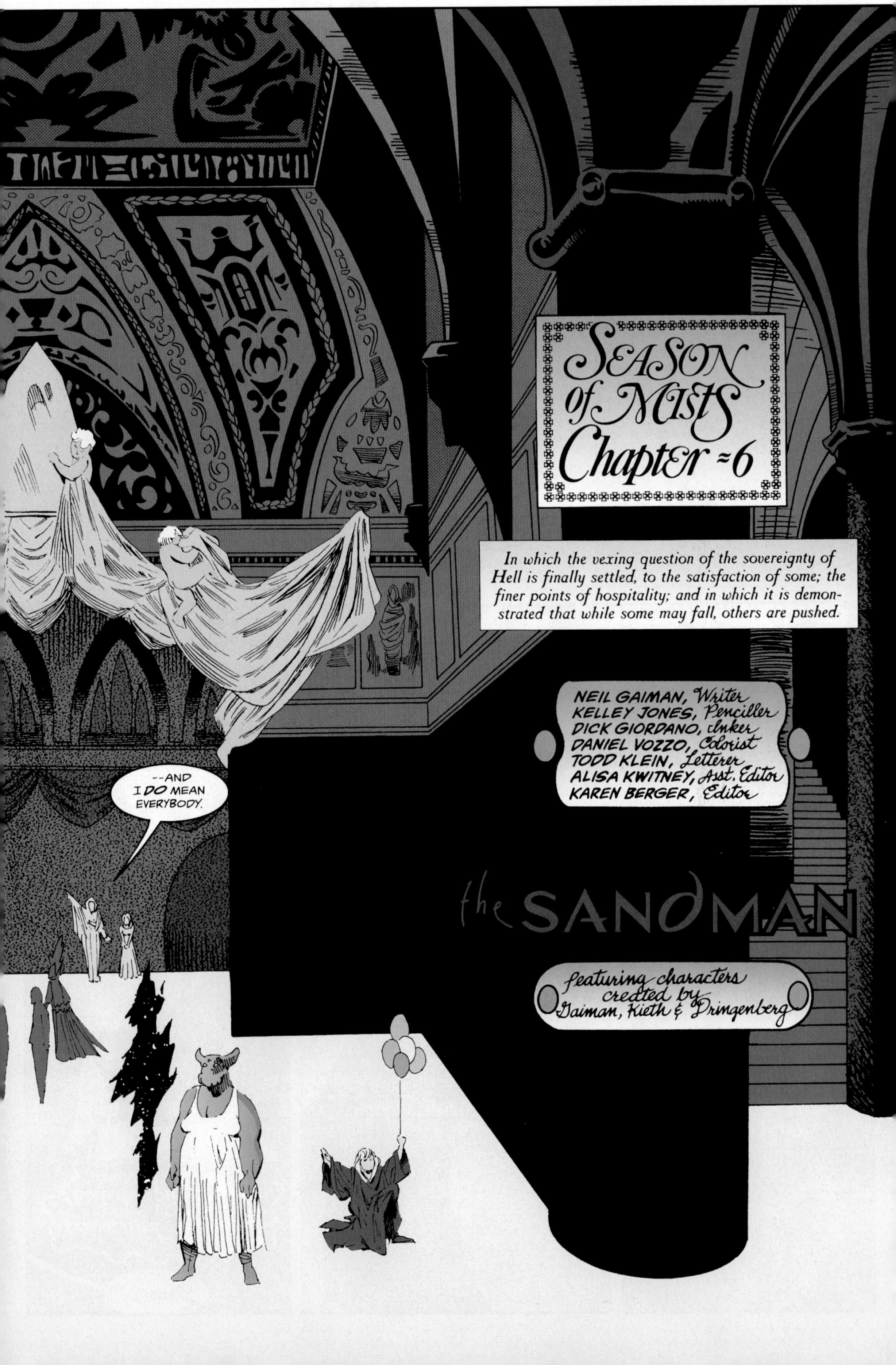
SEASON of MISTS Chapter ≈6
In which the vexing question of the sovereignty of Hell is finally settled, to the satisfaction of some; the finer points of hospitality; and in which it is demonstrated that while some may fall, others are pushed.
NEIL GAIMAN, Writer
KELLEY JONES, Penciller
DICK GIORDANO, Inker
DANIEL VOZZO, Colorist
TODD KLEIN, Letterer
ALISA KWITNEY, Asst. Editor
KAREN BERGER, Editor
--AND I DO MEAN EVERYBODY.
the SANDMAN
featuring characters created by Gaiman, Kieth & Dringenberg

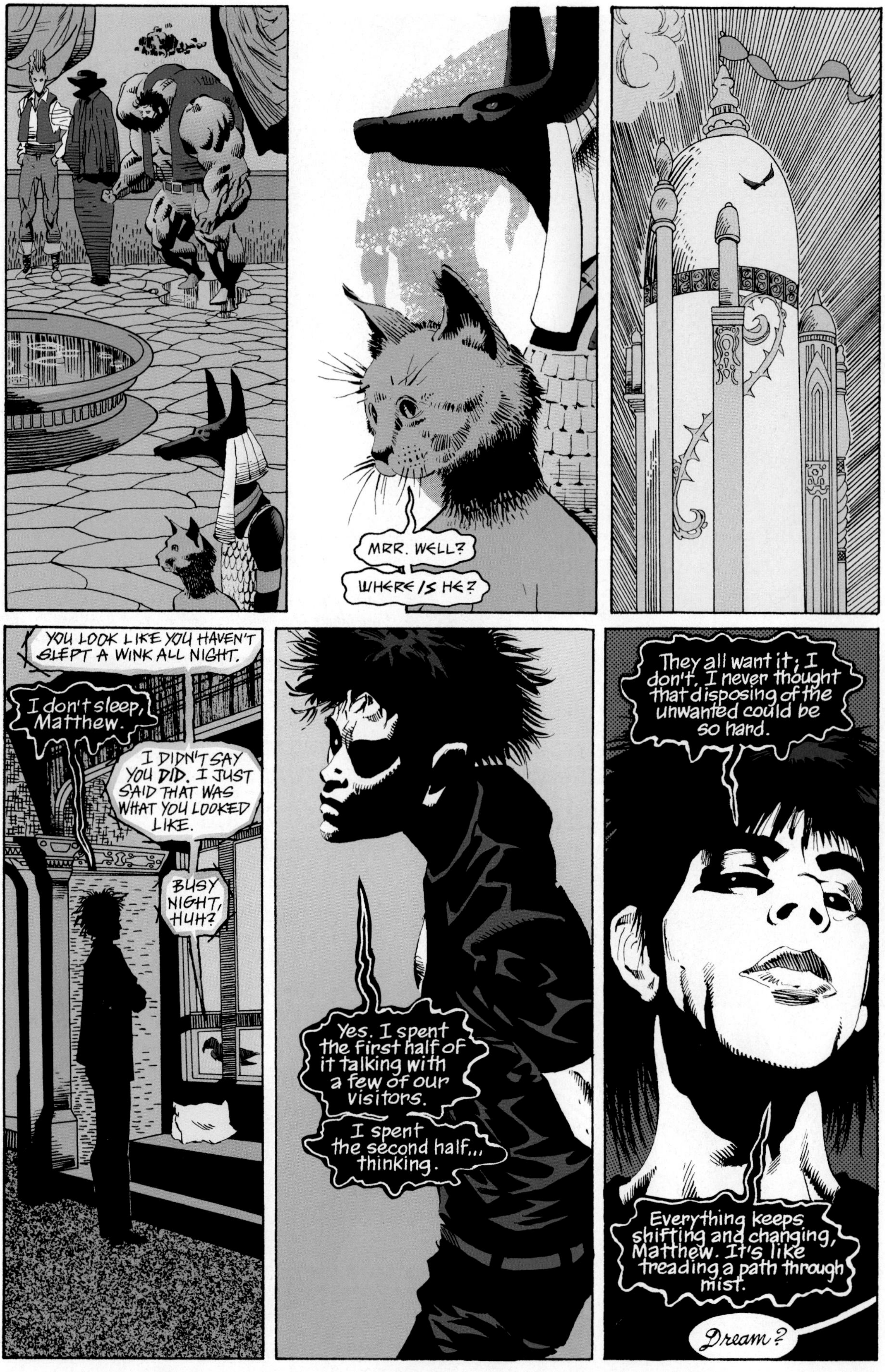
MRR. WELL?
WHERE IS HE?
YOU LOOK LIKE YOU HAVEN'T SLEPT A WINK ALL NIGHT.
I don't sleep, Matthew.
I DIDN'T SAY YOU DID. I JUST SAID THAT WAS WHAT YOU LOOKED LIKE.
BUSY NIGHT, HUH?
Yes. I spent the first half of it talking with a few of our visitors.
I spent the second half... thinking.
They all want it; I don't. I never thought that disposing of the unwanted could be so hard.
Everything keeps shifting and changing, Matthew. It's like treading a path through mist.
Dream?

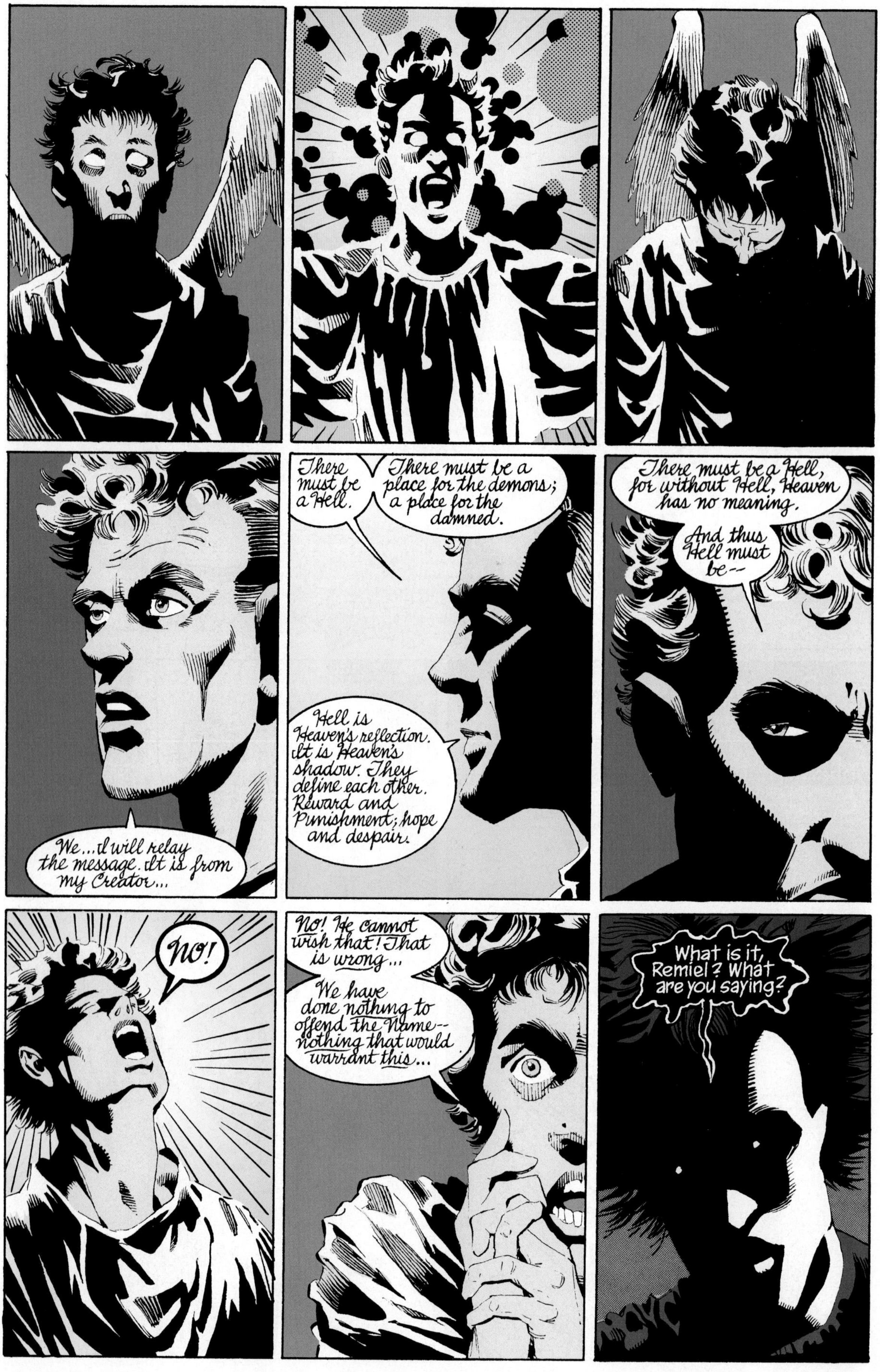
There must be a Hell.
There must be a place for the demons; a place for the damned.
There must be a Hell, for without Hell, Heaven has no meaning.
And thus Hell must be--
We... I will relay the message. It is from my Creator...
Hell is Heaven's reflection. It is Heaven's shadow. They define each other. Reward and Punishment; hope and despair.
NO!
No! He cannot wish that! That is wrong...
We have done nothing to offend the Name-- nothing that would warrant this...
What is it, Remiel? What are you saying?

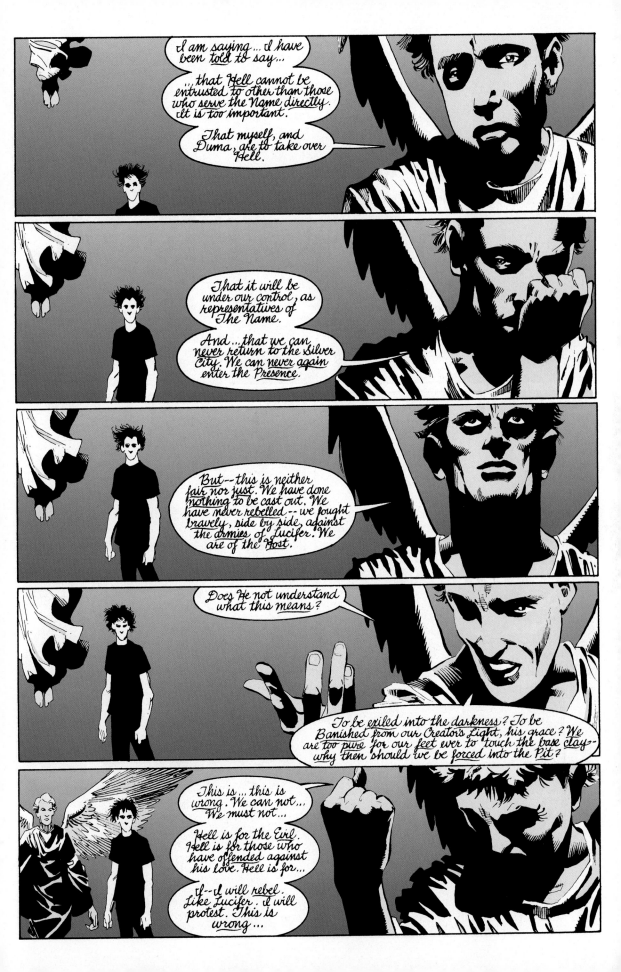

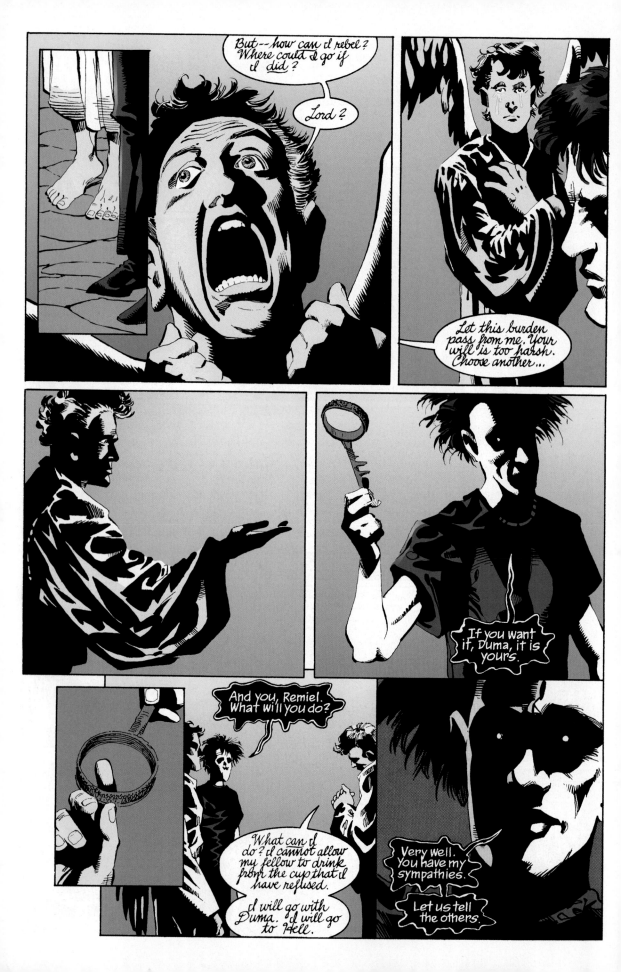

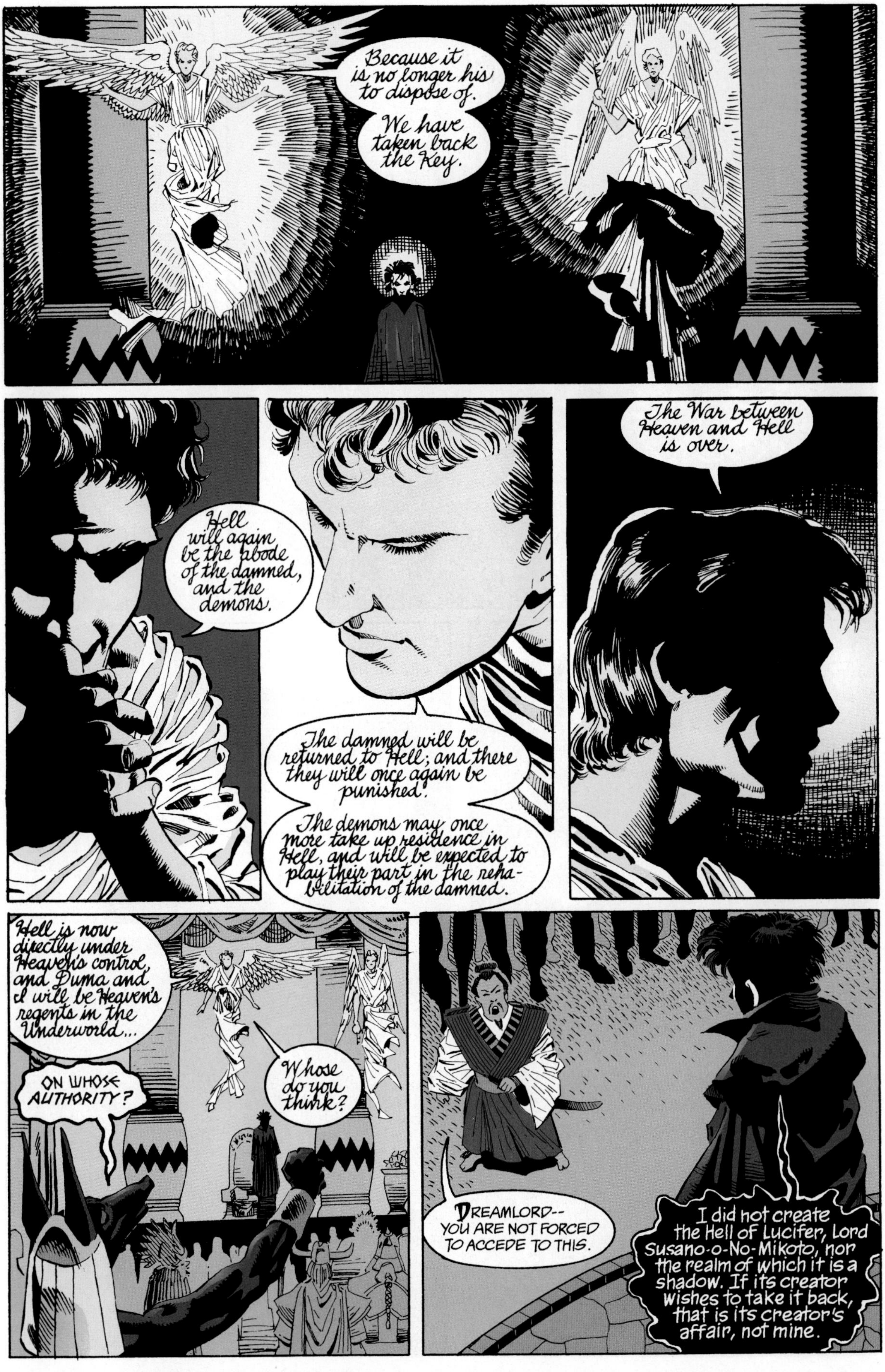
Because it is no longer his to dispose of.
We have taken back the Key.
Hell will again be the abode of the damned, and the demons.
The damned will be returned to Hell; and there they will once again be punished.
The demons may once more take up residence in Hell, and will be expected to play their part in the rehabilitation of the damned.
The War between Heaven and Hell is over.
Hell is now directly under Heaven's control, and Duma and I will be Heaven's regents in the Underworld...
ON WHOSE AUTHORITY?
Whose do you think?
DREAMLORD-- YOU ARE NOT FORCED TO ACCEDE TO THIS.
I did not create the Hell of Lucifer, Lord Susano-o-No-Mikoto, nor the realm of which it is a shadow. If its creator wishes to take it back, that is its creator's affair, not mine.

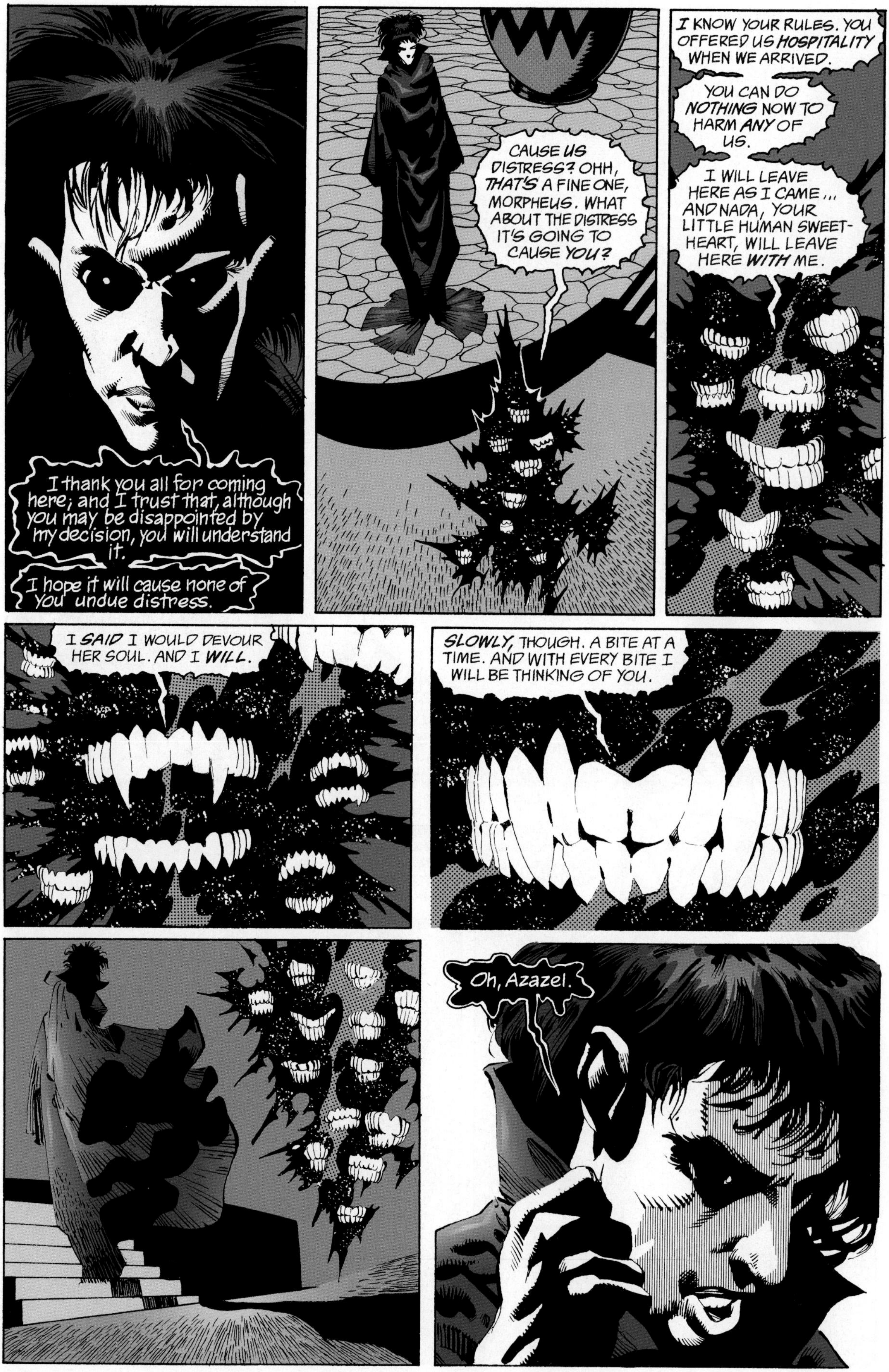

I thank you all for coming here; and I trust that, although you may be disappointed by my decision, you will understand it.
I hope it will cause none of you undue distress.
CAUSE US DISTRESS? OHH, THAT'S A FINE ONE, MORPHEUS. WHAT ABOUT THE DISTRESS IT'S GOING TO CAUSE YOU?
I KNOW YOUR RULES. YOU OFFERED US HOSPITALITY WHEN WE ARRIVED.
YOU CAN DO NOTHING NOW TO HARM ANY OF US.
I WILL LEAVE HERE AS I CAME... AND NADA, YOUR LITTLE HUMAN SWEET-HEART, WILL LEAVE HERE WITH ME.
I SAID I WOULD DEVOUR HER SOUL. AND I WILL.
SLOWLY, THOUGH. A BITE AT A TIME. AND WITH EVERY BITE I WILL BE THINKING OF YOU.
Oh, Azazel.

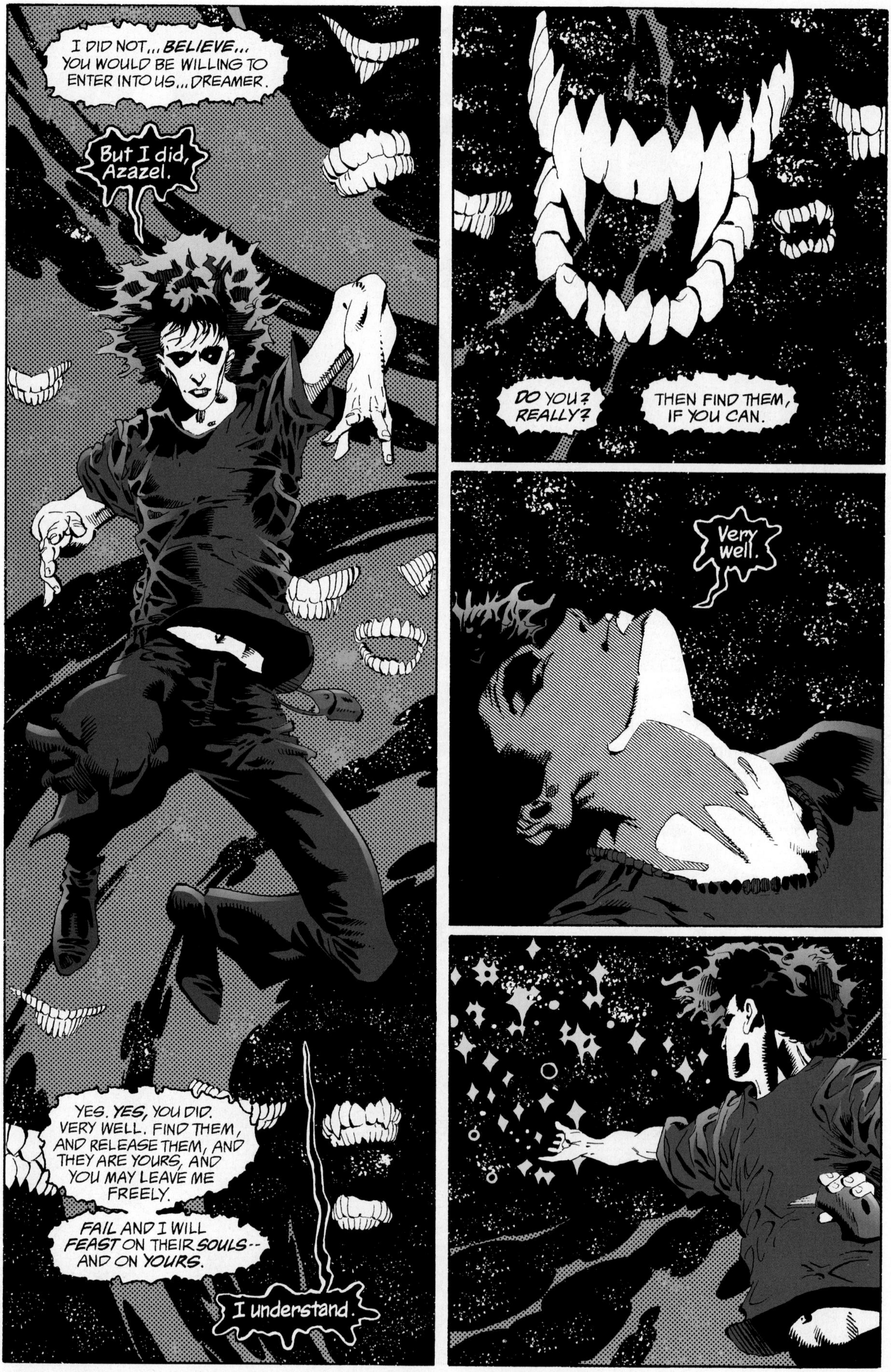
I DID NOT... BELIEVE... YOU WOULD BE WILLING TO ENTER INTO US... DREAMER.
But I did, Azazel.
YES. YES, YOU DID. VERY WELL. FIND THEM, AND RELEASE THEM, AND THEY ARE YOURS, AND YOU MAY LEAVE ME FREELY.
FAIL AND I WILL FEAST ON THEIR SOULS-- AND ON YOURS.
I understand.
DO YOU? REALLY?
THEN FIND THEM, IF YOU CAN.
Very well.

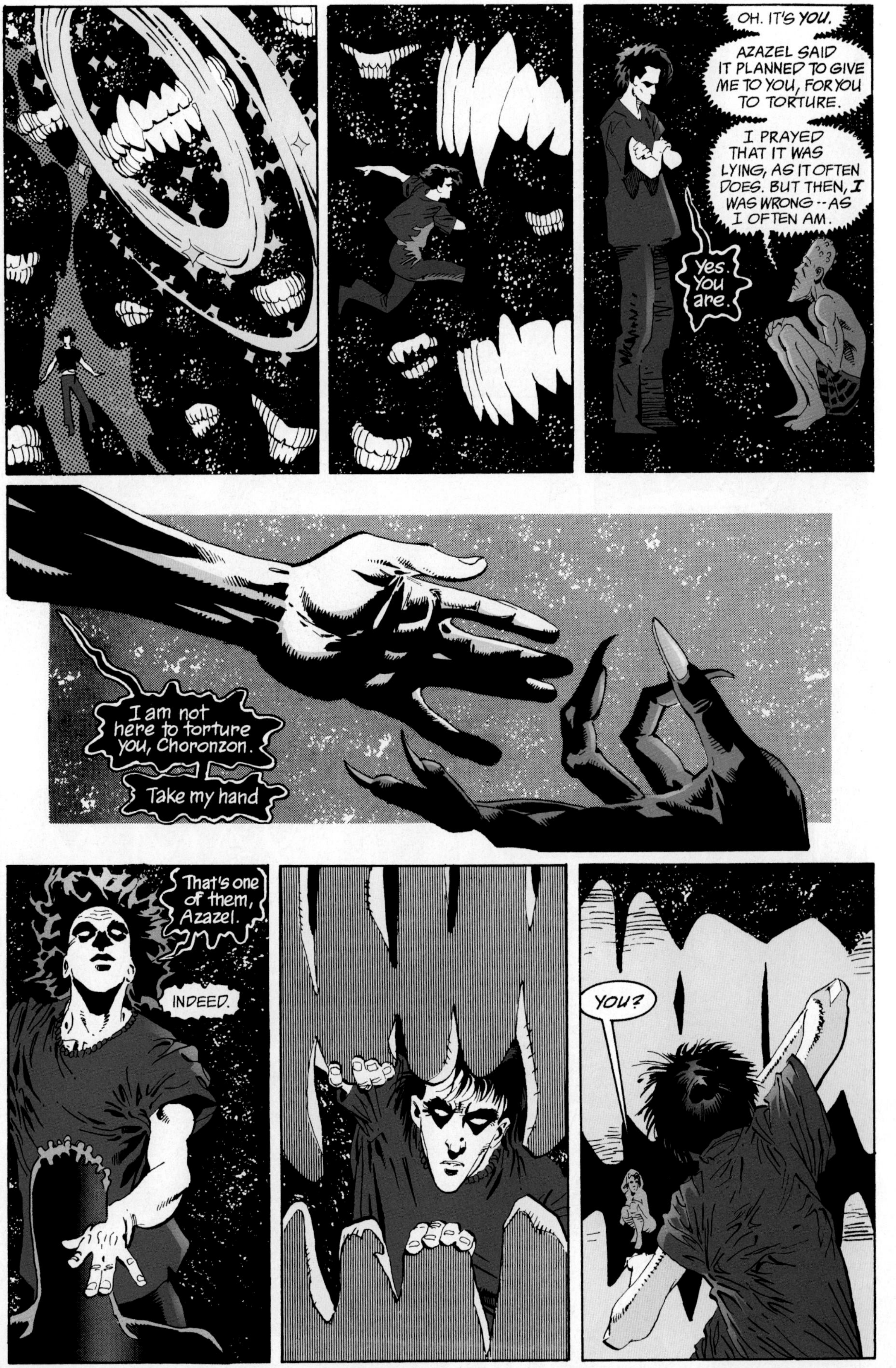
OH. IT'S YOU.
AZAZEL SAID IT PLANNED TO GIVE ME TO YOU, FOR YOU TO TORTURE.
I PRAYED THAT IT WAS LYING, AS IT OFTEN DOES. BUT THEN, I WAS WRONG -- AS I OFTEN AM.
Yes. You are.
I am not here to torture you, Choronzon.
Take my hand
That's one of them, Azazel.
INDEED.
YOU?

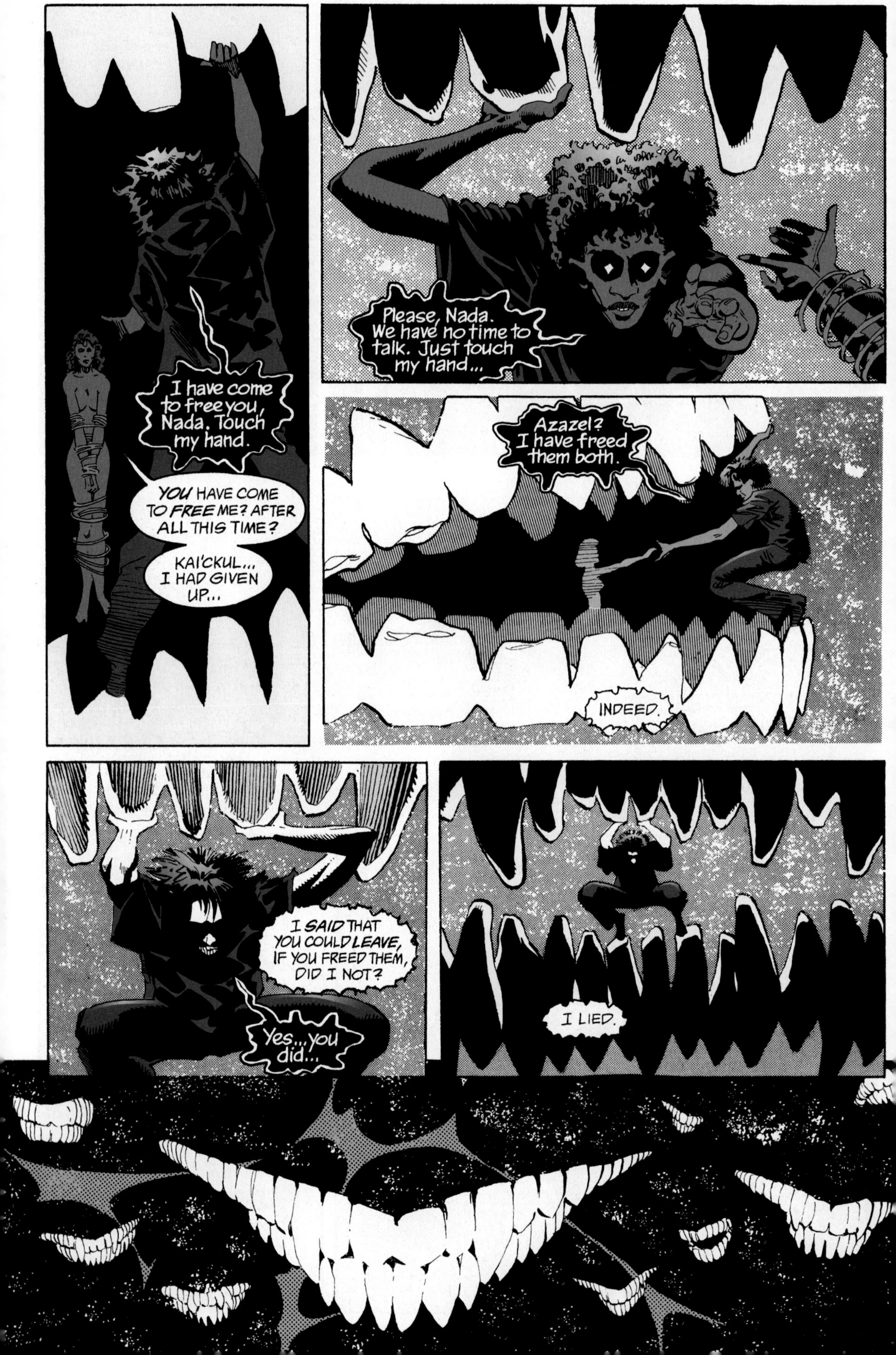
I have come to free you, Nada. Touch my hand.
YOU HAVE COME TO FREE ME? AFTER ALL THIS TIME?
KAI'CKUL... I HAD GIVEN UP...
Please, Nada. We have no time to talk. Just touch my hand...
Azazel? I have freed them both.
INDEED.
I SAID THAT YOU COULD LEAVE, IF YOU FREED THEM, DID I NOT?
Yes... you did...
I LIED.

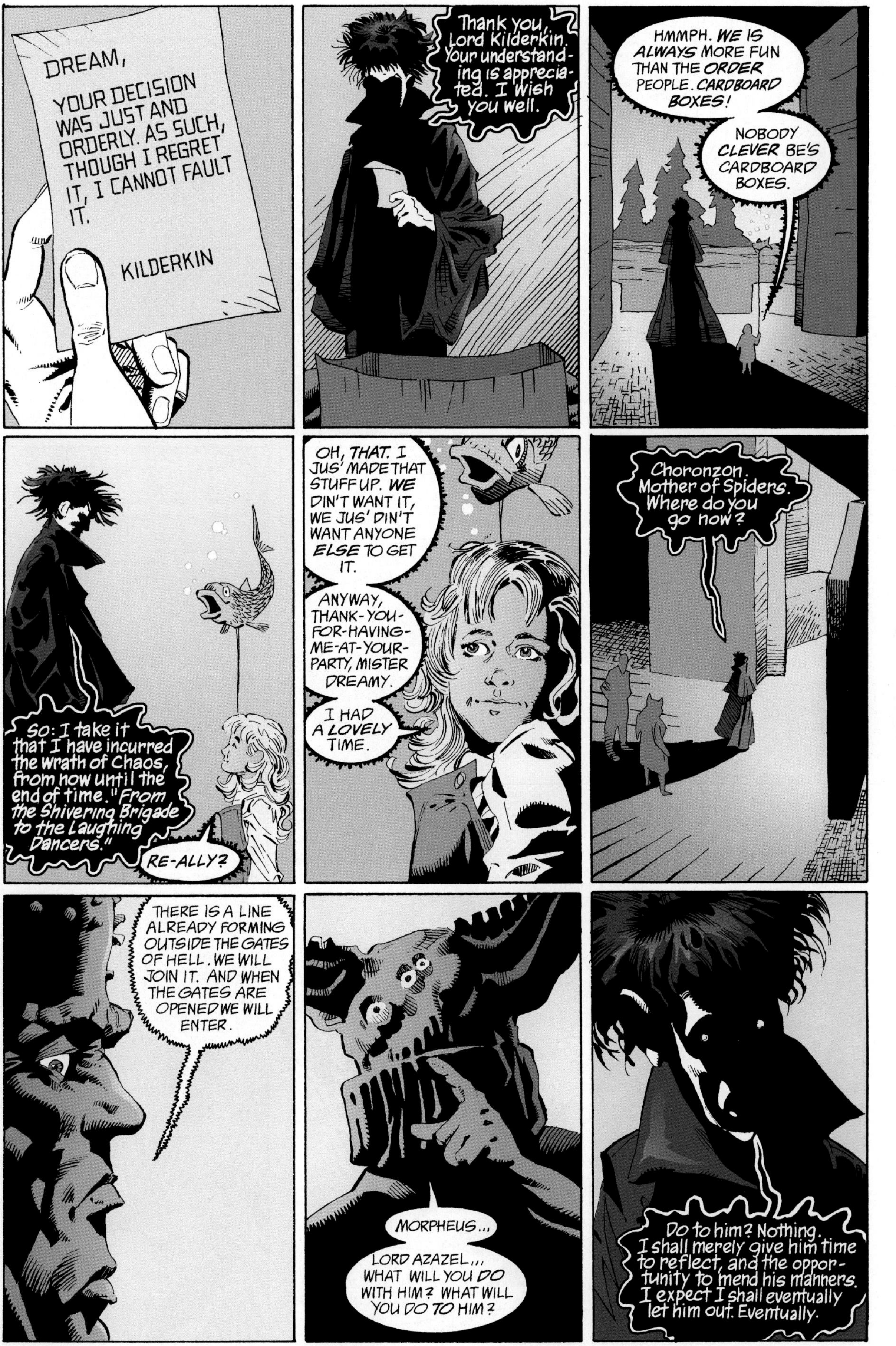
DREAM,
YOUR DECISION WAS JUST AND ORDERLY. AS SUCH, THOUGH I REGRET IT, I CANNOT FAULT IT.
KILDERKIN
Thank you, Lord Kilderkin. Your understanding is appreciated. I wish you well.
HMMPH. WE IS ALWAYS MORE FUN THAN THE ORDER PEOPLE. CARDBOARD BOXES!
NOBODY CLEVER BE'S CARDBOARD BOXES.
So: I take it that I have incurred the wrath of Chaos, from now until the end of time. "From the Shivering Brigade to the Laughing Dancers."
RE-ALLY?
OH, THAT. I JUS' MADE THAT STUFF UP. WE DIN'T WANT IT, WE JUS' DIN'T WANT ANYONE ELSE TO GET IT.
ANYWAY, THANK-YOU-FOR-HAVING-ME-AT-YOUR-PARTY, MISTER DREAMY.
I HAD A LOVELY TIME.
Choronzon. Mother of Spiders. Where do you go now?
THERE IS A LINE ALREADY FORMING OUTSIDE THE GATES OF HELL. WE WILL JOIN IT. AND WHEN THE GATES ARE OPENED WE WILL ENTER.
MORPHEUS...
LORD AZAZEL... WHAT WILL YOU DO WITH HIM? WHAT WILL YOU DO TO HIM?
Do to him? Nothing. I shall merely give him time to reflect, and the opportunity to mend his manners. I expect I shall eventually let him out. Eventually.

To Be Concluded

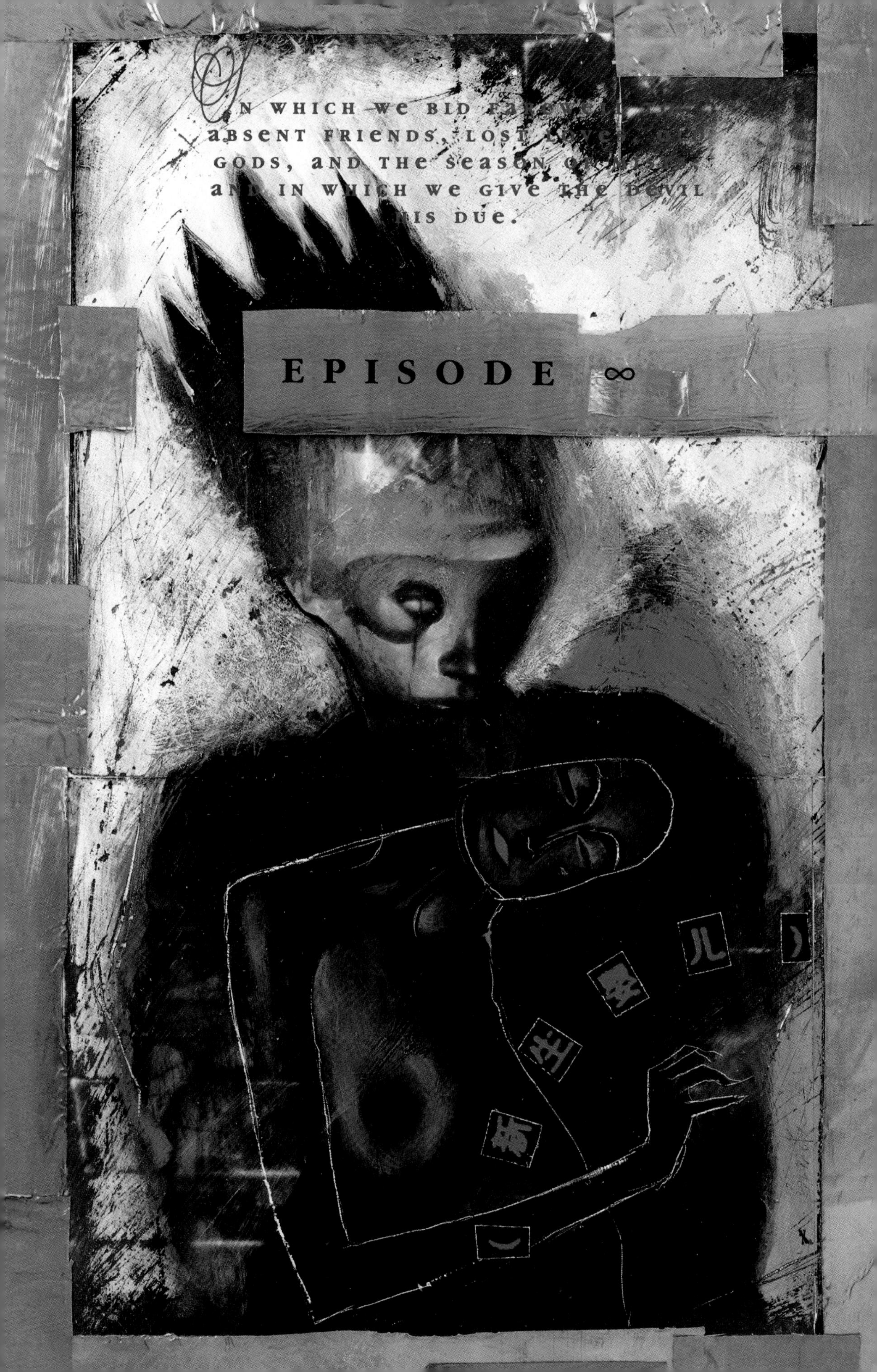
IN WHICH WE BID
ABSENT FRIENDS, LOST
GODS, AND THE SEASON
AND IN WHICH WE GIVE THE DEVIL
HIS DUE.
EPISODE ∞

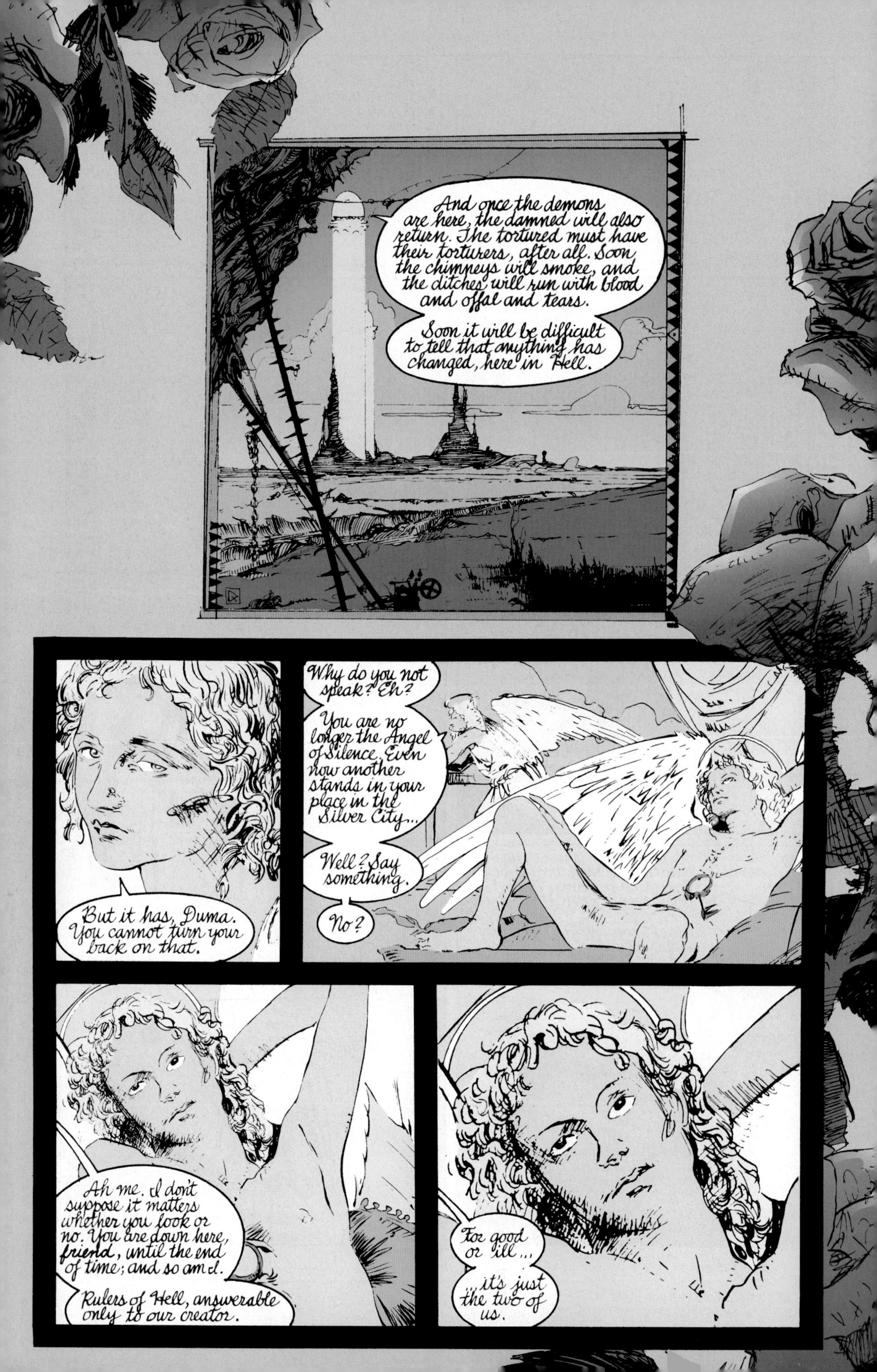
And once the demons are here, the damned will also return. The tortured must have their torturers, after all. Soon the chimneys will smoke, and the ditches will run with blood and offal and tears.
Soon it will be difficult to tell that anything has changed, here in Hell.
But it has, Duma. You cannot turn your back on that.
Why do you not speak? Eh?
You are no longer the Angel of Silence. Even now another stands in your place in the Silver City...
Well? Say something.
No?
Ah me. I don't suppose it matters whether you look or no. You are down here, friend, until the end of time; and so am I.
Rulers of Hell, answerable only to our creator.
For good or ill...
...it's just the two of us.

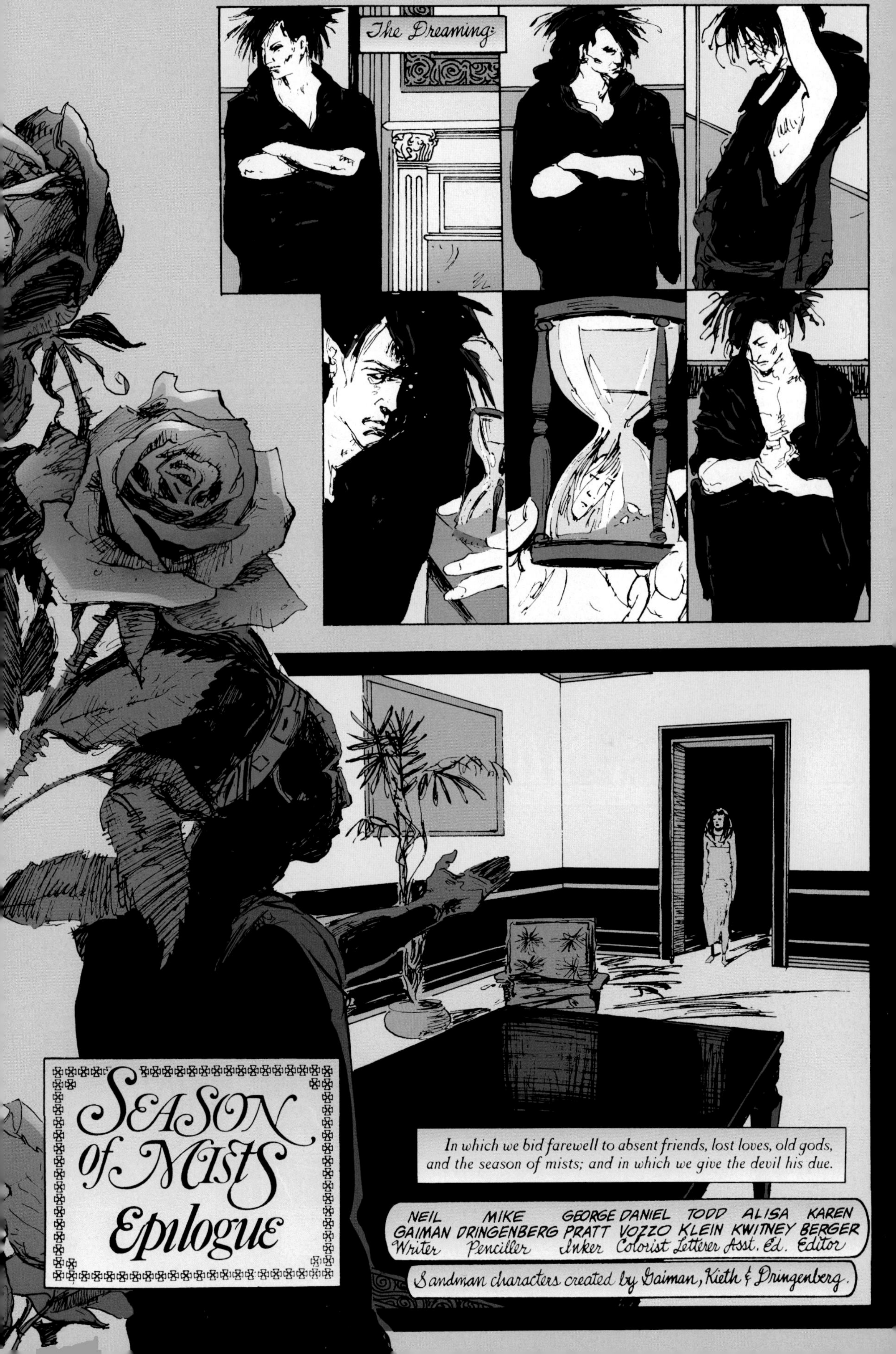
The Dreaming:
SEASON of MISTS
Epilogue
In which we bid farewell to absent friends, lost loves, old gods, and the season of mists; and in which we give the devil his due.
NEIL GAIMAN Writer
MIKE DRINGENBERG Penciller
GEORGE PRATT Inker
DANIEL VOZZO Colorist
TODD KLEIN Letterer
ALISA KWITNEY Asst. Ed.
KAREN BERGER Editor
Sandman characters created by Gaiman, Kieth & Dringenberg.

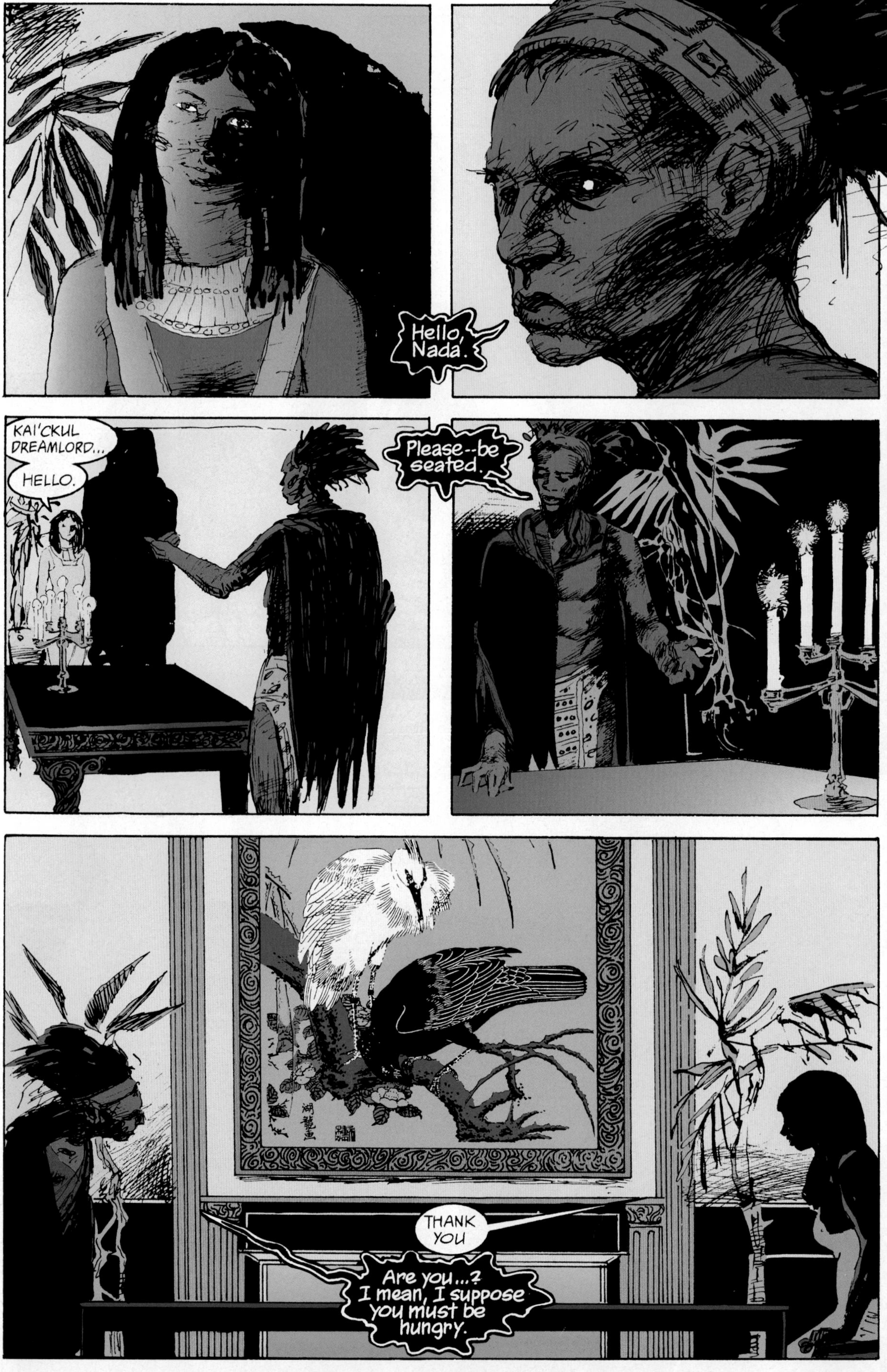
Hello, Nada.
KAI'CKUL DREAMLORD...
HELLO.
Please--be seated.
THANK YOU
Are you...? I mean, I suppose you must be hungry.

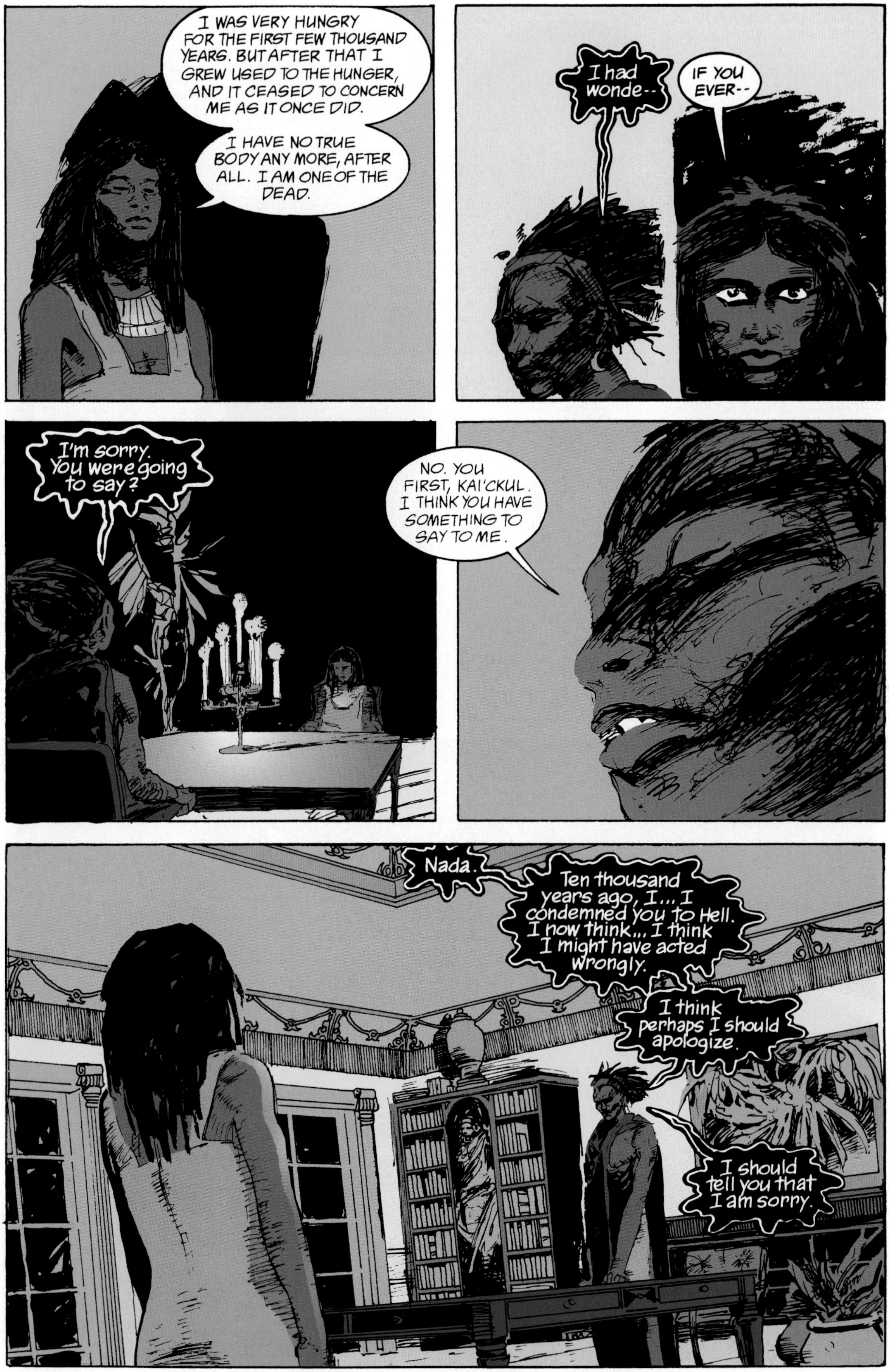
I WAS VERY HUNGRY FOR THE FIRST FEW THOUSAND YEARS. BUT AFTER THAT I GREW USED TO THE HUNGER, AND IT CEASED TO CONCERN ME AS IT ONCE DID.
I HAVE NO TRUE BODY ANY MORE, AFTER ALL. I AM ONE OF THE DEAD.
I had wonde--
IF YOU EVER--
I'm sorry. You were going to say?
NO. YOU FIRST, KAI'CKUL. I THINK YOU HAVE SOMETHING TO SAY TO ME.
Nada.
Ten thousand years ago, I... I condemned you to Hell. I now think... I think I might have acted wrongly.
I think perhaps I should apologize.
I should tell you that I am sorry.

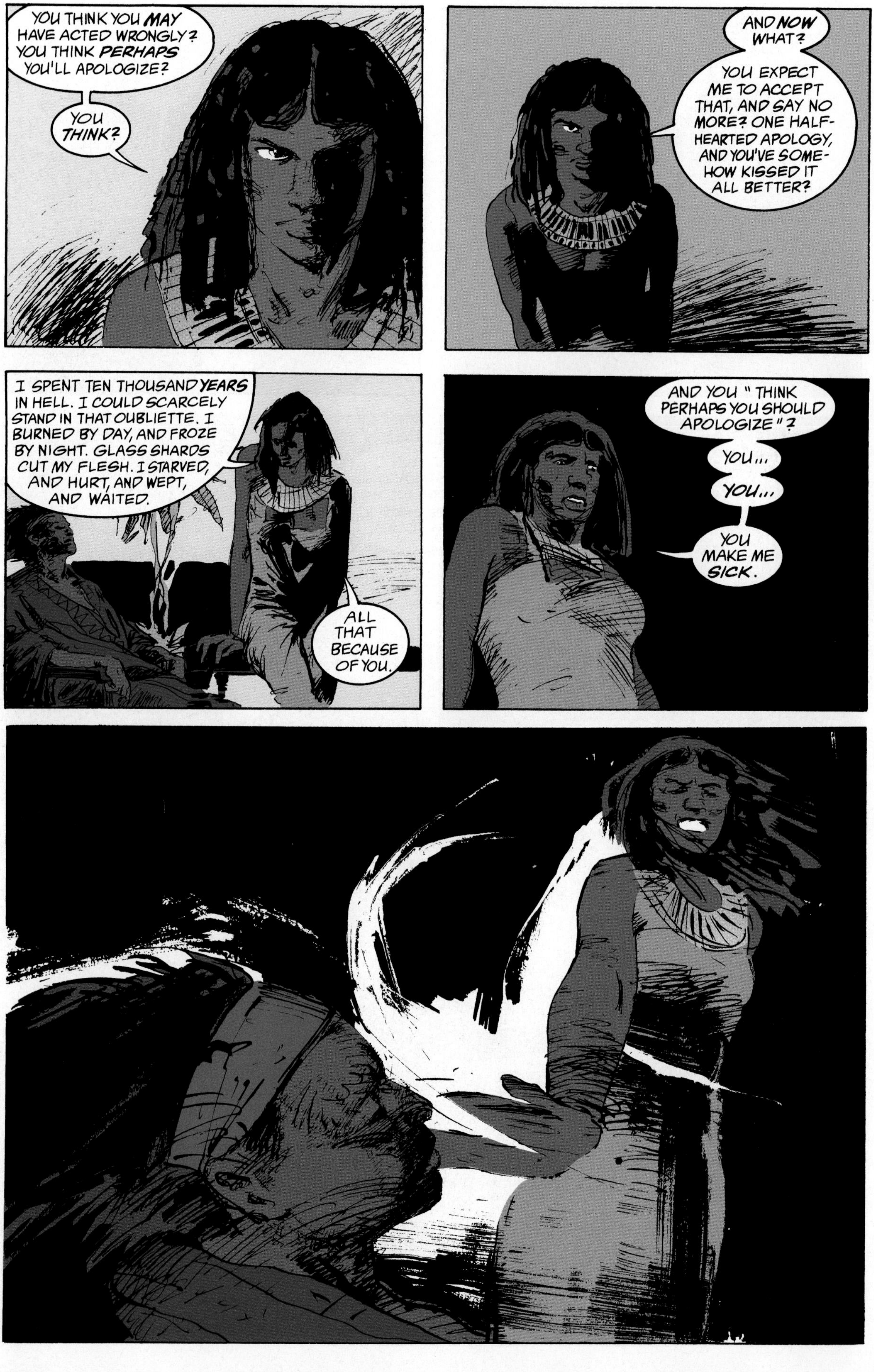

YOU THINK YOU MAY HAVE ACTED WRONGLY? YOU THINK PERHAPS YOU'LL APOLOGIZE?
YOU THINK?
AND NOW WHAT?
YOU EXPECT ME TO ACCEPT THAT, AND SAY NO MORE? ONE HALF-HEARTED APOLOGY, AND YOU'VE SOMEHOW KISSED IT ALL BETTER?
I SPENT TEN THOUSAND YEARS IN HELL. I COULD SCARCELY STAND IN THAT OUBLIETTE. I BURNED BY DAY, AND FROZE BY NIGHT. GLASS SHARDS CUT MY FLESH. I STARVED, AND HURT, AND WEPT, AND WAITED.
ALL THAT BECAUSE OF YOU.
AND YOU "THINK PERHAPS YOU SHOULD APOLOGIZE"?
YOU...
YOU...
YOU MAKE ME SICK.

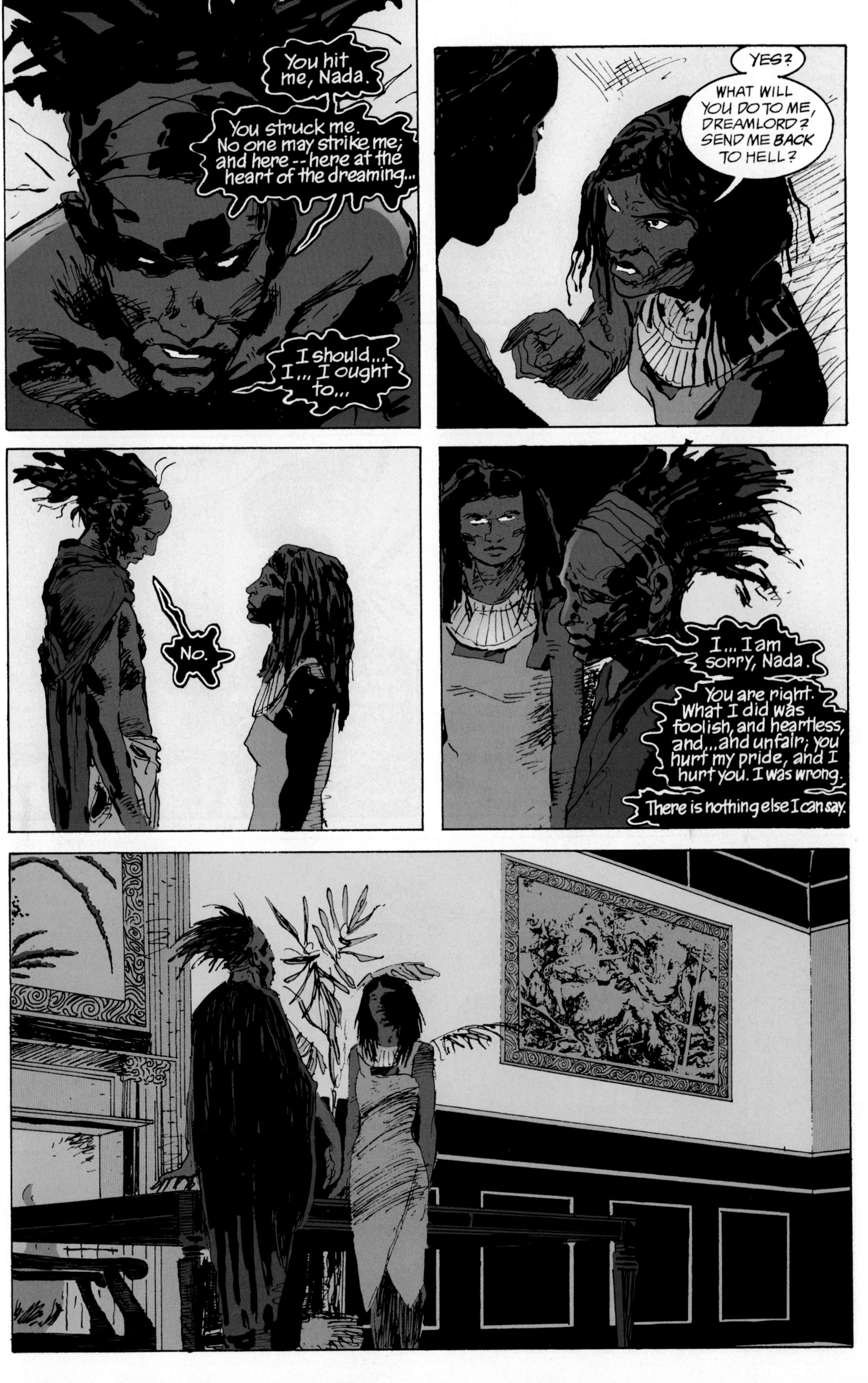
You hit me, Nada.
You struck me. No one may strike me; and here -- here at the heart of the dreaming...
I should... I... I ought to...
YES?
WHAT WILL YOU DO TO ME, DREAMLORD? SEND ME BACK TO HELL?
No.
I... I am sorry, Nada.
You are right. What I did was foolish, and heartless, and... and unfair; you hurt my pride, and I hurt you. I was wrong.
There is nothing else I can say.

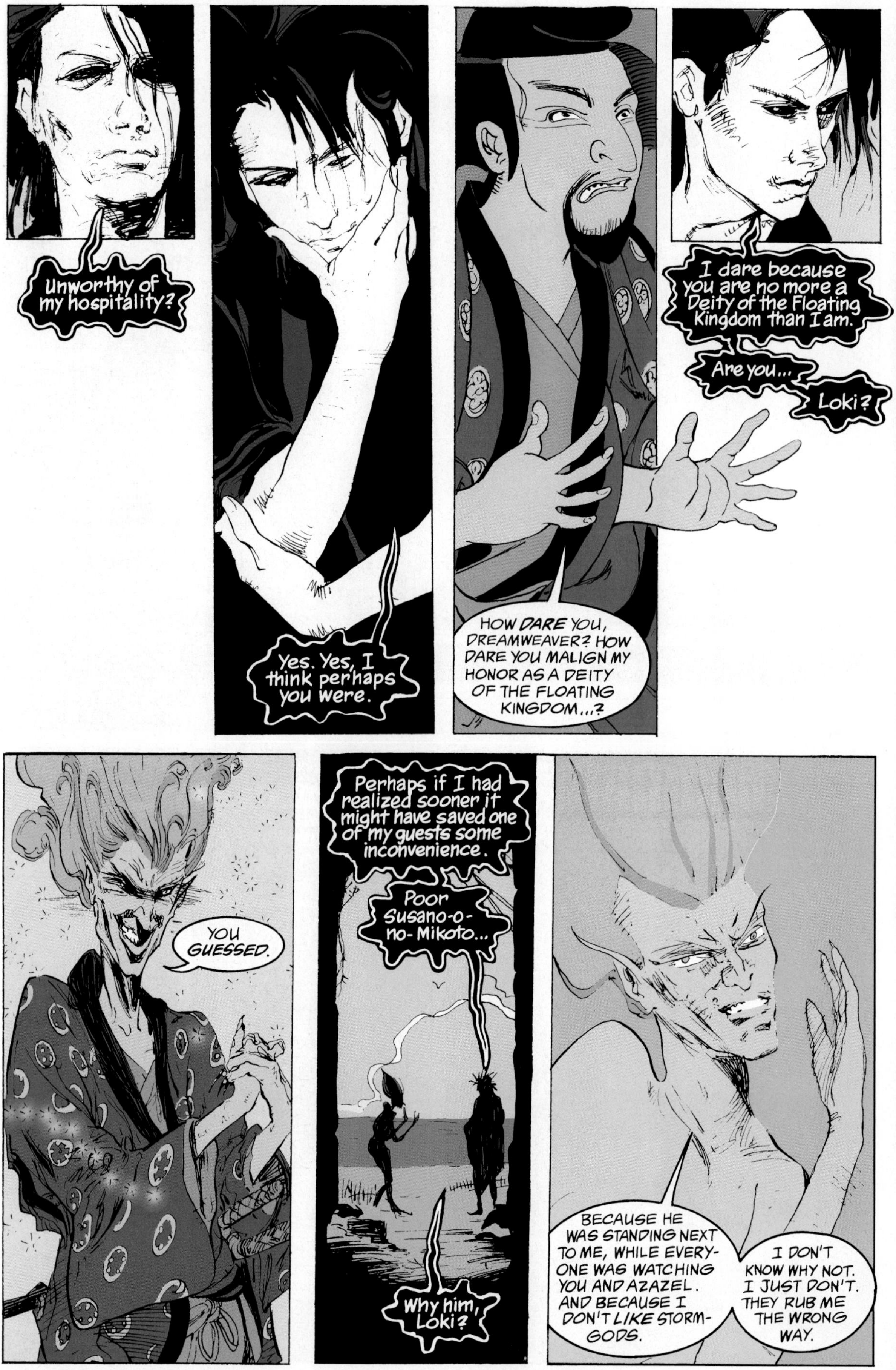
Unworthy of my hospitality?
Yes. Yes, I think perhaps you were.
HOW DARE YOU, DREAMWEAVER? HOW DARE YOU MALIGN MY HONOR AS A DEITY OF THE FLOATING KINGDOM...?
I dare because you are no more a Deity of the Floating Kingdom than I am.
Are you...
Loki?
YOU GUESSED.
Perhaps if I had realized sooner it might have saved one of my guests some inconvenience.
Poor Susano-o-no-Mikoto...
Why him, Loki?
BECAUSE HE WAS STANDING NEXT TO ME, WHILE EVERY-ONE WAS WATCHING YOU AND AZAZEL. AND BECAUSE I DON'T LIKE STORM-GODS.
I DON'T KNOW WHY NOT. I JUST DON'T. THEY RUB ME THE WRONG WAY.

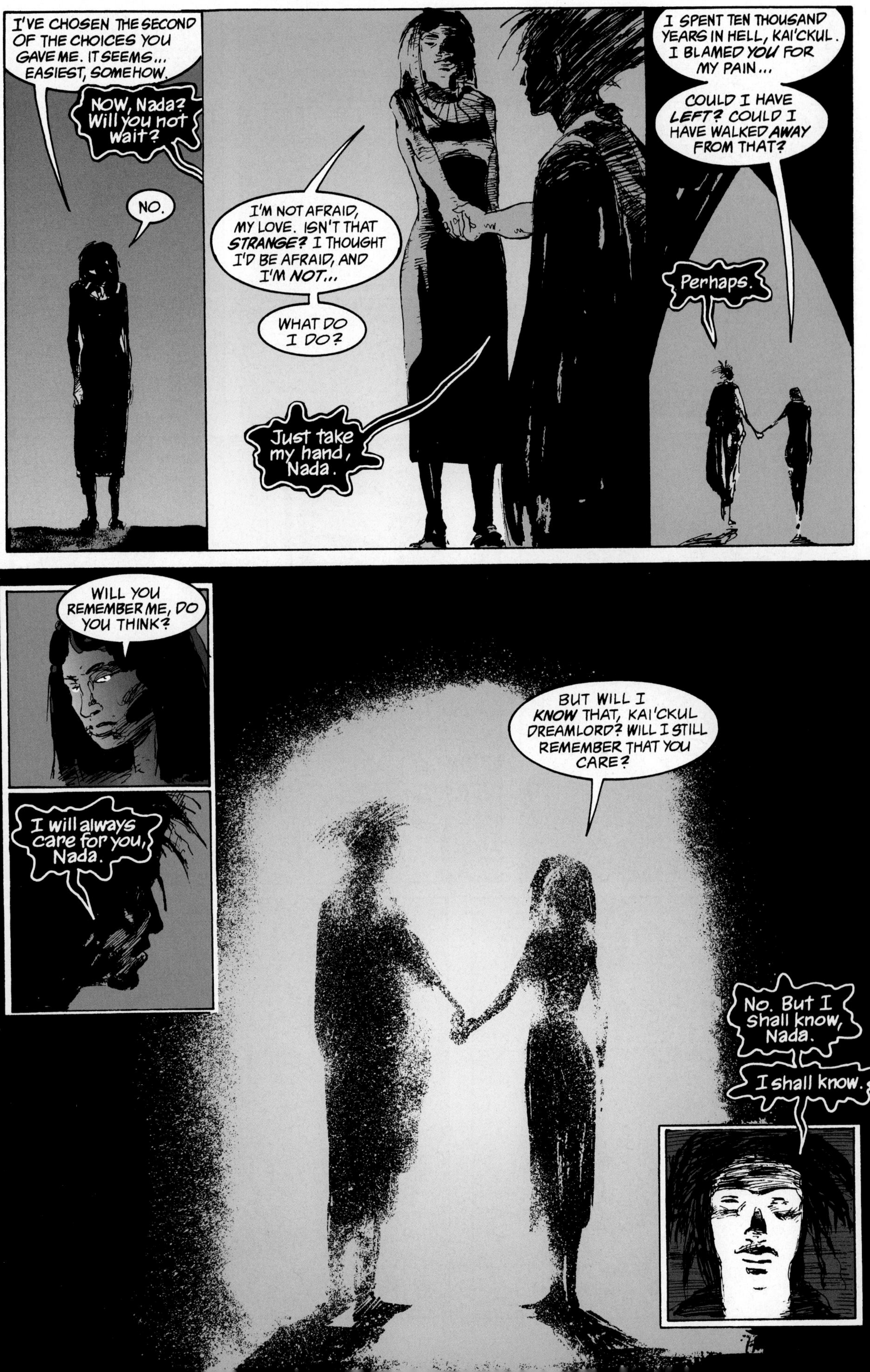
I'VE CHOSEN THE SECOND OF THE CHOICES YOU GAVE ME. IT SEEMS... EASIEST, SOMEHOW.
NOW, Nada? Will you not wait?
NO.
I'M NOT AFRAID, MY LOVE. ISN'T THAT STRANGE? I THOUGHT I'D BE AFRAID, AND I'M NOT...
WHAT DO I DO?
Just take my hand, Nada.
I SPENT TEN THOUSAND YEARS IN HELL, KAI'CKUL. I BLAMED YOU FOR MY PAIN...
COULD I HAVE LEFT? COULD I HAVE WALKED AWAY FROM THAT?
Perhaps.
WILL YOU REMEMBER ME, DO YOU THINK?
I will always care for you, Nada.
BUT WILL I KNOW THAT, KAI'CKUL DREAMLORD? WILL I STILL REMEMBER THAT YOU CARE?
No. But I shall know, Nada.
I shall know.

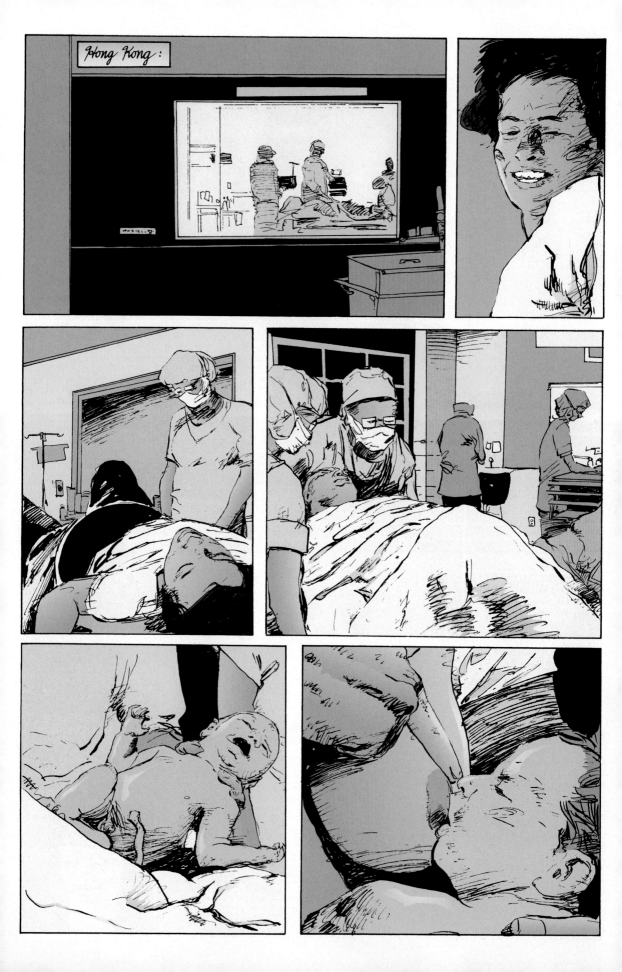

Hong Kong:

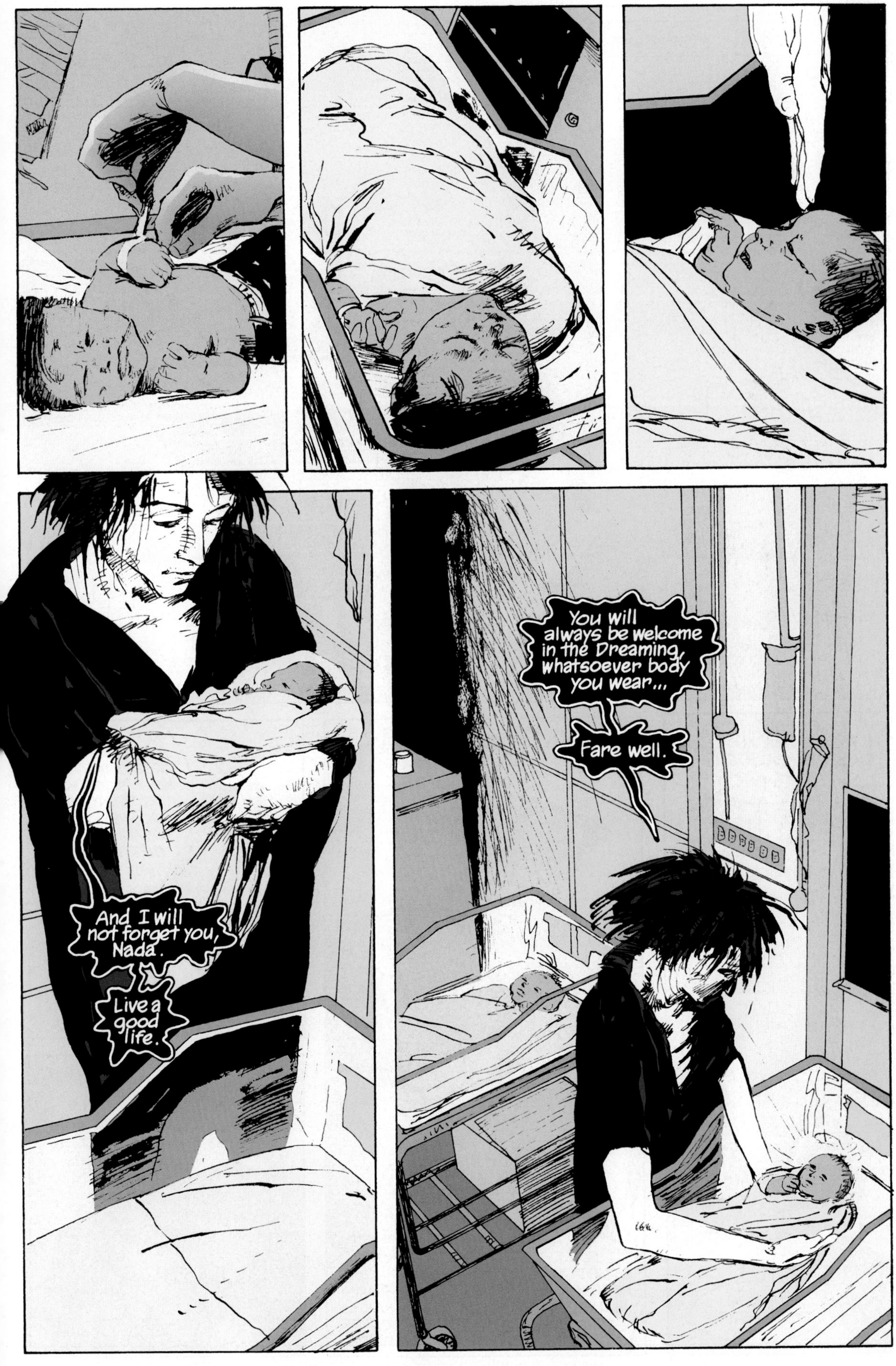
And I will not forget you, Nada.
Live a good life.
You will always be welcome in the Dreaming, whatsoever body you wear...
Fare well.

Perth, Western Australia:

Y'KNOW, I'VE SEEN YOU BEFORE, MATE. DOWN ON THE BEACH. SLEEPING *ROUGH*, ARE WE?

THERE ARE *WORSE* PLACES.

I'LL TELL YOU *THIS* FOR FREE, ANY KID WHO TRIED BATHING TOPLESS 'ROUND HERE TWENTY *YEARS* AGO, WELL, *WE'D'VE* SAID SHE WAS NO *BETTER* THAN SHE SHOULD BE.

IT CAN GETS A A BIT WARM IN THE DAYTIME, BUT CRACK A TUBE, OR GO FOR A DIP, AND YOU'RE RIGHT AS RAIN.

I DON'T COME DOWN HERE MUCH IN THE DAY, ME.

BEACHES ARE FOR THE *YOUNGSTERS*, IN THE DAYTIME. Y'KNOW, STARIN' AT ALL THE YOUNG SHEILAS WITH NOTHING TO COVER THEIR NEVER-YOU-MINDS.

I SUPPOSE THAT WE ARE.

REALLY. DO GO ON.

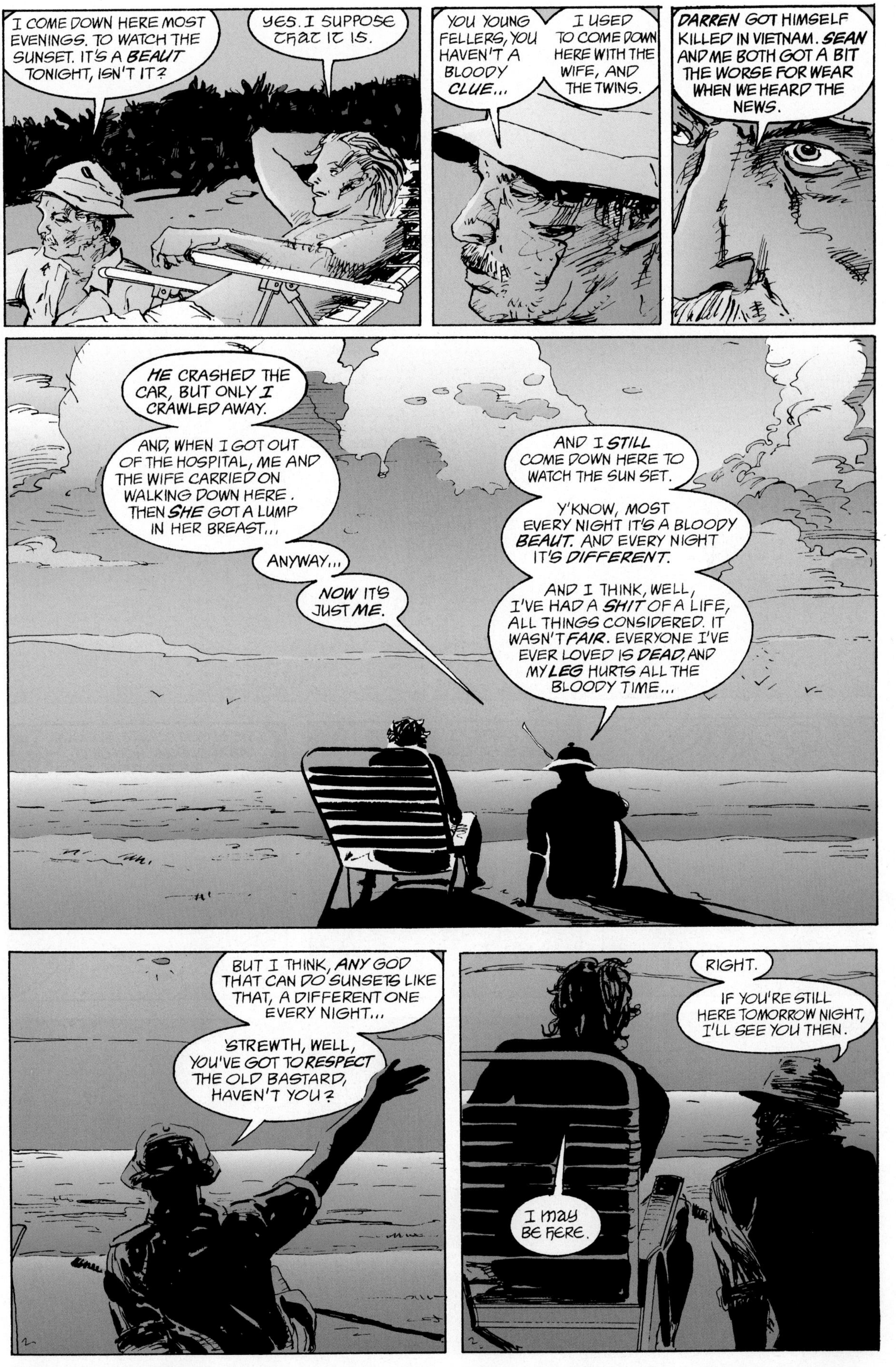
I COME DOWN HERE MOST EVENINGS. TO WATCH THE SUNSET. IT'S A BEAUT TONIGHT, ISN'T IT?
YES. I SUPPOSE THAT IT IS.
YOU YOUNG FELLERS, YOU HAVEN'T A BLOODY CLUE...
I USED TO COME DOWN HERE WITH THE WIFE, AND THE TWINS.
DARREN GOT HIMSELF KILLED IN VIETNAM. SEAN AND ME BOTH GOT A BIT THE WORSE FOR WEAR WHEN WE HEARD THE NEWS.
HE CRASHED THE CAR, BUT ONLY I CRAWLED AWAY.
AND, WHEN I GOT OUT OF THE HOSPITAL, ME AND THE WIFE CARRIED ON WALKING DOWN HERE. THEN SHE GOT A LUMP IN HER BREAST...
ANYWAY...
NOW IT'S JUST ME.
AND I STILL COME DOWN HERE TO WATCH THE SUN SET.
Y'KNOW, MOST EVERY NIGHT IT'S A BLOODY BEAUT. AND EVERY NIGHT IT'S DIFFERENT.
AND I THINK, WELL, I'VE HAD A SHIT OF A LIFE, ALL THINGS CONSIDERED. IT WASN'T FAIR. EVERYONE I'VE EVER LOVED IS DEAD, AND MY LEG HURTS ALL THE BLOODY TIME...
BUT I THINK, ANY GOD THAT CAN DO SUNSETS LIKE THAT, A DIFFERENT ONE EVERY NIGHT...
'STREWTH, WELL, YOU'VE GOT TO RESPECT THE OLD BASTARD, HAVEN'T YOU?
RIGHT.
IF YOU'RE STILL HERE TOMORROW NIGHT, I'LL SEE YOU THEN.
I MAY BE HERE.

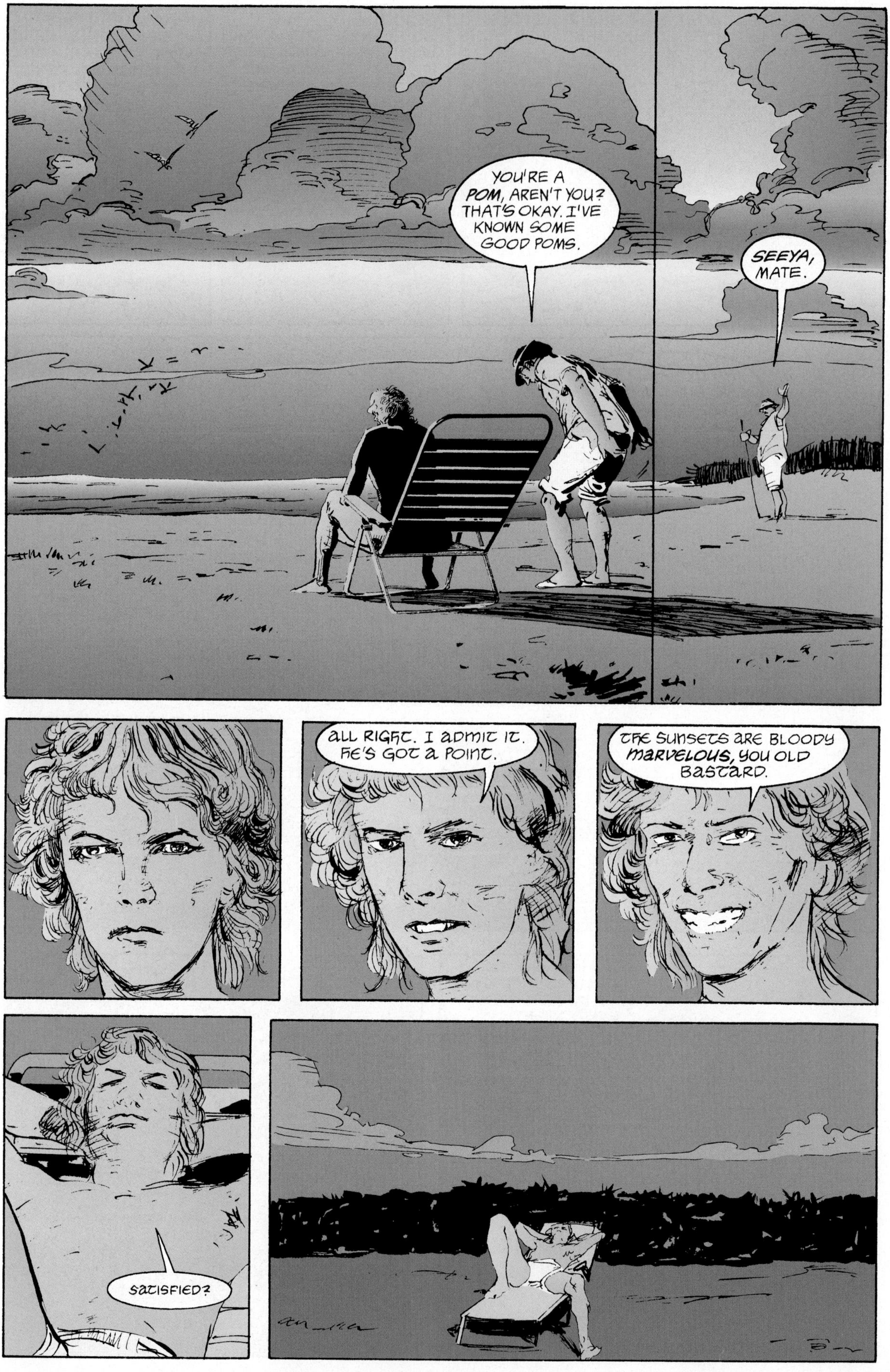

YOU'RE A POM, AREN'T YOU? THAT'S OKAY. I'VE KNOWN SOME GOOD POMS.
SEEYA, MATE.
ALL RIGHT. I ADMIT IT. HE'S GOT A POINT.
THE SUNSETS ARE BLOODY MARVELOUS, YOU OLD BASTARD.
SATISFIED?

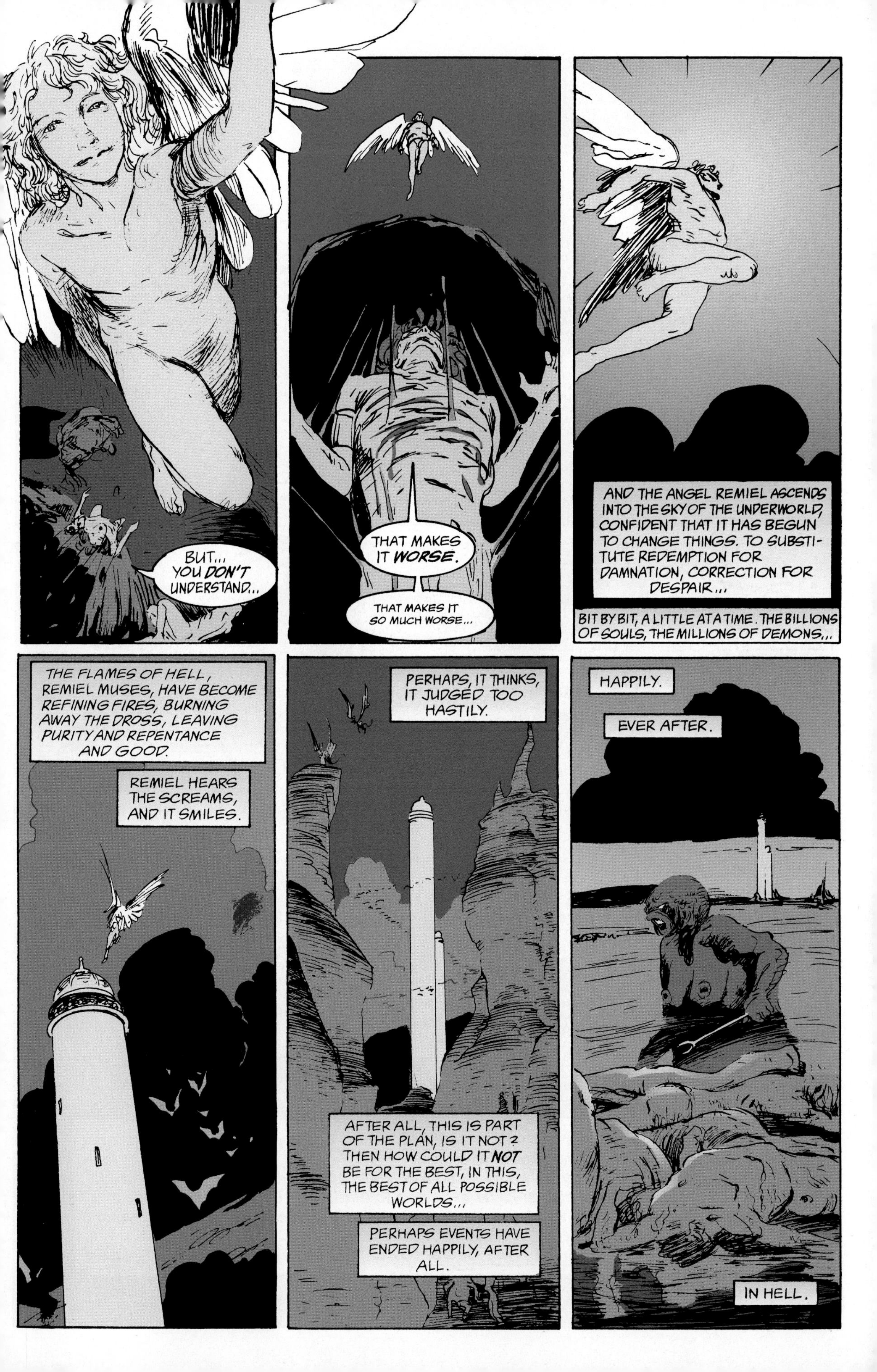
BUT... YOU DON'T UNDERSTAND...
THAT MAKES IT WORSE.
THAT MAKES IT SO MUCH WORSE...
AND THE ANGEL REMIEL ASCENDS INTO THE SKY OF THE UNDERWORLD, CONFIDENT THAT IT HAS BEGUN TO CHANGE THINGS. TO SUBSTITUTE REDEMPTION FOR DAMNATION, CORRECTION FOR DESPAIR...
BIT BY BIT, A LITTLE AT A TIME. THE BILLIONS OF SOULS, THE MILLIONS OF DEMONS...
THE FLAMES OF HELL, REMIEL MUSES, HAVE BECOME REFINING FIRES, BURNING AWAY THE DROSS, LEAVING PURITY AND REPENTANCE AND GOOD.
REMIEL HEARS THE SCREAMS, AND IT SMILES.
PERHAPS, IT THINKS, IT JUDGED TOO HASTILY.
AFTER ALL, THIS IS PART OF THE PLAN, IS IT NOT? THEN HOW COULD IT NOT BE FOR THE BEST, IN THIS, THE BEST OF ALL POSSIBLE WORLDS...
PERHAPS EVENTS HAVE ENDED HAPPILY, AFTER ALL.
HAPPILY.
EVER AFTER.
IN HELL.

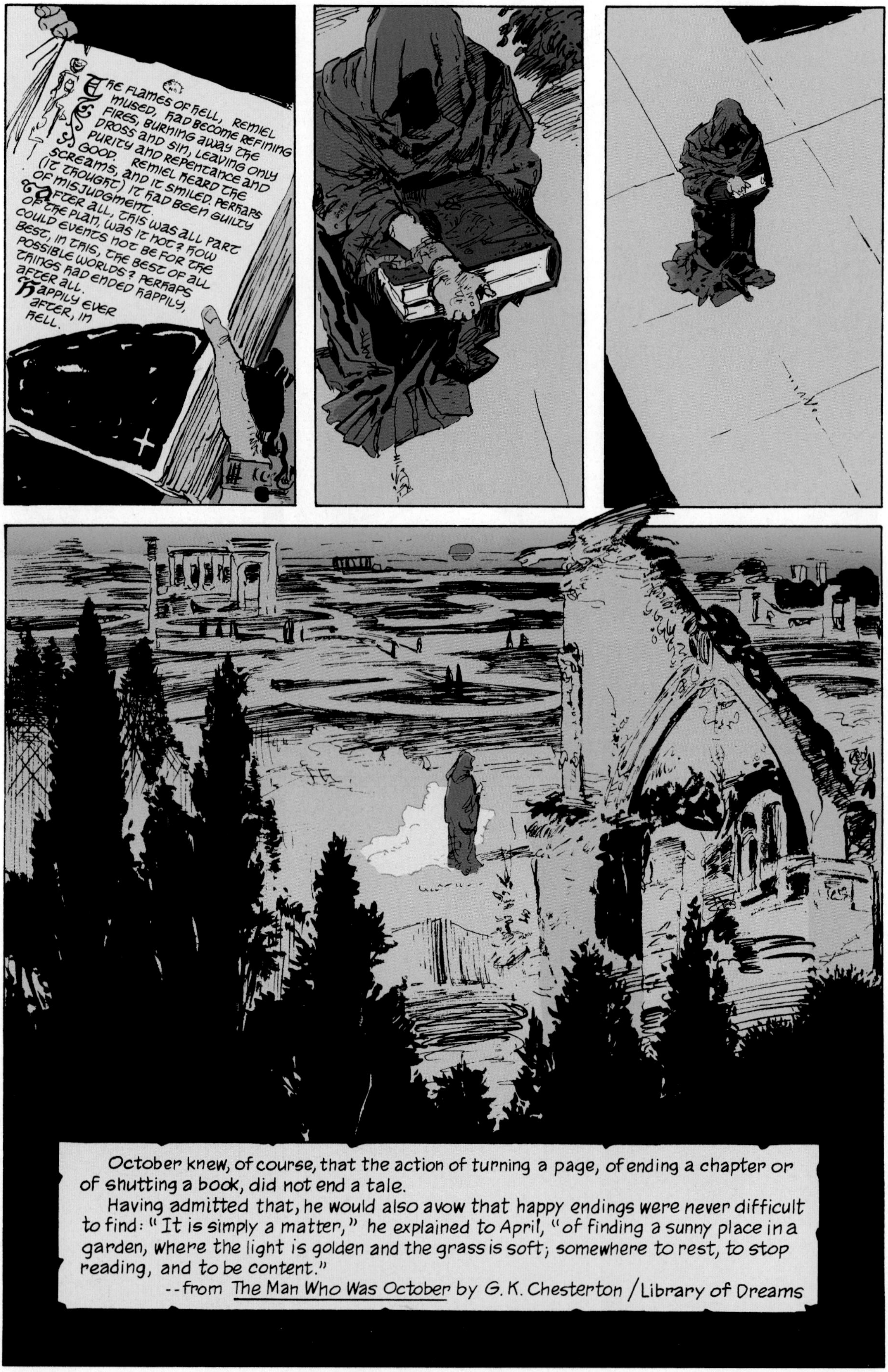
THE FLAMES OF HELL, REMIEL MUSED, HAD BECOME REFINING FIRES, BURNING AWAY THE DROSS AND SIN, LEAVING ONLY PURITY AND REPENTANCE AND GOOD. REMIEL HEARD THE SCREAMS, AND IT SMILED. PERHAPS (IT THOUGHT) IT HAD BEEN GUILTY OF MISJUDGMENT. AFTER ALL, THIS WAS ALL PART OF THE PLAN, WAS IT NOT? HOW COULD EVENTS NOT BE FOR THE BEST, IN THIS, THE BEST OF ALL POSSIBLE WORLDS? PERHAPS THINGS HAD ENDED HAPPILY, AFTER ALL. HAPPILY EVER AFTER, IN HELL.
October knew, of course, that the action of turning a page, of ending a chapter or of shutting a book, did not end a tale.
Having admitted that, he would also avow that happy endings were never difficult to find: "It is simply a matter," he explained to April, "of finding a sunny place in a garden, where the light is golden and the grass is soft; somewhere to rest, to stop reading, and to be content."
--from The Man Who Was October by G. K. Chesterton / Library of Dreams

b i o g r a p h i e s

NEIL GAIMAN
writer

To set certain popular misconceptions to rest once and for all:

1) He was not found wandering the sewers of London as a child during the winter of 1864, unable to say anything more than "Powerful big rats, gentlemen."

2) He was never exhibited in public houses to the curious; only briefly in July, 1865, to selected gentlemen of standing from the scientific and literary community.

3) He did not have a vestigial tail.

4) He did indeed have what most people would commonly understand as "eyes."

5) He was not actually the pilot of the Zeppelin, although he did disappear for good following the explosion.

6) There is quite obviously no "underground kingdom beneath London inhabited by huge, intelligent rodents." And even if there were, any suggestion of Neil's involvement in the mazy territorial negotiations between Londons Above and Below can be considered a joke, and in poor taste at that.

7) He was afraid of neither mirrors nor street conjurers.

8) There were no tooth-marks on the bones.

KELLEY JONES
penciller
episodes 1,2,3,5,6

When he was born, in 1802, Kelley Jones had every appearance of being in his mid-nineties. He astonished physicians by growing younger with each year that passed. This photograph, taken in his seventieth year, appears to be that of a man in his twenties. He died as an infant in 1888, killed in a nursery fire. A recording of his voice reciting Keats's '*To Autumn*' was discovered on the telephone answering machine of a taxi company in Toronto in 1979, but was erased by a temporary secretary who failed to understand its worth.

by NEIL GAIMAN

MIKE DRINGENBERG
penciller
episodes 0,∞

". . . all of the people were coming and I said to them and I said, there's no hope for me here, none of them have faces, always walking, and I never saw any of them before, and they keep touching me in the night, always in the night, sometimes when the rain comes, and no-one sees them but me, grey eyes maybe screaming, and I said to them, and I said to them . . ."

P. CRAIG RUSSELL
inker
episode 3

The details of his black life and dubious death are written in certain books, and the foolish and the curious may seek them out. Nothing could induce us to elaborate here: by comparison Gilles de Rais was an angel in human form, and de Sade a weak and simpering child. The world is well rid of him—if rid of him it truly is.

MATT WAGNER
penciller
episode 4

Matt Wagner was the only man to be elected posthumously to the United States Senate. He served three terms before being narrowly defeated by a living candidate in 1874, whereupon he retired from public life. Until recently his jawbone was on display in the Smithsonian Institution.

GEORGE PRATT
inker
episodes 5,∞

Documented cases of spontaneous human combustion are rare; however, in all the annals of this phenomenon, only George Pratt was able to combust on cue. As a thaumaturgic Music Hall 'turn,' Mister Pratt would ignite on stage, in front of a paying audience, whereupon Millicent Wirth, his lover and assistant, would extinguish the blaze with a patent liquid of Pratt's own invention. This photograph was taken of 'Combustible George' the afternoon before his final performance, in Boston, in 1901. 'Miss Millie's' subsequent trial and acquittal was a *cause célèbre* for many weeks. Fifty years later she filled a bathtub with gasoline and climbed into it, naked, holding a lighted taper.

MALCOLM JONES III
inker
episodes 0,1,2

This photograph of one of Malcolm Jones's three homunculi was originally published in the *Journal of the American Society for Psychical Knowledge*. Measuring no more than six inches in height, these tiny creatures were, it is said, capable of human speech, and were wholly subordinate to Jones's will. None of them survived Jones by more than a week, disintegrating to dried blood, rose petals and ashes.

DICK GIORDANO
inker
episode 6

Impresario, shipping magnate, oil baron, surgeon, and philanthropist. One Thursday morning in November, 1893, Giordano took his usual table at the Savoy Hotel and requested the waiter bring him 'a newspaper, a bootjack, the Bible, a pint of vinegar, a paper of pins, and some barley sugar.' Upon the waiter's refusal to comply with this extraordinary request, Giordano's face dissolved into silent tears. "Aye, me, sir," he said, "you have condemned an honest man to his doom." Thereupon he hailed a cab, and was heard to tell the driver to take him to his office, a journey of no more than fifteen minutes. He was, of course, never seen again, although his tiepin was cut from the stomach of a twenty-five pound sturgeon caught in the Black Sea on the first day of World War One.

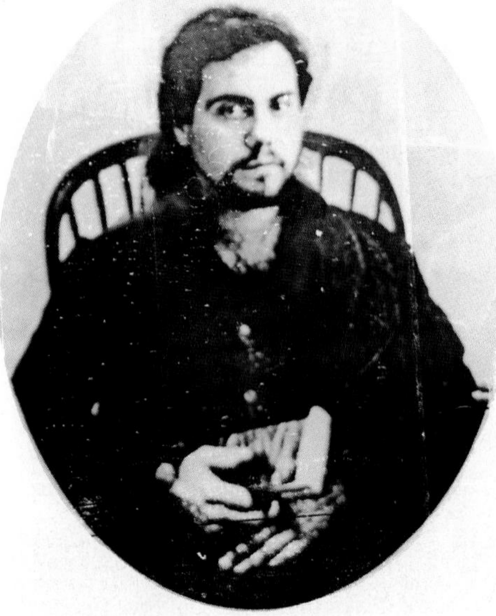

DANIEL VOZZO

colourist

episodes 2,3,4,5,6,∞

Professor Vozzo's handbook, *Ten Thousand Important Questions Resolved for the Modern Gentleman*, issued in monthly parts from October 1889 on, contained essays on such vital subjects as: *"Is dancing, as usually conducted, compatible with a high standard of morality?" "Was the purchase of Alaska by this government wise?" "Does the study of physical sciences militate against religious belief?" "Has our government a right to disfranchise the polygamists of Utah?"*

Not satisfied with resolving these questions, and many others of equal import, by 1894 he began to address such issues as: *"Is there a purpose to existence?"* and *"What is the composition of the Philosopher's Stone?"*

At this time Vozzo began to complain of being followed by women with the faces of animals. All copies of the latter installments of his handbook were bought up by an anonymous cartel, and destroyed, and shortly thereafter Vozzo was removed to a private asylum. He is still there, and he has not aged, although on the advice of a long-dead physician his tongue was surgically removed, and he is permitted no writing materials.

STEVE OLIFF

colourist

episodes 0,1

Best known for his revolutionary embalming techniques. Upon his death in 1897 his collection of perfectly preserved schoolchildren was donated to the Royal College of Surgeons. It may be inspected by prior appointment, although several of the older boys were damaged by falling masonry during the Blitz, and have been removed from the permanent exhibition.

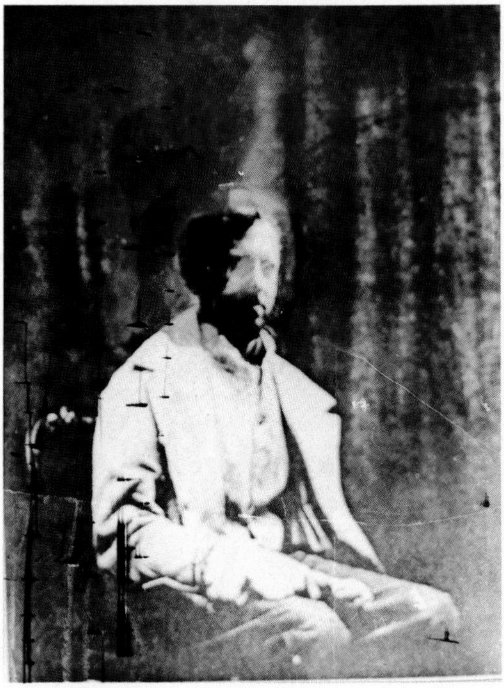

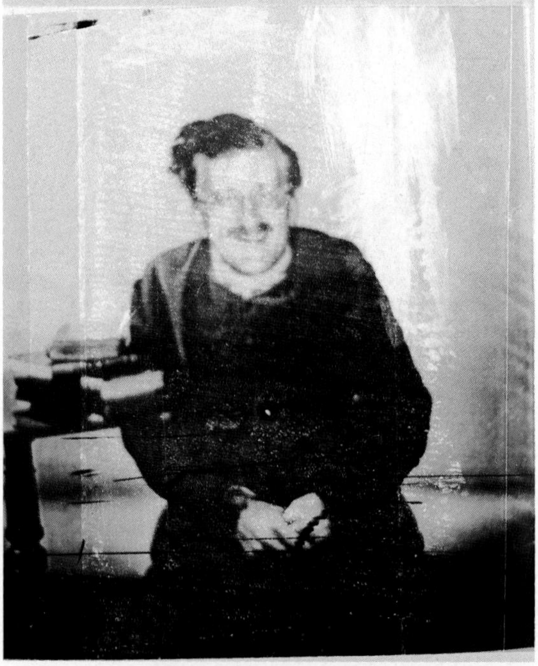

TODD KLEIN

letterer

Was never convicted of any capital crime, for reasons that still remain shrouded in mystery.

KAREN BERGER
editor

They say she done them all of them in. They say she done it with an axe.

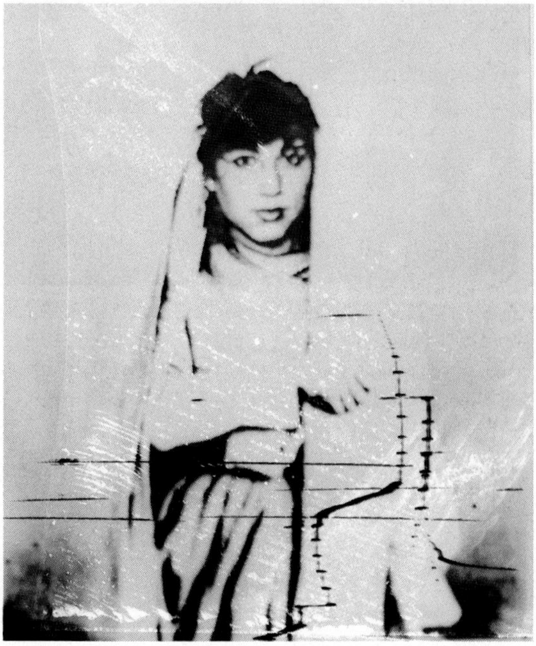

ALISA KWITNEY
assistant editor

According to an old New York folk-tale, Alisa Kwitney appears in a bathroom mirror to people in the final stages of *delirium tremens*, and pleads with them to mend their ways. In another version of the same story she can be induced (by threatening to break the mirror) to reveal winning lottery ticket numbers.

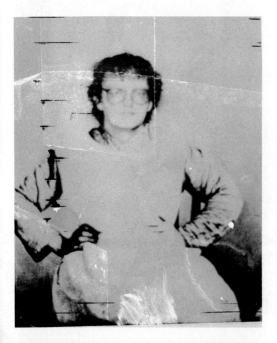

TOM PEYER
assistant editor

Notorious for his cross-dressing during a period when society frowned on such hobbies, Peyer (the illegitimate son of Francis Egerton, the Eighth Earl of Bridgewater and self-styled Prince of the Holy Roman Empire), was arrested at the outbreak of the Crimean War for singing an obscene ballad in a public place while dressed as a washerwoman. The ballad, in the *Parlarie* Argot, went as follows:

> *Nanti dinarly; the omee of the khazi*
> *Says due bionc peroney, manjaree on the cross.*
> *We'll all have to scarper the latty in the morning*
> *Before the bona omee of the khazi shakes his doss.*

DAVE McKEAN
covers and design

This photograph, found in the Hanussen collection, appears at a hasty first glance to be a portrait of a bearded man in a hat, his coat glittering with five brass buttons. A second, and more careful look reveals that this is simply an illusion: we are looking from above at a snowy landscape: the 'coat' is a river, the 'buttons' stepping stones, the 'face' an island, and a fallen tree, the 'hat' a small body of water in the distance. Photographic illusions of this kind were popular with our forefathers; to our more sophisticated eyes, however, the deception is transparent, and once we see it for what it is, we are unable to see the face that once we thought we saw. The seagull in the foreground is extremely blurred, due to the lengthy exposures Victorian photography demanded.

HARLAN ELLISON
introduction

Harlan Ellison is the author of fifty-eight books and is listed in the *Swedish National Encyclopedia*.